TO HR _

THANKS FOR YOUR
SUPPORT AND
FRIENDSHIP.

I ALSO APPRECIATE
THE CIGAR.

I HOPE TO SEE YOU
AGAIN AT HOGSHEAD
CIGAR LOUNGE.

PEACE AND BLESSINGS,

11/28/2015

HUNTING CRIMINALS
TO HIDING THEM

My Journey to and with the United States Marshals Service

SYLVESTER E. JONES SR.

authorHOUSE®

AuthorHouse™
1663 Liberty Drive
Bloomington, IN 47403
www.authorhouse.com
Phone: 1 (800) 839-8640

Published by AuthorHouse   10/15/2015

ISBN: 978-1-5049-2371-2 (sc)
ISBN: 978-1-5049-2372-9 (e)

Library of Congress Control Number: 2015912101

Print information available on the last page.

CONTENTS

From Hunting Criminals to Hiding Them.

My Journey to and with the United States Marshals Service.

DEDICATION

This book is dedicated to four people who I love, admire, and miss very much. All have passed on. I dedicate this book to my Grandfather William A. Jones; my very good friend and police partner during my time with the Markham Police Department, Sergeant Gregory L. Simmons; father figure, friend and colleague, Senior Inspector Julius Turner; and former Director of the United States Marshals Service and Police Executive, Eduardo Gonzalez. All four of these great men served as mentors, friends, and advisors in my journey in life and in law enforcement, including my outstanding and wonderful career with the United States Marshals Service.

William A. Jones was an inspiration and father figure to me in so many ways. As he used to say to me "I put you on the road to success" and he did. He believed in me and encouraged me to be the very best I could be. He helped me get started with the Markham Police Department by loaning me his 45 caliber semi-automatic pistol when I did not have a service weapon. Granddad Jones left this world a week and a day after his 95th birthday on June 27, 2014. We both shared service with the United States Army, as he served from 1941 to 1945 with distinguished service during World War II earning decorations including three Bronze Service Stars and a Philippine Liberation Ribbon.

My Grandfather was the Patriarch of the Jones Family prior to his death as he was a Father, Grandfather, and Great Grandfather. He often had various sayings or quotes which I am certain he picked up from others and his own experiences in his long life such as "I need you like a duck needs a rain coat"; "Winners Never Quit and Quitters Never Win" (Vince Lombardi); "Hang in the Gang"; "I am going to pay him off and lay off him"; and "You can't take no zero and make no hero." Granddad, you will always be remembered and missed by your family and friends who are left behind to carry on. I thank you for being a father figure to me although you were my grandfather. I will always remember, honor, and love you.

Gregory L. Simmons left this world on December 14, 2013, at the young age of 62. As a husband, father, brother, uncle, grandfather, and a friend to many. Greg left many behind to continue his legacy and to remember his many lifetime accomplishments. He was a very good friend and advisor to me. Greg and I spent time together as Police Officers with the Markham Police Department and the decades after. Greg was great police partner and friend. We had each other's back. I thank God for Greg and what he stood for. Greg was a big brother to me and I will always love and miss him.

Julius Turner left this world in December 2001 at the young age of 63. Julius Turner and I hit it off very well in 1992 when I was in charge of the security detail for the first Just the Beginning African American Judge's Conference in Chicago. We became great friends in the years that followed, as we maintained contact after I left Chicago and went to St. Thomas, U.S. Virgin Islands, San Juan, Puerto Rico and the Washington DC area in 1996. Julius, also known as JT or Sonny, enjoyed playing bid whist and golf and I always felt the love and concern he had for me. I thank JT for being a father figure, mentor and advisor. He is still missed.

The former United States Marshals Service Director Eduardo Gonzalez left this world in March 2014 as I was just beginning my campaign for Sheriff of Prince George's County, Maryland. Like the loss of the others mentioned before, I was devastated to hear of his passing. I met Director Gonzalez in Richmond, Virginia, at my second National Organization of Black Law Enforcement (NOBLE) Conference in 1994. I had just received my first Marshals Service promotion after many, many attempts. Director Gonzalez by far was the best director I have served under. He was a great leader and visionary. He treated people with dignity and respect. I received my promotions to GS13, 14, and 15 under this great Director. All directors of law enforcement agencies, both federal and local, should find his playbook or documents of accomplishments, and learn from him.

Director Gonzalez served at the highest levels of local and federal law enforcement and achieved many great accomplishments including leading the United States Marshals Service to be the first federal law enforcement agency to undergo and achieve Law Enforcement Accreditation through CALEA, the Commission on Accreditation for Law Enforcement. Accreditation in law enforcement is very important to law enforcement and communities, as standardized police training, procedures, methods and operations lead to better policing. I thank the late great Director Gonzalez for his leadership, friendship, mentorship and his love. I will always miss and have love for Eduardo Gonzalez.

I have been fortunate to have a number of other people including law enforcement executives who have been instrumental in my law enforcement and military journey. However, my grandfather, the late William A. Jones, my former police partner the late Gregory L. Simmons, my very good friend, mentor, and father figure the late U.S. Marshals Service Senior Inspector Julius Turner, and the late U.S. Marshals Service Director and local police executive Eduardo Gonzalez are four great heroes, leaders, and family men who made a tremendous lifelong impact on me. May they forever be remembered and may they rest in peace.

FOREWORD

Since the 1930s the Department of Justice attempted to rid the nation of organized crime with varying degrees of success. But, not until the 1950s did the Department establish the Organized Crime and Racketeering Section, bringing together in one place experienced trial lawyers who were ordered to direct their attention solely to attacking organized crime throughout the United States. By 1961, when Robert Kennedy became Attorney General, 17 attorneys had been assigned to the Section. In April 1961, I was the 18th and soon the Section grew to over 60 prosecutors. Our function at that time was to serve as Area Coordinators assigned to coordinate federal investigations in a specific geographical area but we were working out of Washington. That led to the creation of Strike Forces, which were field offices in major cities around the country and were staffed not only be prosecutors but also by representatives of the several federal investigative agencies.

The Strike Forces resulted in an increased intensity of investigative and prosecutorial activity, which in turn led to the development of potential witnesses. I say potential because if there was not a mechanism to protect them, they would be murdered, before or after trial. Recognizing that something had to be done led to my developing the Witness Protection Program in the 1960s, which is now known as WITSEC, the acronym for Witness Security Program. To date, over 10,000 witnesses and over

20,000 members of their families have been relocated, resulting in tens of thousands of convictions of racketeers, motorcycle gangs, large narcotics organizations, hate groups and terrorists. In the almost 50 years of operation, no witness who has followed the rules laid down by the Marshals Service has been killed.

The person responsible for that success for almost 10 years is Sylvester Jones, who in this book provides you with a story of a man whose philosophy that every problem encountered must have a solution has well served the criminal justice system. In the pages that follow, you will see how that attitude existed his entire life, resulting in his becoming the person the Marshals Service chose to become the Assistant Director in Charge of WITSEC, which followed his extraordinary success as the Assistant Director responsible for the safety of all Federal Judges.

This book will take you through the excitement of the many cases in he which he was involved from the time he was a police officer with the Markham Police Department, a Deputy Marshal, fugitive hunter and finally reaching the rank to which many aspire.

Now enjoy the exciting story of a true American hero.

Gerald Shur

ACKNOWLEDGEMENTS

There are a number of people I have to acknowledge as I write this book. However, the first acknowledgement and praise is to God. As I grew up, I developed my faith in God and Christ. My faith has only gotten stronger and I have been tremendously blessed. I thank God for his love and blessings as he has been with me on every journey and brought me through troubled times and adversity. God has blessed me to know many people all around the world.

I thank my loving Mother Cherry Jacqueline Claytor. She has been an inspiration to me all of my life and has been a steadfast supporter, advisor and confidant

I thank my children Sylvester E. Jones Jr., Lawrence J. Jones, Erika J. Jones, Sean E. Jones, Justin E. Jones, Ashley A. Jones and my youngest, Morgan A. Jones. My children have made many sacrifices for me to be successful in my military and law enforcement careers. As my older kids know all too well, as I was chasing my careers, I was here and there taking assignments across the country and some assignments or deployments around the world and missed too many special family times. To my children, I say thank you very much for your unconditional love and unwavering support.

I thank my two Aunts Sheila McKinnon, and Rosebud Robinson, who both inspired me to continue to seek higher education. I thank my

Uncle's Ron Jones and the late Robert Jones for their love and support. I also thank Barbara, Katheryn, Sylvia, and Alicia for their support and being good Mothers to our children.

When it comes to my friends, I have many to acknowledge and thank them for their support, love and encouragement. My oldest friend is Eugene Johnson. He and I became friends in the 3rd grade and later reunited in high school where we both played on the football team and became Captains of the team in our senior year. Eugene, I thank you for your friendship, encouragement and love.

Pastor David Ballard, you have been and will always be a lifelong friend. You and I also played football together in high school but for different teams. We helped get each other ready for our games, as I was a quarterback and you a wide receiver. I thank you and your lovely wife Lisa for being lifelong friends. I love you both.

I thank Mr. Eugene Shaw who is a lifetime friend and law enforcement colleague. I played high school football with Eugene. He was my right offensive tackle, and always protected me on the offensive line along with other good offensive lineman. I was a lefty and played quarterback.

I owe a lot to my longtime friend, military and law enforcement colleague and Fraternity Brother Bill Walker. It is because of Bill Walker that I stayed in the military as I long as I did. He and I had served in the same Army Reserve Unit and both assigned by our employers to the Washington DC area. Bill and I always encouraged each other to be the best we could be and were always there to consult and support each other during trying times. Bill was instrumental in me pledging and joining the greatest Greek Letter Fraternity of all time, Alpha Phi Alpha Fraternity. Thanks for being a longtime very good friend, colleague and Fraternity Brother.

To my longtime friend and former fugitive partner Herman Brewer, I thank you for many years of friendship and brotherhood. We have been brothers-in-law in more than one way. I appreciate you and your good counsel especially when we were tracking and finding fugitives. I also extend my appreciation for your review and edits of this book. Thanks for always being there for me.

I want to acknowledge and thank Ms. Doris Harris for treating me like a son as her son, David Walker, and I spent many evenings together tossing the football, playing magnetic football, and going to parties at Mendel High School. David Walker thanks for being a lifelong friend. We certainly had some good times growing up during our high school days. It was a pleasure to be on the football team with you.

My longtime friend, and Fraternity Brother Al Howard, you and I have gone through some tough situations together. No matter what we endured be it war or other life or family matters, our friendship and brotherhood has stood firm. You and I have been like brothers for many years. Thank you for being the person you are.

Edward Scheu my first Chief Deputy and lifelong friend and mentor, thanks for taking a chance on me back in 1987 when I was selected to be a deputy marshal in the Southern District of New York. Had you not reached out to Marshals Service Headquarters, I most likely would not have become a deputy marshal and a number of events and accomplishments in my life would not have occurred. My destiny in our great agency was to start as it did in the great city of Chicago. Also thanks for letting Al Howard and I have tickets for all of those Chicago Bear games when you worked for the National Football League.

Mr. Clarence Edwards, Retired Director of the Federal Protective Service and First African American Police Chief of Montgomery County, Maryland. Thank you for your invaluable mentoring, wise counsel about law enforcement, family and life. It is a pleasure to serve in our noble profession and Fraternity with you. You are an icon in our profession and I am very proud to be a longtime friend and Fraternity Brother.

I acknowledge and thank Mr. Gerald Shur, the Founder of the American Witness Protection/Security Program. Mr. Shur has been an inspiration to many people around the world. Mr. Shur has been of tremendous help to me as I led the Witness Security Program for nearly nine years. I have enjoyed his friendship and wise counsel. Gerry thanks for all of your invaluable assistance not only with domestic operations but also with the International Symposiums on Witness Security/Protection. I also appreciate you participating in this book by writing such a wonderful Foreword.

To my Fraternity Brother, and very good friend L.B. Clinton, I thank you for all you have done for me and for just being a great older brother, not only in the Fraternity but in life. You have always been there for me in some very trying times and I will never forget that. True friends stay by your side in good and bad times. You are certainly a true friend. I thank God for you.

James and Bernadine Howard, you two have been absolutely wonderful friends and more like family to me. I appreciate and love you both. You two have always welcomed me in your home and I have placed my feet under your dinner table on numerous times along with my daughter Morgan. Thanks for always being there for me.

Charles Fonseca thanks for being a good friend, advisor and brother over the many years. It was a pleasure to work with you during my tenure as the Assistant Director for the Judicial Security Division. Your dedicated service as Chief of the Judicial Security Division oversight team is appreciated. You are a true professional and a valued colleague.

Ivan Baptiste, it has truly been an honor and pleasure to know you and to work with you over the many years since we met in St. Thomas USVI. You have been a tremendous advisor, friend and big brother to me and I will never forget our countless talks about family, love, life and business.

I extend love and appreciation to Jean Turner who has been like a mother to me during my time in the Washington DC area. You will always have a special place in my life.

I also thank my good friends who are members of the Bijou Family. Thanks for your love, friendship and support.

There are numerous Marshals Service employees current and retired that I have had the pleasure of working with that have made an impact on me personally and in my career with the Marshals Service. I thank each of them for their friendship, support, and all of their efforts to get the job done, and done well. They are the best of the best.

Donald Horton thanks for your friendship, support and mentoring. I really appreciate the support and guidance you gave me when I followed you as the Chief of Court Security and in my position as Assistant Director for Judicial Security leading security programs for federal judges, prosecutors and court facilities. I also thank you for introducing me to Georgetown Men's Basketball.

I thank Charles E. Day who has authored two books, Call Center Operations: Profiting From Teleservices, McGraw-Hill, Publishing and The Tenth Man: Living Black in Blue, AuthorHouse Publishing. Charles you were very helpful to me with your excellent organizational advice when I was stuck near the middle of my manuscript.

I acknowledge and thank Darryl Ahmad, another law enforcement and military colleague who has been a good friend for over 25 years. Thanks Darryl for your longtime friendship and wisdom.

Congratulations to Chief Darryl Williams on your recent retirement from the Marshals Service after a 30-year stellar career. You have been a good friend and colleague since I met you in 1988 while I was assigned to Miami, Florida for Operation WANT II. You are also another great Alpha Phi Alpha Fraternity Brother. Thanks for your many years of great friendship.

I have to thank my pastor Delman Coates, Pastor of Mount Ennon Baptist Church for his outstanding spiritual and community leadership.

I extend my appreciation to Photography by Tre' Lynn and Rob Morton for the cover photo of this book.

Lisette Taylor thanks for being a very good friend and advisor to me during some very trying times. I appreciate you being there for me, and the fact that you are a great listener. I have certainly benefitted from our special relationship and send much love your way.

I must thank my good friend and colleague Joseph Alexander for his friendship and guidance on numerous matters. Joe, it was certainly my pleasure to work with you when you left the federal courts and worked with me in the Marshals Service in the Judicial Security Division. I thank you very much for your tremendous efforts editing my manuscript for this book. Your superb assistance and friendship has been a blessing to me. Your sharp pencil and edits were on point. You and your lovely wife Dr. Mary Alexander and family will always be very special to me.

Lastly, I thank those who I may have unintentionally omitted from my acknowledgements. I am certainly very appreciative to all of those who have been a good friend to me over the years and those who I have served with in various capacities that positively affected my life and my two service careers.

INTRODUCTION

As a young child growing up on the south side of Chicago, I had three goals or dreams. I wanted to be a soldier, policeman, or a professional football player. I tried all three of my dreams but realized at a young age while in college that being a professional football player was not going to happen. I was a very good athlete and played football as a left handed quarterback at Carver High School in Chicago, Illinois, and for a brief stint as a scout team quarterback at North Carolina A&T in Greensboro, North Carolina. My football career ended after leaving North Carolina A&T, my first college enrollment, as I was homesick and not attending classes. I also had fatigued from the three a day and two a day football workouts. I eventually tried and succeeded at my other two goals or aspirations of being in law enforcement and joining the military.

I considered many factors while deciding to write a book about my extremely blessed and rewarding law enforcement career such as whether I had made a difference, or made significant contributions impacting my agency or the Department of Justice including the law enforcement initiatives I established around the world. In thinking about my career with the United States Marshals Service, I realized that with God's blessings and direction, and the support of many others, I had accomplished a number of significant achievements both domestically within the borders of the United States and globally impacting several other Continents.

Additionally, I have worked with hundreds of professional law enforcement colleagues around the world.

My journey with the United States Marshals Service started in 1987 when I was selected as a U.S. Deputy Marshal with an initial assignment to the Southern District of New York. At the time I was in my 4th year as a police officer with the Markham Police Department. Markham is a small Illinois south suburban town of about 25,000 people located just south of Chicago along the Interstate 57 corridor. From 1983 to 1987, I served the people of Markham as a very good aggressive patrolman and for a short stint as a detective performing the full-range of police duties, which I enjoyed. As a patrolman, I changed shifts every 28 days back then and often worked midnights so I could continue to take classes in the day hours trying to complete my undergraduate degree at Chicago State University. At the time I was married with a family and was also in the Illinois Army National Guard, which I joined as an enlisted Military Policeman in July 1980.

I pushed my start date with the Marshals Service March back four months to July, using my military orders to complete my Military Police Officer Basic Course (MPOBC), which was also scheduled from March to July. I went from being an enlisted soldier to a Commissioned Officer joining the Reserve Officer Training Corps (ROTC) while taking classes at Chicago State University and the University of Illinois at Chicago. The delay gave me time to further consider the job offer with the Marshals Service in New York. The MPOBC was at Ft. McClellan, Alabama. At that time I had a dilemma. I was competing for a sergeant's position at my police department and was skeptical about taking the Marshals' position in New York. I heard rumors and feedback that new Deputies assigned to New York who were not from the area, had a very difficult time trying to make it financially. The rumors suggested that new Deputy Marshals lived four or five together sharing an apartment and were eligible to collect food stamps. Additionally, I was going to take a pay cut to start and the rules of the agency prevented law enforcement personnel from working second jobs. As a police officer, I also worked various second jobs providing security. I was leaning towards turning the job down, although my wife was urging me to take the new job as a major step in fulfilling one of my three dreams.

God is very good and has blessed me tremendously on my journey in law enforcement, particularly my service with the Marshals Service. I was at Ft. McClellan going through the intense MPOBC training when I received a call from a relative in Markham that I had a letter from the Marshals Service. I asked the relative to open the letter and read it to me. To my delight and surprise the letter informed me there was an opening in the Chicago office and asked me if I would accept a change from the Southern District of New York assignment to Chicago. I obtained the name of the contact person on the letter at the Marshals Service agency headquarters, and called right away accepting the Chicago position. I was happy that I could take the job and not have to move to New York City. I found out later that the gentleman who was conducting my background investigation for the agency found out I was being assigned to New York and decided to contact the Chief Deputy in the Northern District of Illinois informing him that I had a very good career at the police department with some very good contacts with suburban police departments. He further mentioned to the Chief that I was considering turning the position down because of the New York assignment and recommended that since the Chicago office had vacancies, the Chief should contact agency headquarters to see if I could be reassigned to the Chicago office, which the Chief agreed to do. I was very close to not joining this great agency. However, as I have come to understand over the years, what God has in store for you is your destiny.

I reported to the Chicago office of the Northern District of Illinois on July 12, 1987. This was just a couple of days after being away from home at Ft. McClellan, Alabama, for four months. In the ensuing couple of days, three other new deputy marshals along with myself who were all assigned to the Chicago District office, were on our way at government expense to the Federal Law Enforcement Training Center also known as FLETC in Glynco, Georgia. I resigned from my police department and was without a badge and gun after four years of having both. My journey with the Marshals Service starts at this point.

CHAPTER ONE

Growing Up in Chicago, My Favorite Town Joining the Illinois Army National Guard as a Military Policeman

I was born in Chicago, Illinois, in 1960 to a very loving teenage mother. My mother lived with her parents and siblings on the south side of Chicago near 35th and State Street. My mother has always been a sharp witty person. She found work while continuing with high school as my late loving grandmother and my two aunts looked after me. My mother had two more sons in the next three years. She had three boys and was working at the United States Post Office and soon thereafter, rented an apartment for her family. My grandmother and two aunts continued to look after the three of us little guys while my mother worked. I barely knew my father and remember him visiting a few times when I was three or four years old. When I was four my mother married for the first time, and she and her husband had four children, two boys and two girls. I was the first born of seven kids and had the responsibility of looking after my siblings, as I was often left in charge when I was of age. As I grew up with my siblings, we shared some very good memorable times. We were very close.

As a youngster I was always a very good athlete and a pretty good student. I actually feel my first desire to be a part of law and order was as a Patrol Boy in the 6th, 7th, and 8th grade. I remember being a Patrol Boy at Bass Elementary School near Ogden Park on the south side of Chicago, Illinois. The gym teacher Mr. Turner was in charge of the Patrol Boys. We got out of school a little earlier than everyone else to assume our posts and assist our classmates to cross the streets. Mr. Turner was always fair as a gym teacher and coordinator of the Patrol Boys and Girls. He usually kept a fiberglass paddle that he used if students were out of line. I remember he never did more than a flick of his wrist, applying the paddle to our rear ends. There was not much movement, but you could feel a little sting. Just enough paddle to let you know, you needed to straighten up. I think I got the paddle at least twice. My introduction to Professional Hockey was Mr. Turner. He toke the Patrol Boys and Girls to the stadium to see the Chicago Black Hawks. The Black Hawks were a very good team back then in 1971. The team had some very good top-level players such as Bobby Hull and Stan Mikita. I was also a big fan of the other Chicago Professional teams: the Bulls, Cubs, and White Sox. I still am a huge fan of my hometown sports teams, as any of my good friends will tell you.

When I moved on from Bass Elementary School going to the 7th grade I went to Lowe Upper Grade Center. Lowe Upper Grade Center was also on the south side a few miles south of Bass. I also served as a Patrol Boy. At the start of the 8th grade, I entered an election for the Patrol Operation to become Captain. The Patrol Boy Captain was the ranking position, and had two walking Lieutenants walking with him/her to check Patrols. I did a little lobbying with my Patrol colleagues and to my pleasant surprise I was elected to Captain and had my two walking Lieutenants with me as we checked Patrol Posts. My term as Patrol Boy Captain was shortchanged as my family moved from an apartment to a house farther south in Chicago and I had to enroll at West Pullman Middle School. I was one sick puppy, as I did not want to leave my coveted Captain's post at Lowe Upper Grade Center.

West Pullman was a nice school and I made friends quickly. The house we moved in was about five blocks from West Pullman. I met some of my best friends while living at the new house on South Wallace Street. One of my oldest and very good friends, David Ballard, lived across the street and he and I hung out together playing sports, chasing girls, and locating fruit trees to raid as we enjoyed peaches, plums and grapes. The obvious problem was the fruit trees or grape vines were in other people's yards. We eventually got past raiding fruit trees, and played high school football for different teams. I was a pretty good run option and passing quarterback, and David was a pretty good receiver. David and I often practiced together to remain sharp with passing and receiving. We remain close friends.

I also met other very good lifetime friends playing football at Carver High School on the far Southeast side of Chicago near Altgeld Gardens, a community-oriented, low-income housing development. I took the bus from South Wallace Street to the high school. Taking that bus ride was sometimes very interesting, as guys from Altgeld Gardens got on the Chicago Transit Authority bus in Altgeld Gardens and beat people up. I had seen a few such one-way fights where a few guys jumped guys on the bus. This was mainly on the ride home. Thank goodness I was never bothered by the thugs on those bus rides to and from school.

In high school I reconnected with my old friend Eugene Johnson. Eugene and I saw each other at a study hall where students were playing chess. We started talking and saying we knew each other, which we did. We both joined the football team and were captains on the team our senior year. I learned how to play the game of chess during study hall sessions. I watched guys play to learn how the chess pieces moved. After several sessions of watching games, I decided to give the game a try. I lost my first chess game quickly in four moves, known as the "Fools Mate" as it is the least amount of moves a player with no game or game strategy could lose.

I returned to play again, this time losing in seven moves. I kept playing, learning from my mistakes and losing by 13, 17, 21 moves. Then I started to win games. I started defeating the same guys who beat me in chess in four and seven moves and soon they were no longer competition. My chess game kept getting better. In my sophomore year, I joined the school's Chess Team. I played on the Chess Team for three years and in my junior year our team went to the State playoffs and did very well. After leaving Carver High School, I was listed in the school's trophy showcase as the player who won the most chess games, along with the player who scored the most basketball points, retired professional basketball player Terry Cummings, who got drafted by the Milwaukee Bucks and ended up playing a number of seasons with the San Antonio Spurs.

In my junior year in high school, I made the varsity team as the backup QB, sometimes getting playing time. I worked out a lot lifting weights and was one of the stronger guys on the team. I lifted weights to beef up as we ran the run-oriented, wishbone option offense. I needed to be strong and steady, as I was often hit and tackled by defensive ends, linebackers and lineman. In my senior year I was the starting QB and had a very good year. My name was often listed in the Chicago Sun Times Sports section in the high school statistics column for leading in scoring touchdowns. I remember in a game during my senior year against King High School, while running the wishbone option to the right, a pretty good sized defensive end closed in on me as I turned at the edge of the line of scrimmage hitting me head on. It was quite a collision. We both fell to the ground. I immediately got up and returned to my huddle, which was my routine when taking hard hits. The large defensive guy remained laid out on the ground unconscious. He needed what is called smelling salt to come to his senses. In the huddle my teammates who blocked for me asked me why I was smiling after taking such a hit. I responded that my weight room conditioning was paying off, and called the next play. We won that game by running the wishbone run option all over King High School, and scored rather easily off of the option hiding the ball and making good decision reads on the defense. I was interviewed after the game and named the Chicago Sun Times' Player of the Week.

We had a good football season my senior year, making the playoffs. We lost in the second round of the playoffs on a statistical tie against Harrison High School. On the final offensive series we had, we moved the ball very well and scored a go ahead touchdown, only to have it called back. The referees disallowed the score as one of my best offensive linemen was flagged for being off sides. This lineman told me he was getting back at a guy he was battling on the scrimmage line, even though the play we ran and scored on was on the other side. Many people at the game thought our team won on statistics as we moved the ball very easily and the teacher keeping the statistics got into a little skirmish with one of our bench players. Our team was very good and we felt we should have gone on to the championship game and could have won it. That game still bothers some of us who remain close friends. Other very good longtime friends from my old high school football team are David, Brian, and Steve. We remain in contact and are very good friends.

In October 2009 I was invited back to my former high school and inducted in the Carver Military Academy Hall of Fame at a ceremony at halftime of the school's Homecoming Game for career and life accomplishments.

My organized football dream did not last after high school. I served a short stint as a scout team QB in the fall of 1978 at North Carolina A&T. I do remember scoring a running touchdown during one of the practices on an upper classman defensive player who went on to play many seasons as a professional football player in the National Football League. After I scored that touchdown on the practice field in college going around this defensive player on a run option play, the big guy told me after the play that I should not have scored that touchdown on him, and he would teach me a lesson. I did not score on him again as he made sure to contain me.

I left A&T before the semester ended and returned to Chicago. I was not attending classes and the football practices were exhaustive. Also, more of an issue was the fact I was homesick and missing my girlfriend back home. I called my mother and informed her I was coming home. She told me to stay to the end of the term but I let her know I had my airline ticket and was flying home. I flew home on my first airplane flight and found a job pumping gas. I enrolled at South Suburban Community College in South Holland, Illinois, and joined their football team. I was probably a little arrogant thinking I was a better athlete and player than members on the team, although I was not starting and left that school as well. My high school girlfriend had moved on during my short stay at A&T. I was hurt from that relationship and moved on as well. I kept working at the gas station and met my first wife while working there. I noticed her getting off a bus a few times while working, and one day started talking to her. Within a year I was married to her. Shortly after getting an apartment as a very young 19 year-old married guy, I met another longtime friend Willie Campbell.

Willie Campbell and I became friends and started hanging out together. One day Willie mentioned to me he had signed up to join the Illinois Army National Guard and was assigned to the 933rd Military Police Company near downtown Chicago. He informed me the unit had a number of policemen in the unit, and his uncle, a Chicago Policeman, was in the unit and had recommended Willie join the unit. Willie further mentioned he was soon going to basic training and advance individual training at Fort McClellan, Alabama. He said that after training, he returned and was in the unit with his uncle who was a sergeant in the unit. Willie also said that as a member of the 933rd Military Police Company, he had a two-week paid annual training requirement, and received a monthly check for monthly drills at the Armory. My wife was pregnant with our first child who was born in a few months. As a young working man with a low paying job, and trying to make it financially with an expanding family, joining the Army National Guard sounded very interesting to me. I did have an interest in the military and could learn to be a Military Policeman. I was about to pursue one of my three goals or desires I had while growing up: joining the military. I joined the 933rd Military Police Company in July 1980.

Willie left for his training about a month before I was leaving. We ended up in training battalions next to each other and saw each other on occasions. He was in Alpha Company 10th Battalion and I was in Bravo Company 11th Battalion. I learned plenty while going through the two-part training. Basic training was quite an experience with plenty of physical training and psychological mind games at the hand of our Drill Sergeants. I attended Basic Training at Fort McClellan in February 1981 about seven months after joining the 933rd MP Company. I attended the monthly drills for the seven months before I left for basic training. The seven months of training at the armory before going to basic training came in handy as those of us who went through those drills and marching training did well when taught to march by our new "Fathers and Mothers" we came to call Drill Sergeants. The training was demanding and stressful. I remember arriving at Ft. McClellan, Alabama, and staying with other new recruits at the reception station. As new trainees, we stayed at the reception station and received orientated on what we were about to endure.

We also received what we needed for training such as uniforms and boots. I woke up at 5am in the morning each of my three days to the sound of recruits running and singing military cadences. I thought that in a few days, I would be up running very early while it was still dark. On that third day, us new recruits got our duffle bags and boarded large buses to go to our new training units. The buses arrived at the base and parked. We could see nothing but a bunch a Drill Sergeants with their brown hats standing around. The bus doors opened and two or three Drill Sergeants boarded the bus and started yelling and ordering us off the bus, telling us to get our duffle bags and get off the bus. Once off the bus, the rest of the

Drill Sergeants were yelling and ordering us new recruits to get in line. They were yelling, telling us where we had to go to get linen for our bunks also making us run to get our gear. We had to run everywhere it seemed and all of the time.

On one day we were going to a training site and thought we were going to be transported by the large cattle trucks they used for distance trips. We were surprised when we were told we would be using our leather personnel carriers or LPCs to get to the training. We now knew we would be marching in our boots to get to the training site. During basic training, we were up early and most of the time we trained until late in the evening. There was not much privacy living in an open bay bunking area with 40 new roommates. I decided to attend Sunday church service, as I knew I would need my spiritual focus, along with my physical strength to complete the training. I decided I would be the first person down in the parking lot each morning during basic training for PT or physical training. I got out of bed before everyone else in the barracks, used the restroom with a little privacy as everyone else were sleep, and got down to the parking lot and started stretching and warming up.

When the Drill Sergeants arrived early to wake the troops up they found me warming up in the training parking lot and were impressed. I did this every day we had PT. When we graduated basic training, they gave us passes to go off post if we asked. Many of us had family that attended the basic graduation and looked forward to spending time with family. My wife and toddler son Sylvester Jr. attended the graduation. We spent the weekend together at a local Anniston, Alabama, hotel. I returned to the base on Sunday night to prepare for the start of Advanced Individual Training (AIT) where we learned our military occupational specialty also known as MOS. AIT taught us what we needed to know to be Military Policemen. It was very good training. The training was self-paced, allowing us to speed up a little and take tests when we felt we were ready. We were graded on a Go or No-Go grading system meaning you passed or failed and needed to get more training and re-test if you failed any tests.

Near the end of AIT, my unit First Sergeant informed me that he and other Battalion Sergeants were impressed with my motivation and skill-level. He asked me if I wanted to go on active duty instead of returning to my National Guard Unit. He related I could pick any duty station where there were Military Police stationed. I asked him if that included Schofield Barracks in Hawaii and he said yes. I gave this a little thought, but thanked him, letting him know I wanted to return to my National Guard Unit back home. I finished the Advanced Individual Training a few days early and was ready to head back home. I went to the travel office to book my flight back to Chicago and was told that it would be a day and a half before I could be booked for a flight. I did not want to wait and decided to take a Greyhound bus ride home. This was a 20 hour-ride, but I was ready to leave and thought the ride would be nice. As I was leaving Ft. McClellan with my duffle bag on my back, my Platoon Drill Sergeant called me over and asked me if I was going to say goodbye before leaving. I said goodbye, shook his hand and went on my way. I had an interesting four months at Ft. McClellan, and was thinking to myself, that I never wanted to come back. However, I returned to Ft. McClellan as an Officer in seven years.

CHAPTER TWO

Chasing My Dreams and Goals
Joining the Markham Police Department

I returned home to Chicago from Basic Training and Military Police Advanced Individual Training in late May 1981, rejoining my family and my job working for a company in downtown Chicago known as BMA or Bank Marketing Association, a training and marketing private corporation for banks. I rejoined the 933rd Military Police Company as a squad member in a platoon. I learned plenty of things about soldiering from the seasoned sergeants in my unit, and got to serve with my good friend Willie. Willie and I usually drove together to our monthly drills, as we lived nearby each other. I had moved to the South Suburbs of Chicago. Willie also lived in the South Suburbs. I attended drills, which brought in extra money. I also attended the unit's 2-week summer camps. I was pleased to know that employers are required by law to allow employees to attend National Guard and Reserve duty.

I cannot recall the name, but one of my superiors mentioned to me that I should consider being an Officer. That was very interesting to me as I have a competitive side. I started to look into the requirements of becoming a Commissioned Officer and soon found out that I could enroll again in college, and join the Reserve Officer Training Corps better known as

ROTC. After completing that training program, I was commissioned an Officer with the initial rank of Second Lieutenant. This was very exciting to me, and I decided to give college one more attempt and enrolled at Chicago State University on the south side of Chicago. I soon found out that while Chicago State had an ROTC program, all Military Science courses had to be taken at the University of Illinois' Chicago Circle Campus located in downtown Chicago. This was not an issue because my employer BMA was also downtown. I took my Military Science courses during my lunch break or after work while putting in the hours required at work to maintain my full time status. My supervisor who I will name as Claudia was very supportive.

I was now a Cadet in my Military Police Unit, which changed my status to a hybrid status. I was no longer an enlisted member of my unit and not an Officer either. As a Cadet my rank was a silver small circle. I remember some of the sergeants in my unit called ROTC Cadets "dot heads." I was a very proud dot head as unit members did treat me a little better, and I had more freedom during drills. I was able to maintain good relationships with my good friends who were enlisted. Since I had completed Army Basic and Advanced Individual Training, my ROTC requirement was two years and not the four-year requirement for those with no military training. ROTC students in the first two years normally had ROTC enlisted ranks, if you were in the advance last two years you had Cadet Officer rank structure. I was a good Cadet. In my second and last year I was promoted to Cadet Captain. This promotion gave me three dots on my hat and uniform. It was at this time that I met one of my lifetime and very close friends, William Walker. William was one year behind me in ROTC. William will be mentioned a number of times in my story as our military careers and law enforcement careers have crossed paths for over three decades.

As I was working for BMA and entering my fourth year with the organization after being promoted during my third year to supervisor of shipping and receiving, I became a little frustrated when a colleague and friend, I will name as Tim, was promoted to supervisor of another section in the office. Tim's promotion was after my promotion. We both reported to the same supervisor who I will name as Claudia. There were some office discussions that Tim was making much more money than me although we were both supervisors, and I was senior. I approached my supervisor Claudia and asked her if it was true that Tim made more money than me. I had a good relationship with my supervisor. Claudia told me it was true and said that Tim's section was more technical than running the shipping and receiving room.

A good friend and colleague at the company informed me about the pay disparity between Tim and I. This pay issue may not be viewed as that important, but it was about to change my life and career as my frustration over the pay issue pushed me to look for another job. I applied for a number of positions at different organizations including the United States Post Office, the Illinois State Police, and with the Markham Police Department in South Suburban Markham, Illinois. I took exams for all three of these organizations and passed. I was interviewed by all three organizations and called first by the Markham Police Department. I accepted the offer from the Markham Police Department to become a Police Officer. I was now about to complete the second of my three childhood goals: joining the military, becoming a Police Officer, and being a professional athlete playing football. Obtaining two of my three goals was not bad. By this time I figured out the professional football goal was not obtainable.

I knew the City of Markham existed because my Grandparents William and Rose Jones moved there when I was about eight years old moving from State Way Gardens in Chicago. My grandparents bought a home in Markham where my grandfather resided in almost to the day of his death in 2014. I resigned from BMA, and my second job at Forest City Enterprises, in Burbank, Illinois. I worked for Forest City Enterprises as a

Forklift Driver and Utility person in the evenings, and weekends to make extra money for my family.

I moved my family to Markham, rented a home, and left for the Police Academy in October 1983. Many Suburban Police Departments sent their officers to the Police Training Institute or PTI, a 10-week resident law enforcement program that focused and taught the full range of law enforcement tactics, techniques, search and seizure, arrests, pertinent Illinois law, weapons training, and shooting. The Police Training Institute was held on the campus of the University of Illinois in Champagne, Illinois. It is a very nice facility with very good instructors. I enjoyed the training at PTI and did my best to excel in the various aspects of training from physical fitness to shooting, and the legal exams. All training areas were ranked, and students competed for top honors in shooting and overall scoring. On most weekends I drove home, which was a little over two hours, to spend a quick weekend with my family. My family had grown as I now had my wife and two sons. My second son Lawrence was born in 1982. I returned to PTI on Sunday evenings to get ready for my next week. I was in pretty good shape from my military training and the physical fitness training was pretty easy for me.

I remember my PTI Firearms Instructor often told us that as Police Officers, we needed to be ready and alert. He mentioned four stages of alertness or readiness and said that if you are in Phase I, or the white phase, you are totally relaxed and obviously not alert. He related that if you are in Phase II or the yellow phase, you are relaxed but somewhat alert and aware of things. He further stated that if you are in Phase III or the orange phase, you are alert, aware, and checking things out and ready to respond to situations. Lastly he related if you are in Phase IV or the red phase, your weapon was out and in the ready, in an intense mode expecting danger. I have always remembered the four phases my Instructor told me about, and have tried to use the phases in my career and home life.

I graduated from the Police Training Institute at the top of my class and returned to my home and police department. We had to purchase our own handguns and if you qualified with a shotgun, you could sign out a police shotgun for your shift. However, that weapon had to go back to the police station, you could not take it home. I did not have my own weapon at the time so my grandfather let me borrow his 45-caliber Colt semi-automatic pistol until I made enough money to buy my own duty weapon. In a few months I purchased my duty weapon, a 357 six inch barrel blue steel Colt Python. It was a very nice duty weapon and it shot well. I had a very rewarding career with the Markham Police Department and developed several longtime friends including my very good lifetime friend, the late officer/Sergeant Greg Simmons. I started with the police department with a Field Training Officer or FTO who I will name as Sam. Sam was a very good and detailed officer who retired as a Sergeant. I learned a lot from him.

I was on probation for my first year on the force. I remember my first day at the department I was summoned to meet the Chief of Police. The Chief, who has since passed on, told me I would make it as an officer if I watched out for the three "B's." I asked the Chief what are the three B's. He told me booze, broads, and bucks. I thanked him and always remembered the three B's. I soon learned that many police officers fall susceptible to one or all of the three B'S.

As I was released to patrol duties without my FTO and driving my own assigned squad car, I was very proud and took great pride in my uniform. Markham Police Department officers had to wear hats when outside of the car. Our sergeants got on us when they saw us out of the squad car without our police hats on. I was still performing my military duty attending drills and the two-week summer camp. People around town often saw me in either Army fatigues or my dark blue police shirt and light blue police pants and matching light blue tie. I responded to the full range of calls for assistance or assigned calls such as burglaries, robberies, domestic violence and car theft. Early on in my career with the Markham Police Department, I responded to a call with another more senior officer, my very good friend Greg Simmons. There was some kind of disturbance and Greg and I responded. Usually with a disturbance or domestic violence or other potentially dangerous calls, two units or more were dispatched. Greg and I arrived on the scene and were told about a man who was causing problems. We approached the fellow and to my surprise he turned around with a closed fist striking me in my right jaw with a stinging blow, and took off running south down the street. I was upset about this blow to a uniformed officer, and took off running behind him. Greg got in his squad car to also pursue the fellow. I caught this guy and he tried to fight me again. This time he scored no blows and was physically restrained by me after a very physical wrestling match. As Greg approached, I had this guy handcuffed and he was apologizing to me with the statement "I am sorry sir for hitting you." He was taken to the station and charged. I had found out that this particular guy was known for burning homes down and later was arrested, convicted and sentenced to prison for setting fire to the home of one my colleagues on the police force, almost killing him. The officer told us that the reason he got out of the burning house alive was that one of his dogs led him out. He lost his second dog in that fire. Officer Greg Simmons and I often worked midnight shifts together, and handled a number of violent offenders and cases. I will discuss a few of these cases and situations, as I think some of the cases or situations are interesting, and may be even funny as I look back.

While serving as a police officer, and national guardsman, I was also trying to complete my undergraduate degree at Chicago State and complete my ROTC requirement to become an officer. The police department was very good about allowing me time off to attend to my military requirements. I worked a lot of midnight shifts so I could take my college classes during the day or evenings at Chicago State. I had finished my Military Science requirements at the University of Illinois'

Chicago Circle Campus, which included Advance Training Camp in 1982, the year before joining the police department. ROTC advanced training was a requirement before becoming an officer at the Second Lieutenant rank. ROTC advance training was eight weeks at Ft. Lewis in Seattle, Washington. Thousands of Cadets from the same 4th ROTC region attended this session. I completed the intense training, and upon completion of my second year in ROTC in December 1983, I received my Commission as an Officer. I was now a Second Lieutenant and no longer called a "dot head" or Cadet. I was a police officer with Markham PD and a Second Lieutenant assigned as a Platoon Leader in the 138th Military Intelligence Battalion in the United States Army Reserve. Professionally, 1983 was a very good year for me.

Working in the police department was very rewarding and interesting. At the time and during my four years we changed shifts every 28 days. This was very tough on the home life, as officers rarely got one of the few rotations with weekends off. As police officers, we worked just about every holiday. Spending quality time with our families was sometimes difficult. I had a very busy schedule, and missed a number of family gatherings. Most officers dreaded making arrests at the end of shift because we had to complete the arrest paper work and reports, and get the documents approved before we went home. We also had to appear in court at the initial appearance for the subject arrested. This might mean we needed to return in the morning after an afternoon arrest, or stay over for the hearing after a hard stressful midnight shift. I had one goal each day of each shift: to get home safe and sound. I kept at the forefront of my mind the four phases of readiness and alertness that my range instructor told me about at the Police Training Institute. I usually stayed in the yellow and orange phases while on duty. I often traded my assigned day shift to work the midnight or afternoon shift so I could finish my undergraduate college requirements during regular school hours. I learned many years later that my former police department went to a 90-day shift rotation, which in my view provides a much better quality of life for officers and their families. I was happy for my old police colleagues that the old 28-day shift rotations had ended.

The midnight shift is where my good friend and police colleague Greg and I worked many of the shifts when I served with Markham PD. One of the things officers were scolded for was a stolen stripped car located in their zone during the midnight shift, or shortly thereafter. That happened to officers including me. However, when we patrolled aggressively, auto thieves looked elsewhere and did not drop a stripped stolen car in our zone. I was in a few car chases with auto thieves and tried to make it clear to a local group of car thieves who stole cars in the southern end of Chicago and the south suburbs, that they ran a significant risk of getting caught messing around in any zone I was working. Some auto thieves got up and out early in the morning to meet and plan their miscreant activities with the stolen car business. On one midnight shift, I located a garage some auto thieves were using to strip cars. The garage had two stolen cars in it that had not been stripped of parts. The two cars were recovered and returned to their owners in good condition. The only damage to both vehicles was the steering column. The steering columns had been damaged when the auto thieves stole the vehicles. I was very proud of my police work, and praised by my superiors and colleagues for my efforts.

I was a pretty good shot on the range with my duty weapon. One of the Department Range Officers who was the coordinator of the Markham Police Department Shooting Team approached me and asked me if I wanted to join the shooting team. I was more than happy to accept the offer and joined the team. Being on the shooting team was nice and it allowed me extra time to shoot on the range practicing for tournaments. I stayed on the shooting team until I left the Police Department. Our team competed in several shooting tournaments in the Chicago area, competing with other police and sheriff's departments. In 1984 and in 1985, I received shooting trophies in the Mid-Mark Top Gun Shoot Off for 1st Expert. In the 1984 Mid-Mark Team Top Gun competition, the Markham Police Department Team won the Top Team Shooting Trophy. The team was comprised of four officers from the police department. Being a good shot assisted me later, as you will find, in my career with the department when I responded to a situation involving a truck company strike where vicious dogs were inserted on the grounds of the truck company to attack people still working.

While serving as a police officer in Markham, I had the privilege and honor of being elected the first President for the Markham Police Department Fraternal Order of Police or FOP, Lodge 199. Our Department had formalized an FOP lodge joining many other FOP lodges in Illinois and across the country. I served as the presiding officer of our meetings, and enjoyed my tenure working on a number of labor related issues affecting our department and officers. I still have my presiding officer gavel to this day, which I am still very proud of.

Getting back to patrol duties, Officer Greg and I met when we could during our midnight shifts for a cup of coffee and to discuss police business along with whatever was on our minds. If either one of us needed a break from action, we parked in one of our many isolated locations we termed as "holes" and let the other know where we were using a code. On occasion, we both met at a location to get a break. We often backed each other up, and responded to a myriad of calls catching bad guys in the act or as they we trying to get away. I remember one call of a burglary in progress, where several units responded very quickly to the aid of a lady homeowner. We arrived so quickly we caught the guys in progress and returned the lady's items that were being carted off. She was so happy and thankful that she wrote a nice letter to our Police Chief mentioning our names and our quick response describing how we caught the bandit red-handed. I received and still possess a number of these letters, but always remembered what my Chief told me about all the "atta-boy" letters I received. My Chief told me that if I received one "all-shit" complaint, all the "attaboy" letters would be wipe away. I tried to limit the "all-shit" complaints, and enjoyed the "atta-boy" letters.

While working midnights, I responded to a number of bar fights. Our town's local bars and pubs stayed open to 4am. A number of residents, and a number of officers including myself did not like that the bars and pubs were open to 4am. The extra hours the bars were open often resulted in driving under the influence arrests. However, we mostly had to deal with drunken, and disorderly bar patrons trying to or actually whipping up on someone.

On one midnight shift, as soon as we checked in for work, we were told to hurry up and head to the east side of town to zone 384 to a major bar fight or brawl. The entire afternoon shift was at this bar trying to stop the brawl. However, according to 911 callers into the police station, the afternoon shift was getting the worse of the brawl. As I was getting my gear and leaving the station, one of the police dispatchers was taking a call and the caller said our afternoon shift needed more officers. I traveled to the bar with lights and siren to assist my afternoon shift colleagues. Upon my arrival, I noticed several of my colleagues battling bar patrons and some of the officers on the ground taking blows and giving blows to violent bar patrons. I immediately started pulling bar patrons off of our officers and quickly restrained them. I did this about three or four times reestablishing control of the situation and telling all of the patrons who were not under arrest to go home because we were closing the bar. One bar patron who was not arrested started telling the patrons that they did not have to go home or anywhere. I instructed this loud mouth to go home. The guy started telling me he was not going anywhere, and that he was a Marine and could handle himself well. I moved to arrest him and he took off running, but he did not get far before I caught up with him and arrested him. Order was restored.

On another midnight shift I was driving to my usual zone area 384 on the east side of town from zone area 385 where the Police Station is located, and observed a three car accident on a main road as cars appeared to be fleeing the parking lot of a bar. I called in the accident, checked for injuries and noted none, and was then assigned to back up the zone 385 car at a bar fight near the location I was at. When I called in my arrival and entered without a second unit, what I observed was right out of a movie. There were broken bottles and glasses everywhere. Tables were broken and upside down. Men seemed to be hiding or crouched down behind their ladies. The bouncer, a pretty nice size guy, was against one of the walls bleeding from the face. There was one rather large African American male standing like a champion with everyone appearing to be afraid of him for some obvious good reason. I had my nightstick in my hand and asked what was going on. One petite attractive African American lady approached me and related that the big guy asked her to dance, she refused and he then started causing a scene. She further related that the bouncer tried to control the situation and the big guy punched him in the face. I was still in the lounge by myself trying to let some time lapse for the regular zone car to arrive and assist me. I directed the big guy who had beat up several people to step outside and grabbed his elbow. He immediately said, get your "effing" hands off me. His friend in the bar told him to step outside and that he did not need further issues. The big guy did step outside. The zone car arrived. The zone officer was a more senior white male. I briefed the zone officer of the situation, and he reached to grab the big guy's arm. The big guy told the officer to get your "effing white hands off of me" and went to swing at the zone officer. I caught the big guy's arm preventing him from hitting my colleague. We wrestled with the guy to restrain him. I put restraining techniques on him, we cuffed him, and I transported him to the police station.

After arriving at the station, I instructed the arrestee to exit my squad car so I could take him into the station. He told me he was not getting out the car and said "f**k you" saying the full words to me. I was fed up with this guy, and decided to lock him in the car and go into the station to my locker and get my mace. I returned and asked him one more time to get out of my squad car and he again told me "F me." I used some mace on him and he immediately asked to get out of my car. I took him into the station and processed him. I also assisted my colleague the zone officer who had to take statements from the nine victims the big guy beat up, including the bouncer who also came to the station to give a statement. As I resumed my patrol duties, I had to leave the windows down as I had mace still in my squad car. I kind of regretted using mace but felt I had no choice. The arrestee was convicted of nine counts of battery related to the bar brawl. We later learned the big guy was the owner's nephew who was visiting the establishment from Chicago.

I recall another midnight shift where I responded to a bar fight or altercation. In this particular instance, the perpetrator was a white male in one of the town's white bar establishments. He was belligerent, cursing and it appeared he had the bar under siege. I asked patrons what had happened and they told me he had fought with two patrons and was belligerent and cursing at everyone including some of the female patrons. I instructed this guy to step out. He told me he was not going anywhere and started cursing me. I went to remove him from the bar and he started to fight me. I restrained and hand cuffed this guy pretty quickly. I left the bar with this arrestee to a standing ovation from all of the patrons in the bar.

I will discuss one last bar situation and move on. On another midnight shift, I was called to a shooting at a local popular nightclub and bar where blacks frequented. I arrived on the scene and noted a local town troublemaker and bully who appeared to be shot and bleeding. A few people were standing outside of the bar nearby the victim who was shot. I asked these bystanders what happened and was told the victim was causing problems with another guy, bullying the guy, when the other guy pulled a handgun and shot him. I was told the shooting occurred inside the bar and the victim ran outside and collapsed. I asked about the shooter to get a description to call it in, as the shooter had fled the scene. More squad cars arrived along with an ambulance. I went back inside the bar observing people washing blood off the wall and people still dancing to loud music and drinking. I directed the DJ to stop the music and ordered the club closed over the objection of the club manager. The department's duty detectives arrived which was the case when major crimes involved murder or serious injury. That night was the last time the local bully would bother anyone as he died at that club succumbing from the gunshot.

There was one midnight shift situation that still bothers me when I think about it. I was working one of the west zones and received a call about two or three in the morning to respond to a call of a woman sitting in a car on the driver's side with the door open on Interstate 57 north of 167th street which was Illinois State Police jurisdiction. On occasion, it took the Illinois State Troopers patrolling the highways some time to respond to situations, and my department would be called to respond or assist the Troopers as they covered plenty of ground and their back up units may be far away. As I got on the highway and pulled up to the vehicle, I observed an African American woman sitting in the driver's seat, her head bent to the left and her left leg outside of the open door. I approached using careful tactics not knowing if anyone was in the trunk or back seat. I noticed her to be unresponsive and from my view appeared to be deceased. She had what appeared to be a gunshot wound to her lower abdomen. I called in what I had observed to our dispatch and requested an ambulance and the estimated time of the State Police. As the State Police arrived, two other Markham Police units responded. This scene and situation was turned over to the State Police and their crime scene units. To this day, I have never found out if this case was ever solved. At times, I still see the picture of this beautiful young woman and victim sitting in that car.

I worked my share of afternoon shifts as well. The afternoon shift was 3:45 pm to 11:45 in the evening. The summer months seemed to be the busiest as more people would be out and about. In the cold months in the Chicago area, people tend to be in the house more. The afternoon shift presented the usual type of calls and patrol duties such as shoplifting arrests, responding to alarms at homes and businesses, robberies, domestic violence and other family issues, responding to accidents, traffic control, parking enforcement and writing traffic tickets. I remember a number of interesting cases or situations. One afternoon shift I observed an erratic driver on one of the town's main streets. The vehicle had out of state license plates. I made a traffic stop, called it in and approached the driver and observed him to be under influence of something. I placed him under arrest and called to have his car towed. Our department policy called for an inventory of the vehicle contents. This vehicle was modified in the interior of the unit and the trunk. I discovered over 40 bags of marijuana in the car, which was seized and placed in evidence. My department contacted the Drug Enforcement Administration to find out if they wanted to take the case, which they did. When I went to court for the court hearing the case had been removed and I was not ever contacted about the case, which I thought was interesting.

On another evening shift while assigned to zone or area 385, I was assigned to a call of an unwanted individual on top of a garage who would not get off at the owner's request. I arrived at the location along with a backup unit shortly thereafter to assist me, and was briefed of the situation. I observed the guy sitting on top of the garage and asked him to come down so the matter could be resolved. He told me he was not getting off the garage roof. I again asked him to get down and asked what his problem was. He again stated he was not coming down and we should leave him alone. I told the guy the owner did not want him on the roof, and that he was trespassing. The guy again refused to come down and said we should leave him the "f" alone. I pleaded with the guy to get off of the top of the garage roof, telling him I did not want to climb up to get him. I let the guy know if I had to climb onto the roof, he would certainly be arrested. He still refused to come down from the roof of the garage. I had to climb to the top of the garage roof, and gave this guy some assistance getting off the roof. He was arrested and charged with trespassing and disorderly conduct. I must admit that after pleading with him to get off of the garage roof, I was frustrated as I had to climb to the top of the garage roof to physically get him down.

The population of the City of Markham is mainly black and white. As a uniformed police officer, I was a witness to racism. I remember on one afternoon shift I responded to a call of a woman laid out on the ground in the middle of a street on the west side of town. The west side of town is where most of the white population lived. This area also included a small portion of the black population. The east side of town has a population that is pretty much all black. I arrived on the scene to see a white female laid out in the middle of the street. I pulled up with my lights activated to render assistance to what I thought was an injured lady. I walked up to this lady to see what the situation was and asked her what was wrong. She immediately got up and said: "get away from me nigger." I responded by asking what did you say to me? She then said you heard me and repeated her nasty comment. I said a little something to her that was not that nice, and left the scene calling in that it was an intoxicated lady and she was out of the street.

In 1985 while in my second year with Markham Police Department, I had my third child. Erika Jones was born, my first daughter, and I was very excited. After Erika was born, my good friend and colleague on the police force Greg, along with some other officers on the Department and I went to a cop friendly watering hole or bar to celebrate her birth. We had a great time celebrating. It was a night to remember, to say the least. I was very happy, and enjoyed both of my careers although the shift work at the Police Department made it difficult to spend quality time with my family.

I was assigned another call of a disturbance in zone 385. A white female who met me at the door asked, "don't you all have any white officers working this area?" The lady further stated "I do not want any "nigger cops coming to my house." I said a little something to her that was not that nice and left her home. I contacted the police dispatch station that said the caller did not need assistance. I resumed my patrol and about five minutes later I received a call from my Sergeant to return to the station. My Sergeant, who was a very good supervisor who I will name as Sergeant B who was white, informed me that the lady at the house where I was assigned to respond, called and said that I said something that was not nice to her. Sergeant B asked me if it was true what the woman or now complainant said as far as my comments to her before I left her residence. I told him it was true. He asked me why I said what I said and I told him what she had said to me. That was the end of the matter. I worked a lot of shifts with Sergeant B and he knew I was a very good responsible and respectful officer. I heard Sergeant B passed on a number of years ago. He was a very good police professional.

Another Sergeant on the department was Sergeant OT. Sergeant OT was a jovial but witty guy. Some of the African American officers said to me that Sergeant OT usually assign African American officers to the east side of town with the notion that we could better handle police matters involving our community. I found that Sergeant OT tended to assign blacks officers to the east zone where the majority of black residents lived. I remember one time a few officers gathered at a meeting location in town with Sergeant OT for some kind of briefing or information update. We were discussing a situation, and Sergeant OT tore a very small piece of paper about an inch long an inch wide from his notebook. He gave the small piece of paper to me, and told me to "write down everything you know about law enforcement on this paper and try and fill it up." We all got a good chuckle as I was the junior officer and I got the point, that I was the junior officer.

Domestic violence cases were usual calls during the afternoon shifts. I responded to a number of these calls and was always very careful as I was trained that these calls could get very tricky, and both individuals, the complainant and assailant, involved could turn on you. This happened on one occasion where I was dispatched to a domestic violence call. I arrived to the residence with my back up unit and observed a woman who was physically assaulted with visible bruises to her face and her clothes disheveled and torn. The husband was hiding in the house and after we located him, and were arresting him, the abused woman attacked me jumping on my back stating in a loud voice "do not arrest or hurt my husband." Unfortunately, we had to arrest them both. The lady was released and the husband held overnight for a court hearing.

I recall a situation while working the day shift in zone 384 involving a large trucking company in an industrial area. The trucking company was experiencing a labor strike. I received a call to respond to the trucking company as there was an incident involving dogs inserted on the grounds of the plant. I arrived, called in my arrival time, got out of my vehicle and was immediately met by trucking company officials including the plant security officer. These officials were explaining the situation that two rather large Doberman Pinchers were inserted on the grounds of the plants and attacking people. As I was getting this briefing, I observed the two dogs in hot pursuit of a man who was running right at us. This man was in trouble and I could visibly see blood coming from the crouch area of his trousers. I quickly thought to myself that the dogs were about to catch this man and finish him off. I immediately drew my 357 colt python revolver, targeted the lead Doberman and fired one round which dropped the dog. A backup officer arrived, drew his weapon and fired at the second Doberman and missed. The security officer who was to my right suddenly drew his weapon and fired across me. I was very upset by his actions, as he shot across me. I fired another shot that dropped the second Doberman. I immediately scolded the security officer for shooting across me, letting him know that was not a safe thing to do. My shooting skills as I mentioned earlier were pretty good as it can be a challenge to shoot at and hit moving targets. I had no problem with my target acquisition. I called in for an ambulance for the injured plant employee who was still bleeding profusely with blood dripping from his crouch area. I radioed for canine assistance to remove the carcasses of the dogs as I knew the dogs had to be examined for rabies since one or both of the dogs had bit and drew blood from this victim. I obtained all of the relevant information for my report and left the scene once everything required of me was done.

I had an interesting coincidence while back on the campus of Chicago State the very next day from the dog-shooting incident during one of my Saturday classes. I noticed the last name of my Ethics Professor was the same last name of the dog attack victim. I explained to my professor at a break in the class that I assisted a gentleman at a trucking plant the day before with the same last name as his who was attacked by dogs. The professor informed me that the man was his brother. He told me his brother was doing okay and thanked me for my service and assistance to his brother. The Ethic's course was not an easy course. I was happy as I received a B grade. My Professor and his brother were not from the United States and the names were not common which drew my attention and made me mention the name to my Professor. I had a couple of other dog incidents while a police officer at Markham. I answered a business alarm call one evening in zone 385. I responded before my backup unit arrived. On all alarm calls two units were dispatched. While inside the gate of the premise, I heard a dog barking loudly and charging very hard at me. I noticed that the dog was a large German Shepherd. My weapon was already out as I was answering a burglar alarm call. I yelled at the dog in a very loud voice saying "come on, keep coming at me and I will blow your "effing head off." I knew I had to mean business and the dog had to understand I would deliver on my statement. This dog started applying the brakes trying to stop and a cloud of dust appeared. The dog did stop and did an about face going in the other direction. I was very happy I did not have to shoot this large and intelligent dog. I secured the gate and called in that the business was secure and resumed my patrol duties.

On another business burglar alarm call, I entered the premise prior to my backup unit arriving. My gun was out due to the nature of the call, but I felt a presence behind me and thought to myself that I may be done in. I turned around and observed another large dog, which had sneaked up on me. As soon as I made eye contact with this dog, it started to growl and I knew it would attack me. I raised my 357 colt python up to the level of the dog's head and talked to the animal. I told him in a firm loud voice what I had told the other dog "come on, keep coming at me and I will blow your "effing head off." This dog must have also sensed that I was all business and dropped his growl and went about his business. I decided I should wait for backup before entering a premise on these business burglar alarm calls, because I really thought someone had the drop on me.

I had knowledge of a small organized drug group where there were two brothers leading the group who lived on the southeast side of town in Markham. Some residents who lived nearby the two brothers told me they had seen the guys and other associates selling drugs out of, and nearby, their home. These residents told me they did not want to get involved with having to be a witness. They also said they did not want their names associated with the information they provided. I let them know I understood and respected their wishes. I shared this information with other officers in the department and conducted extra patrols in the area where I observed some of the group's early morning suspicious activity. I stopped the brothers on occasion for suspicious activity and traffic violations and let them know I was aware of some of their criminal activity. I also mentioned to them I would do my job and arrest them if I caught either of them selling drugs in town and would report their illegal activity with the Drug Enforcement Administration.

Subsequent to my encounters with the brothers, I met with a young man who lived in the area near the brothers. This young man who was a friend of a couple of other guys in the community that I knew fairly well, and also friendly with the two brothers, told me he had heard that the two brothers were very upset with me stopping them and looking into their drug business. This young man further let me know that the two drug-dealing brothers were talking about placing a contract on my life. I thanked the young man for the information and asked him to pass a response back to the brothers and their associates. My message was that if they send someone to target and try and kill me, they better not miss. I was on high alert. I further told the young man to let the brothers know that after I took care of the person they sent for me, I was coming straight for the two brothers to take care of business with them and it would not be pretty. As far I as I know, the message I sent to the two brothers and their associates resonated, as I never had anyone target me or attack me and the two brothers drug activity in my city curtailed.

As I mentioned, I was very busy serving as a police officer, serving in the Army Reserves, working on my undergraduate degree and being a husband and father. I was at Chicago State University conducting business when I bumped into my longtime and very good friend William Walker. I had not seen Bill in a while, and there was a good reason for that. He had been busy himself. We were both in the Army Reserves and both serving as police officers. William Walker or Bill as most of us call him had worked as a Railroad Police Officer in Chicago. I was excited to tell him I had joined the Police Department in Markham and proudly displayed my badge and credentials. Bill related that my credentials were "very nice." He then stated "you have police powers in the whole state of Illinois, wow that's great." I should have known I was being setup for something. I thought Bill was giving me a little praise.

At this point Bill displayed his new Drug Enforcement Administration credentials showing me he was now a DEA Special Agent. He read a few words from his credentials that said he was authorized to enforce crimes against the United States of America. Bill knew and I had to admit that his very nice credentials made my Markham badge and credentials look inferior, which of course it was. I gave him a few choice words and we both went our own ways. We saw each other an hour or two later while still on campus and had a good laugh about the credentials "show down." Bill and I kept in touch over the years and grew together professionally and personally, as this book will further depict. We have supported, challenged and competed with each other for many years and always with each other's best interests in mind. Bill is a very good lifelong friend and brother as well as a few other guys I will talk about.

Getting back to the Markham Police Department, on another afternoon shift, I reported to the squad room for duty along with other members of the afternoon shift. Some of us noticed a flyer on our bulletin board, which was an announcement about openings in the United States Marshals Service. The announcement was titled "Wanted Deputy U.S. Marshals." Two other officers and I were trying to figure out what the announcement was about as we had heard of U.S. Marshals, but thought the agency expired with the end of the Wild West. The two officers that took the Marshals Service exam with me did not pass. However, I did pass. At this time, my family grew in December of 1986 as my 4th child and 3rd son Sean Jones was born.

The hiring process for the Marshals Service took nearly 8-months. I went through an extensive background check as a part of the process. I continued to perform my job as a police officer and duties as an officer with my Reserve Unit. While assigned as a detective for a brief stint, I was involved in the investigation of a home invasion from Oak Lawn Police Department, another South Suburban Illinois Police Department. I was living in the town of Hazel Crest, Illinois, which borders Markham, Illinois, to the south. There was a police broadcast of a crime with a description of the car. While driving home near my apartment complex, I just happened to observe a car fitting that description. I used my radio to call in the license plate and the location of the vehicle, informing the dispatcher that I thought this was the vehicle involved in the home invasion. I asked for back up from both Hazel Crest Police Department and my department. The vehicle in question was parked near my apartment complex. I followed and parked nearby and called in my exact location. Two individuals got out of the vehicle and I approached them with my badge in one hand and weapon in the other ordering them to place their hands on the car. The backup units from my department and Hazel Crest Police Department arrived to assist. This was the vehicle involved with the home invasion and there was property from the Oak Lawn residence inside in plain sight. The individuals were arrested and turned over to the Oak Lawn Police Department as their detectives arrived to take custody of the suspects and the property. I received a nice certificate of Honorable Mention from Oak Lawn Police Department for my efforts with the case.

I enjoyed my nearly four years as a police officer with the Markham Police Department. I learned a lot about policing and communities. I understood the importance of local businesses in communities as businesses contributed to the well-being of the town or city. While working as a police officer in Markham, I also worked part time security jobs at one of the town's junior high schools during basketball games and also provided security at the town's shopping mall. These jobs helped with paying the bills for my growing family. I actually enjoyed working security at the basketball games, watching the youngsters play ball.

As my background investigation to join the Marshals Service was getting close to being completed, I was still happy working with my good friends and colleagues on the police force. My background investigation to become a Deputy United States Marshal was being completed by a Senior Deputy Marshal in the Chicago office who was also a military reservist and a great guy. As he was working on my background he spoke with me on occasion, keeping me posted on the status of his work. I told him I was testing for the Sergeant position with my department and even at my patrolman's salary, I was going lose money at least initially by accepting the job as a new Deputy Marshal. I was not at the time sure about joining the Marshals Service and taking an assignment out of the area. I asked the Senior Deputy Marshal about details of the job of a Deputy Marshal, and he referred me to other new Deputies working in the Chicago office to talk with them to get a feel for the job. This is when I first met another colleague and lifelong friend, Herman Brewer.

Herman was relatively new on the job having started the year before me. I called him and introduced myself telling him I was an applicant for the job as a Deputy Marshal. I asked Herman about the job, and what his thoughts were about the job since he was already on the job. Herman was very frank and told me "it is not a bad job if you do not mind sitting in court with prisoners for the first couple of years and transporting prisoners." I thought about what he said and had a bit of trepidation, as I was use to the freedom of rolling around in my police squad car, making arrests and chasing car thieves. I was getting a little tired of the bar fights and thought a change may be a good thing. Now my concern was if I hired by the Marshals Service, where was I going to be assigned. I wanted Chicago or the Northern District of Illinois, but knew the agency placed new hires where they needed them.

While patrolling another zone, 386, I met a young man who was interested in joining the police department. He asked me about the department and I briefed him on the job and how to come on board. This young man came on the Markham Police Department as I was leaving to join the United States Marshals Service. Years later, he also followed me to the Marshals Service and we continue to be friends and colleagues. I received a notice of hiring from Marshals Service Headquarters to start the academy in March 1987. I accepted the job offer. My assignment was to the Marshals office in the Southern District of New York. Although I accepted the job offer, I knew I had some time to reconsider. I was not sold on moving my family to New York City as I did not know anyone there and knew it was very expensive to live there. I also had a requirement to complete my Military Officer Basic Course at the United States Army

Military Police School, which at the time was located at Fort McClellan, Alabama.

Both the Marshals Academy and the Officer Basic Course were at the same time. I figured the Marshals Service would be amenable to letting me attend their next training class, which started in July 1987. My Military Police Officer Basic Course was four months and would end three days before the next Marshals Academy and Criminal Investigator School located at the Federal Law Enforcement Training Center in Brunswick, Georgia. I wrote the Marshals Service Headquarters submitting a copy of my military orders to Fort McClellan asking for the July class. I was relieved and happy to receive written notice that I was assigned to the July class, which meant I had more time to contemplate the job offer in New York, which I was having difficulty making a final decision. My research into the prospect of working in New York did not help me much, as I found out that new Deputy Marshals assigned to work there had to partner as roommates living four to an apartment. These deputies were eligible to receive food stamps because of their starting salary, and the high cost of living in New York. I knew if I accepted the assignment in New York, I could not afford to move my family there.

CHAPTER THREE

Transition and a New Beginning with the United States Marshals Service

I had a very busy year in 1987. I completed the 4-month Officer Basic Course at Fort. McClellan, Alabama. I also joined the United States Marshals Service completing the four months of training at the Federal Law Enforcement Training Center in Glynco, Georgia. While at Fort McClellan, Alabama, I received a call from a family member back home in Illinois. I was told I had a letter from the U. S. Marshals Service. I asked the family member to open the envelope and read the letter. The letter was from a lady from the personnel office at Marshals Service Headquarters. It informed me there was an opening in Chicago and asked if I would like that assignment instead of the Southern District of New York in Manhattan.

I was elated, obtained the contact information for the lady, and called her the next day accepting the offer to be assigned in my hometown of Chicago. The Senior Deputy Marshal working on my background investigation had convinced the District Chief Deputy Ed Scheu to contact Marshals Service Headquarters to ask that I be assigned to fill a vacancy in the Chicago office. Chief Ed Scheu and I got to know each other quite well over the years, and remain very good friends. I am very grateful for the efforts of the Senior Deputy Marshal for all of his efforts to get me assigned to the Chicago office. After I completed my Military Police Officer Basic Course, I returned home for a three day weekend before heading to Glynco, Georgia, for the Marshals Training.

The training started with an eight week Criminal Investigator course. This course was intense and studying was very important. Our class had a couple of class coordinators assigned from the Marshals Service who assisted us trainees, making sure we did all of the requirements the Marshals Service had for us when we were not in the Criminal Investigator classes. We were also introduced to our physical fitness instructor who I will name as Mr. Fitness who was very intense. He was with us each day in the mornings for our runs and in the evenings for our afterhours training. He made us all take aerobics. Some of us in the class, me included, thought aerobic training was a joke. It was not. It was hard physical training and we usually finished a day's training with a sweat pile under us and our t-shirts soaking wet. I arrived at the Federal Law Enforcement Training Center (FLETC) in top shape. I had just completed another 4-month intense training program with the Army. To finish my Officer Basic Course, my class had to run 10 miles with our team chief who was an Army Major that loved to run. The Major appeared to enjoy running us lieutenants even more. After my Officer Basic Course, I was ready for the Marshals Service physical training program. I am a huge fan of Mr. Fitness who retired a number of years ago. Mr. Fitness was in tremendous physical shape and did his best to make sure he taught us to be prepared both physically and mentally for the job. Mr. Fitness loved his job and is, in my thoughts, a legend for what he accomplished during his many years as a fitness instructor at FLETC.

When my Marshals training class conducted our first physical fitness assessment, I came in second on the run out of 48 students. The one student who beat me was a long distance runner. Eventually as we continued to train and run, more of my classmates improved their fitness. I had no problem with sit-ups or pushups as I always could do those exercises from my days playing football. My Marshals class was a very good class. A large number of our class members were former police officers or sheriff's deputies. There were three other guys from the Chicago area in my class, two were assigned to the Chicago office which is the main office in the District, and the third guy assigned to the sub office in Rockford, Illinois, about 80 miles west of Chicago. We all looked forward to the weekends while at the academy, but made sure we studied during the week and on weekends, as the legal exams were very tough and we only had one test to fail. If we failed a second test, we were on your way home. The legal exams focused on legal and illegal searches and seizures in homes and vehicles. I remember failing one legal exam by a question or two. I think it was the second exam. So I had to make sure I had no further mishaps with those exams. Thank God, I did not. One of our classmates failed a second exam. This student was moved out right away, and there was no saying goodbye.

Our weekends for the most part were spent on St. Simons Island, which is very close to Glynco, Georgia. The Island had several nice bars and clubs. We usually jumped in a car with a classmate who drove down or took a cab to go out and return, which worked out well since we were enjoying the libations and the time off. I went home one of the weekends to spend a little time with my kids. As I mentioned, 1987 was a very busy year for me with two 4-month training requirements. Everyone with the exception of the one guy who failed the second exam completed the Criminal Investigator course and went on to the next phase of the 4-month program, the Marshals Academy. This course was about eight weeks and focused more on the Marshals Service and being a Deputy Marshal. Both of the Criminal Investigator and Marshals Service training courses were very good. I enjoyed the training, which included a lot of shooting on the range and driving courses. The Marshals Service program at FLETC was well known and respected. The Border Patrol 22-week training program in my assessment was the second best training program next to the Marshals

Service. I had heard a number of people say the Marshals Service and Border Patrol programs were very tough programs with good discipline and training.

We lost one other classmate just a few days before graduation and our departure from FLETC. We had completed all of our training requirements to graduate and there were plenty of celebrating and partying. One of our classmates had been warned about too much partying in a prior situation, as this student had been late for class after a late night of partying. The student was out celebrating the end of training, and missed a few hours on the last day of training before graduation. This was a sad situation as the decision makers decided not to graduate him and sent him home on the eve of the graduation. All of our families who were coming for the graduation had arrived for the much-anticipated event. The student who had missed time on the last day of class was being dismissed from the training program. He also had family arrive for the graduation. However, it was very sad as this student did not graduate. The graduation was very nice and very special.

The Director of the Marshals Service at the time, Mr. Henry Hudson, gave the graduation commencement speech and gave each of us our United States Marshals Service credentials. Each of us stopped on stage obtained our credentials and got a picture taken with the Director. We were all very proud and happy to complete this major law enforcement course. My wife arrived the night before the graduation from Chicago to attend the ceremony. After four months without a badge and gun, I received both and started a new career with a federal law enforcement agency. I could not wait to tell my good friend Bill Walker that I was now authorized to enforce the laws against the United States of America just like he was.

As a new Deputy Marshal in the Northern District of Illinois, Chicago office I was assigned to the General Operations section like all new Deputies. As my good friend Herman Brewer told me months earlier, I was looking at a year or two of what we call "hooking and hauling prisoners." I worked on various court hearings and trials with federal pretrial detainees.

Some court cases were very interesting and some were not. I picked up a very good understanding of court language and demeanor. Many cases at the time were drug related. A number of other cases had notoriety because the defendants were celebrities or politicians who got into trouble for the love of money. The district office like many other Marshals Service districts offices had a list posted with names of deputies for rotation to travel on special assignments. These assignments were for three week details to other districts to assist with major or high threat trials. We were assigned to court security duty, prisoner transportation teams or the prisoner security teams on these special assignments. I looked forward to the assignments, as the out of town assignments broke up the monotony of being in court hooking and hauling prisoners in my home district.

My first special assignment was to the District of New Jersey. I was assigned to a mob trial providing court security. I assisted the prisoner teams. We secured the mob guys bringing them back and forth to court. The defendants were traditional Italian mob guys just like I had seen on television. The trial was held from Mondays to Thursdays. On Fridays, deputies like me assigned to assist with the trial, were assigned to work with the district's fugitive team, which I enjoyed. On each of the Fridays working the detail, I partnered with a deputy marshal assigned to the warrant or fugitive squad helping to find wanted fugitives. On one of the Fridays, I was assigned to work with a Jersey City Police Sergeant. This guy was a very well known policeman and we traveled to various communities from low income housing to more elaborate areas. This sergeant was a very cool white guy who loved the cold weather or so it seemed. It was January 1988, and he kept his windows rolled down and wore short sleeves. He told me you could not hear the noises of the streets if your windows were rolled up. I knew he was right, but it was cold and I rolled my window partially up. I learned a lot from this sergeant. His policing was a very good example of community policing. He knew his community, and his community knew him, including businesses. I was just beginning to learn and enjoy one of the job duties of a deputy marshal; hunting fugitives. The mob trial lasted for a number of months. After I returned home to my district, I found out that the mob guys were all acquitted of all charges.

Getting back to the district office in Chicago, it was business as usual. Back to hooking and hauling prisoners from jail facilities to the courthouse, and returning them to the jail facilities. The Chicago office had several sections or units. One unit was the General Operations squad, and another was the Warrant Squad. The third unit was the Special Services squad, which handled seized assets working with other federal agencies to conduct seizures of illegally obtained assets from drug dealers. Herman Brewer and I were called upon quite often to do the jail runs. At the time we were new or junior deputies. As I mentioned, Herman was on the job almost a year before me. The jail runs included securing and moving prisoners back and forth from the Bureau of Prison's Metropolitan Correctional Center to the federal courthouse. There was a roster for jail run duties. Two deputies were assigned for two weeks to come to work early to go to the Metropolitan Correctional Center or MCC and collect prisoners for the day and bring them to the courthouse. Chicago was a busy district and sometimes we needed to make two or maybe three jail runs with the van or bus to move the prisoners to the courthouse for court hearings. After getting the prisoners to the courthouse, Herman and I usually got coffee before getting ourselves ready to assist with court hearings and taking assigned prisoners to court. Along with court hearings, there were a number of trials. Deputies were assigned to lead and participate in high threat trials.

If you were on the jail runs, you would not be assigned to participate in a trial as you needed to be ready to start getting the prisoners out of the courthouse back to the MCC as the pretrial hearings ended. After months and into the second year of being assigned to court and jail runs, Herman and I started to get a little perturbed as we wanted to experience work in the other sections. Some new deputies came on board and were assigned to the other sections or programs in the district office. New deputies were also receiving better work vehicles or government owned vehicles. Initially, Herman and I were assigned old vehicles from the district vehicle inventory. Herman and I were told by the Acting Supervisor that we had to share a vehicle. This Acting Supervisor who was a journeyman Caucasian deputy marshal was not very inclusive and fair when it came to minorities. Herman and I were assigned older vehicles that were in our opinion unsafe. I remember Herman letting the General Operation's Supervisor know that the Acting Supervisor was assigning us unsafe vehicles to drive and if we had an accident, Herman was going to file a lawsuit. The comment Herman made about suing the Marshals Service did get the attention of the Supervisor and we got a safer vehicle to drive. Herman had some experience in automotive maintenance enabling him to be selected as the district's Motor Officer. He was getting very tired of the second-class treatment by the Acting Supervisor and the Supervisor of the General Operation's section we were both assigned to. I was also tired of this treatment, but had not endured it for quite as long as Herman. Herman filed a grievance stating it was not fair that we could not get assigned to the other units in the office. I signed and supported the grievance as well.

Within a few months, Herman and I were assigned to the Warrant Squad for a 6-month rotation. This was in 1988. I was happy with the assignment as working warrants was about conducting fugitive investigations and making good contacts. This is where I derived part of the title of this book: "Hunting Criminals to Hiding Them." Herman and I were told that there were two top deputies in the Warrant Squad and they were the best in the district at tracking down and apprehending fugitives. Herman and I were on the 4th warrant squad. We were eager to show everyone what we were made of, that we were the best at hunting, finding, and arresting fugitives. We were assigned case files where the fugitives could not be located and arrested by the top district fugitive hunters. These fugitives eluded our district fugitive investigators for many months and in some cases years. We knew this was a challenge and thought to ourselves that we could find these "so-called" hard to find fugitives, and bring them to justice. We got busy working on these supposedly difficult cases. We started working the streets, establishing good contacts with the Chicago Police Department Gang Units assigned to the area we were working. We developed very good contacts with various utility companies and state organizations. We developed good sources of information on the streets and started making arrests, clearing out our warrant caseload. We also received better government owned vehicles to drive as we continued to do well hunting and finding these hard to find fugitives.

Some of the cases we worked on included a female fugitive with over 20 aliases. This fugitive was very elusive. The warrant team assigned to her case had been trying to locate and arrest her for over two years and made no progress. The warrant team that had this case challenged Herman and I saying if they could not locate and find this female fugitive, that there was no way Herman and I, as the new guys in the unit, could find her. What they apparently did not know was that Herman and I had many years of experience living in and understanding the city streets of Chicago. We had a vigorous determination to do our jobs and do it well. We spent only a few days investigating and locating the female fugitive. We arrested her, demonstrating to the more experienced senior fugitive team labeled as the best warrant team in the Chicago Marshals Service Warrant Apprehension Unit, that we were about our business and up to any challenge when it came to hunting, finding and arresting fugitives.

There was another case that a more experienced fugitive investigative team had been tracking for over two years. This fugitive was wanted for drug trafficking by the Drug Enforcement Administration. Herman and I were asked to help with this case. We were more than happy to assist and enjoyed the challenge of working the streets tracking these so called "hard to find fugitives." It took us about one week of hard work to locate this fugitive. We worked many hours in the early mornings and in the late evenings to hunt, and locate these fugitives. In this particular case,

Herman and I were a little tired from our day's efforts and knew we were close to locating the fugitive but decided to call it a day. We went to a local liquor store on the south eastside of Chicago where Herman grew up. We went in the store to purchase an adult beverage and while in the liquor store, our fugitive walked in to also buy a beverage. Herman and I noticed him and we looked at each other and said "that is our guy."

We arrested the guy on the spot. The fugitive was in possession of several bags of crack cocaine. He stated: "I thought you guys might be Marshals, but decided that you two could not be Marshals as many of us on the run know the Marshals do not work after 5pm." We told the fugitive there were some new Marshals on the job and we worked all kinds of hours. We transported him to the Federal Bureau of Prison's Metropolitan Correctional Center (MCC) and signed him into the facility. Herman and I finally had a chance to enjoy our beverage, meeting some friends at one of our favorite hangouts, an automotive repair garage on the southeast side of Chicago.

Herman and I worked on another major fugitive drug case where our investigation took us from Chicago to Gary, Indiana. Gary, Indiana, is close to the southeast suburbs of Chicago. We had developed a good address for the fugitive and went to Gary to investigate. We were certain we had good leads on our guy. I was ready to go arrest the guy right away and take him back to Chicago. Herman was more reserved when it came to our team dynamics. We were both very good investigators, but I think I was a little more aggressive when it came to arrest actions. Herman was more analytical. Based on Herman's recommendation, we decided to contact the local district Marshals' office and our supervisor to let them know we developed very good information on the fugitive. We let them know we were going to conduct an arrest attempt the next morning. The local Marshals' office in Gary related they had looked into the fugitive's whereabouts and did not think he was in their district. The local district Marshals did not come out the next morning to assist with the arrest attempt. Herman and I got up early and went back to Gary, Indiana, located our fugitive and arrested him. We transported the fugitive to the Northern District of Indiana Marshals office that morning and the district warrant supervisor and other staff were very surprised that we had located and arrested this dangerous drug fugitive in their district. It appeared to me that the warrant supervisor had second-guessed his decision not to participate in the arrest planned in their district.

Hunting and catching federal fugitives was both challenging and exciting for Herman and me. We usually celebrated early morning arrests by going to a downtown Chicago breakfast steakhouse where we had steak, two eggs, toast and coffee for $3.95 each. Herman had told me about this restaurant. The restaurant was only a few blocks from our office in the Dirksen federal building. Having that breakfast was our celebration after our very good work which sometimes included the hunting, locating and arresting of as many as three fugitives in one morning.

Herman and I tracked down and arrested several more federal fugitives in the Northern District of Illinois and were very proud of our work and accomplishments. The Warrant Supervisor was shocked that we were hunting, tracking and arresting these difficult cases with positive results in short time. One evening after we had tracked down and arrested another fugitive, Herman and I spoke with a fellow Marshals Service employee about our good work capturing fugitives. This employee asked us if we knew whether or not any of the many cases we had worked on and made arrests, were actually assigned by the warrant supervisor to our caseload. We responded that we did not know for certain. We further stated that after we started making numerous arrests, we were told the cases were assigned to us. This colleague who we were speaking with, was a nice guy that we enjoyed communicating with, started laughing at us. We asked him what was funny and he said that none of the cases were assigned to us. He further stated that the cases were assigned to other fugitive teams assigned to the warrant unit, and they were receiving all of the credit for our hard work. Herman and I were not happy with this revelation about the case assignment process, and could not wait to meet with our supervisor to express our displeasure with being used. We knew the warrant unit cash bonuses were supposed to go to the team with the most arrests. We also knew we had more arrests than the entire warrant unit and we were looking forward to receiving our cash bonuses for our good work. The next morning we met with the warrant supervisor and let him know we were aware we were being used and not getting credit for our hard work and accomplishments. The warrant supervisor was a little surprised we had caught on to the situation. We let the supervisor know that we would not have worked like we had been on cases that were not assigned to us. Herman and I reminded the supervisor that he told us there was a senior warrant team that was the best in the district. However, we now knew they were not the best, and that this team and other teams were benefiting from our good work. We finally started receiving assigned cases and we verified that the cases were assigned to us by checking the National Crime Information Center before going out hunting, tracking and arresting these individuals. Herman and I continued our good work by making even more arrests using our combined investigative skills and experiences.

I located a large bulletin board and started posting the pictures of the fugitives we were tracking and arresting. The large bulletin board was impressive, as it was getting filled up with pictures of those we arrested. I admit it was a bit cocky, and I often said that "We are the A Team" referencing the television show the A Team, and I said there was no B or C teams. Herman and I were very good as partners working the streets of Chicago and the suburbs clearing up district warrant cases. After six months we were reassigned out of the Warrant Squad. By moving us from the warrant squad prior to the issuance of the cash bonuses for the top district fugitive hunters, we were no longer in a position to receive cash bonuses. That was how the warrant supervisor was able to give one of the other fugitive teams the cash bonuses for locating and arresting the most fugitives. Herman and I clearly had the most fugitive arrests for our district office. I was assigned back to the General Operations section and Herman got a break, and was assigned to the Special Services Unit where he was involved with work in seized assets. On occasion I was called out to assist the Special Services Unit with large-scale seizures. Some of these federal investigations culminated with large-scale arrests along with seizures of property. Some of these cases involved several districts as the criminal organizations had sophisticated criminal operations in a number of cities across the country. The arrests and seizures were conducted simultaneously. I found myself assisting with the seizure of an Art Gallery, or seizing nice homes and exotic cars. I enjoyed the diverse roles and missions of the Marshals Service.

I learned a lot from just sitting in court. I learned and understood the terms and language used by the judges and attorneys of both the prosecution and the defense. I was able to know many of these court officials, some of which were very skilled at their profession. I have a friend and former colleague from the Markham Police Department who was going to law school while serving on the police department. He worked a lot of midnight shifts, just as I did so he could attend his law school classes. This colleague mentioned to me that I should consider law school as well. While sitting in those courtrooms learning about court operations and the law, I recalled those conversations with my former police department colleague. I seriously thought about going to law school and spoke to a couple of judges I liked and enjoyed working with about law school and asked for recommendations if I were to apply. They agreed. I was very interested and looked into Kent Law School in downtown Chicago. I learned that Kent Law School had a minority law school program where if admitted, a person could get tuition assistance for the first year if they did well the first year. The following two years of tuition were the responsibility of the student. I gave some serious thought about going to law school, but did not pursue the trade. The thought of going to law school has frequented my mind over the years.

During my probationary year with the Marshals Service, which ended in July 1988, someone in the office posted a bulletin or notice from the Illinois Film Commission. This notice stated that the Illinois Film Commission was seeking law enforcement personnel to work as actors. The notice required those interested to take a small photo, fill out a form and send it in for consideration. I was contacted twice to participate in the filming of a movie. The first notice was for me to come to the filming location in Chicago and if selected, the pay was $75 a day for four or five days to be on the set. I was called to play a uniform Chicago Police Officer in a non-speaking role. I decided to decline this role, as standing around all day for a week for a non-speaking role for $75 a day was not appealing to me. The second offer I received from the Illinois Film Commission a couple of months later did appeal to me. It was for a speaking-role playing an FBI agent in the movie, "Midnight Run." The filming paid $475 a day for four or five days, and I was definitely interested. I went to my acting General Operations Supervisor to get the time off to participate in the movie. He told me he could not let me have the time off, as we were too busy at the time. I knew we were not busy. It was obvious to me that this guy was intentionally blocking me from this opportunity. I thought about taking off, and going to the film set anyway, but knew I was on probation, and would be disciplined for going and maybe even terminated.

Taking this chance with my Marshals Service career was not an option and again I knew what the acting Supervisor was doing. I did watch the movie Midnight Run, and noted that the role I was going to film for was that of the partner to the famed actor Yaphet Kotto. Yaphet Kotto who I watched in movies as a very young man, was the lead FBI agent chasing a character played by Charles Grodin. The movie also featured another famed actor, Robert Deniro who was also chasing Grodin as a Bounty Hunter. I have always admired Deniro as one of the world's greatest actors.

The movie Midnight Run was released July 20, 1988 - the same month I got off of my probationary period from the Marshals Service. I have often wondered what my life would have been like if I had been selected for that role and not continued to follow my dreams working in law enforcement. I was aware of another law enforcement officer who had tremendous success with the movie industry. Actor Dennis Farina was able to take a leave of absence from his police department to give acting a shot. Dennis Farina was a Chicago Police Officer when he landed movie roles in Code of Silence and the movie Midnight Run along with a television series. He never returned to law enforcement, and has had a nice television career. I met Mr. Farina many years later in Washington DC at a National Police Week dinner while I was assigned to Marshals Service Headquarters as a Chief Executive.

After my one-year probationary period, I took an active role in trying to make sure other minority deputy marshals were treated fairly with respect to receiving equipment and assignments. I tried to make sure I was able to compete with my peers, as experience was a critical part of advancement in the Marshals Service. I spoke up and raised issues and concerns to our district Chief Deputy Ed Scheu. Chief Scheu was starting to see what kind of employee I was. He was a former military man having served in the Marines. He supported my military assignments. I had left the 138th Military Intelligence Battalion and joined the 308 Civil Affairs Group, an Army Reserve Unit I served in for many years. The 308th Civil Affairs Group supported active duty military units in Germany. I traveled to Germany two to three times a year usually for three week military assignments. Chief Scheu supported these assignments even though other supervisors and acting supervisors did not. I had a busy schedule. However, for the most part I had weekends off with the exception of my monthly Reserve duty of one weekend each month. As a police officer as I mentioned earlier, I worked shift work and was hardly ever off on weekends. My life and finances were shaping up for me, as I was starting to pick up promotions both in the military and in the Marshals Service.

In July 1988, my wife and I were blessed to have a boy we named Justin. This was my 5th child. I was very happy and also busy trying to take care of my expanding family. In August 1988, I applied for and was selected for a 10-week fugitive operation in Miami, Florida. The Marshals Service Enforcement Operations Division had fugitive operations around the country selecting locations that were described as strategic in the fight against drugs and other violent crimes. Unfortunately, the areas were mainly urban areas in Chicago, New York, Los Angeles, Atlanta, Dallas and Miami. These targeted cities in my view, resulted in the arrests of many minorities. I always took law enforcement operations seriously. If I was issued a court ordered warrant, no matter who was wanted, I was on the case. I was excited to be selected for this 10-week fugitive operation. The assignment provided paid overtime resulting in extra needed money for my family. I was certain that my previous good work with the Chicago district Warrant Squad aided me in my selection for this operation.

The operation was called WANT II. Additionally, I was on per diem receiving funding for my meals and expenses while staying in the Embassy Suites in Miami close to the airport. As a part of my assignment, I had to fly to Atlanta, Georgia, and meet another deputy marshal working the assignment in that city, pick up an unmarked Crown Victoria, and drive it to Miami. I picked the car up and drove it to Miami from Atlanta south on Interstate 75. I arrived in Miami in a little less than 10 hours. This vehicle was assigned to me for use during the 10-week fugitive operation. This assignment proved to be quite interesting and challenging. I was assigned a partner who was a Sergeant working with the Metro Dade Police Department. He was a former Special Weapons and Tactical member with his department. We were both very aggressive law enforcement officers and ended up making a number of significant arrests for our Miami unit.

During my first few days in Miami, I was at the Embassy Suites' Happy Hour with other colleagues enjoying some of the libations and met another guy who was also there for the same reason. He gave me his name and said he worked for IBM. I gave him a false name that came to mind and said I worked for Xerox. We continued with the evening and in the next morning we saw each other as we were having breakfast dressed in our tactical gear. We both laughed knowing we gave each other some phony business with the false names and jobs. We again introduced ourselves exchanging true names and jobs. He was with the Drug Enforcement Administration on assignment from Chicago and I was also on assignment from Chicago. It was quite a coincidence. I was anticipating a great 10-week assignment. I did call my good friend Bill Walker and told him about my encounter with one of his DEA colleagues. Bill and I enjoyed a good laugh about the matter as well.

I received a number of cases with little or vague information on the fugitive cases. Most were Drug Enforcement Administration drug cases. It was difficult to develop additional information on these cases to locate and make arrests. I used all of my skills from working on the Warrant Squad in Chicago to develop information on these fugitives and make arrests. Things were slow initially, as the Team Chief who was from the Western District of Washington in Seattle reviewed our progress each week. Our team chief had to make weekly reports to the Enforcement Operations Division at Headquarters. My Metro Dade County partner was getting frustrated that we had not started making arrests. That soon ended as information was developed on a couple of cases, and we made a couple of arrests. The warrant team chief was happy at our progress. My partner and I were happy as well. Our Miami team was made up of some very good fugitive investigators. I met some very good friends on this assignment.

I recall a case where I was able to develop information on a drug fugitive locating him on his job. It was a 20-year old Drug Enforcement Administration case. The DEA file and background Form 202 did not have much information in it. The files on these cases had very limited information, normally just a name and a description. I had to do a lot of background work checking records to develop additional information. I was able to find a photo and additional information. I arrested this Colombian fugitive on his job at a Nursery in Jupiter, Florida. He had been employed successfully for several years, had quit the drug trade and was living a regular life. However, the problem was that he was still wanted, and I had the warrant and now had him. I located another fugitive from a DEA case that was 17 years old. Again the DEA file and Form 202 did not have much information in it. I conducted the same background work as the afore-mentioned 20-year old case. I did locate this fugitive at his home in Boca Raton, Florida, with his wife and kids. Like the other fugitive, he had stopped selling drugs and settled down with a family, was living a new life and had moved on enjoying his new life and family. However, as in the other case, I had a warrant and I now had him. I arrested him with the assistance of my Metro Dade partner. I did feel bad for his family, after seeing his wife and children who were unsuspecting of the past of the fugitive. I was a cop reared from Chicago, Illinois, from a small town police department making arrests in South Florida, an area I had never been before. I was conducting investigations and working with police departments all over South Florida. I was making arrests in towns and areas I had never heard of before such as Boca Raton, Davie, Jupiter, Coral Gables, Hialeah, Liberty City, Fort Pierce, Port St. Lucie, Key Largo and West Palm Beach.

I remember one morning I woke up and under my room door was a notice from the hotel management. The note stated that in the evening there was going to be filming at the hotel of a scene from Miami Vice. Miami Vice was a prominent television show at the time and there was going to be noises of gunfire at the hotel. The Embassy Suites hotel management knew they had a large group of law enforcement personnel staying at the hotel and did not want us responding to the sound of gunfire with our own weapons. I did hear the sound of shots fired that evening. I saw the actor Edward James Olmos in the hotel restaurant that day. My days on this 10-week fugitive operation were usually long from 5 or 6 am to 6pm and sometimes later. We usually tried to make the hotel Happy Hour from 5:30pm to 7:30pm to wind down discussing the day's events. If we were working on a case that we thought was a high threat, we would let other fugitive team members know.

For known high threat fugitive cases, several fugitive teams got together for the take down of a dangerous fugitive. The law enforcement officer assigned to the case developed an arrest plan. Having several fugitive teams for the known high threat cases was good as we had three or four cars rolling out at 5am to go make an arrest. One morning a group of us were rolling in our vehicles on a major Miami highway. My partner and I were in the lead vehicle and we were working on one of my cases. My car was pulled over by a Highway Patrolman. Of course all four cars stopped and the Trooper was delighted to know we were all good guys as he ended up stopping a convoy of eight cops heading to arrest a very dangerous drug fugitive. After a brief stop and talk, we were back on the highway trying to locate and arrest our man, which we did.

One of the more senior deputy marshals on this assignment from the Washington, District of Columbia area had a saying he used when we located and arrested someone. He told them "You Know What Time It Is?" This particular deputy had located one of his assigned fugitives and found out this fugitive was on a flight coming from the Cayman Islands to Miami, Florida. We had made contact with American Airlines and had a plan to make the arrest once the plane landed. Our plan called for having our squad cars on the tarmac and entering the airplane as it arrived. We asked the flight crew to keep all other passengers in their seats and then request our fugitive to stand and come forward to the front galley of the airplane. We followed our plan as the Flight Attendant called the name of the fugitive and requested he come forward. The fugitive complied gathering his belongings, and moved to the front of the airplane. We escorted the fugitive off the plane and arrested him.

The lead deputy on the case told the fugitive "You Know What Time It Is?" and handcuffed the fugitive. We went to our squad cars on the tarmac and left the area. This was a drug case requiring some very good fugitive work. This 10-week assignment was very exciting, educational, and definitely expanded my view of fugitive operations. My work on this assignment resulted in me being known as a very good fugitive investigator to colleagues working at Headquarters in the Washington, DC area. I was continuing with my love affair working warrants, hunting and finding bad guys and making arrests. I went home only once for a visit to spend time with my family. My wife came down for a visit and we rented a car driving to Key West for a nice weekend visit. I was very happy with my career working for the Marshals Service.

In 1989 I had another very interesting Marshals Service assignment that took me to another part of the country. I was assigned a 3-week assignment to work the Pittston Wild Cat Coal Miners Strike in the Tri-State area of Virginia, West Virginia and Tennessee. A federal judge in the Southern District of Virginia had issued a federal court order against the striking coal miners. Local county authorities were deliberately failing to make arrests of coal miners who were breaking the law, interfering with the coal mining company's right to continue to operate by using an alternate work force or so called "scab" employees to conduct the company's work. This was a very interesting assignment to me as the Marshals Service was working hand-in-hand with the Virginia State Police to enforce the federal court order. The Marshals Service entered into an agreement to have deputy marshals partner and ride with Virginia State Troopers conducting patrols to enforce the court order. The Troopers were on two week rotations while the Marshals Service rotation was our usual three week special assignment. Each deputy marshal ended up having two Virginia State Troopers to work with to complete our 3-week rotations.

I remember flying into Roanoke, Virginia, on a connecting flight from Atlanta, Georgia, on a commuter flight. I was picked up by a deputy U.S. marshal from the Roanoke office and taken to the hotel where all of the detail personnel were staying, both Troopers and Marshals Service personnel. It was a very secure hotel as everyone was on shift work and usually there were always some law enforcement personnel moving around. Law enforcement vehicles were parked all throughout the hotel parking lot. The next day I was picked up by the same deputy marshal who picked me up from the airport and taken to the Roanoke office for briefings on the assignment. I received my shift assignment, which was the 12-hour day shift. I was assigned my partner from the State Police and he had only one week left on his rotation. We conducted our patrols and made a number of stops and investigations of coal miner striker's activity.

I learned about whittling and jack rocks, two terms I had no idea about prior to my assignment to the coalfields of Southwest Virginia. As far as whittling, I observed striking coal miners using a knife to slice small pieces of tree branches or wood. I asked them what they were doing and one of them responded saying "boy we are whittling." I told them my boy days were over a number of years ago, and not to address me as boy but Marshal Jones. They actually respected my point on the issue and called me Marshal. One of the miners subsequently tried to make a joke. He said the following to me "how do you get a group of black kids to stop raping a white girl? He concluded the joke by saying, "throw them a basketball." I told the old guy who they called St. Nick that was not a nice joke and not funny. I went back on patrol with my Virginia State Police partner. I did see St. Nick again later on my assignment and arrested him for violating the federal court order. St. Nick who was somewhat heavy and had a full white beard, was leading a group of striking coal miners to the street to block vehicles, carrying temporary workers to the plant.

After the first week my Virginia State Trooper partner went back to his police district and I met my new partner a canine Trooper. His canine partner was a Rottweiler, one of my favorite dogs. We worked the next two weeks together on patrol duties trying to maintain law and order for this strike. One day while on patrol with my partner and his canine partner riding in his state police marked patrol car, someone from near the road threw a Molotov cocktail firebomb at us. Molotov cocktail bombs are considered an incendiary device consisting of a bottle filled with a combustible liquid with a fuel soaked rag stuffed in the neck of the bottle. Thank goodness the Molotov cocktail did not hit us but exploded right in front of the car. We both exited the vehicle to try and catch the person who ran up a hill into a forest area. My State Police partner was chasing the unknown subject with his canine and I was running parallel to them in the forest area. We did not catch the person and did not want to leave the patrol car too far out of view. We returned to the car and cleaned up the bottled debris. I remember one day I was off for the day and went into town. I recall being told that there were three corners near where I was standing that involved three states: West Virginia, Virginia and Kentucky. I actually stood on all three corners, in three states, within a minute or two of walking distance. This was neat to me.

In 1990, I went on another Special Assignment to the Northern District of Georgia in the Atlanta area. The Marshals Service had responded with 24 hour protection details for all 11th Circuit Federal Judges in response to the mail bombing in Alabama that killed the Honorable Judge Robert S. Vance at his home after opening a package he thought was from someone he knew. I was assigned to the 24-hour protective detail of one of the 11th Circuit judges for three weeks, working the 12-hour day shift including providing protection for the judge at his home and courthouse chambers. I enjoyed this detail as I have always enjoyed serving the federal court and court officers, especially judicial officers. The Marshals Service Court Security Division was the division in charge of the security details for all of these appellate court judges. I had no idea at the time that in years to come, I was going to be selected to lead all Court and Judicial Security functions and operations for the Marshals Service. I was learning my job and doing the best I could to protect the judge and his family when they went out for functions or just out to eat.

After I complained a number of times to my district management about not being provided with opportunities to lead or supervise details in the Northern District of Illinois to gain invaluable security experience for my promotion package, I was selected to lead and supervise the first "Just The Beginning Judicial Conference." This conference was coordinated in large part by the Honorable Judge Ann Claire Williams who at the time was a United States District Court Judge in Chicago after a very successful career as a prosecutor. I will discuss the Just The Beginning Conference in detail a little later.

CHAPTER FOUR

Working the Hunt
My Assignment to the Organized Crime
Drug Enforcement Task Force
And the Ghost Case

In the summer of 1989 after rotations to the Northern District of Illinois Chicago office warrant squad and then back to the General Operations section handling various court matters, including a very successful assignment to Miami Florida working Operation WANT ll, I was assigned to work in support of the Regional Organized Crime Drug Enforcement Task Force (OCDETF). I was partnered with another deputy marshal who I will name as SB. SB and I were to work with the OCDETF Coordinator in Chicago to find and apprehend dangerous drug fugitives who were associated with organized criminal elements or groups. This was an interesting assignment as we were dedicated to this assignment full time. Not only were we to work on these new cases, but we also had to maintain our regular district fugitive assigned cases, as many deputies maintained warrant cases when not assigned a court matter. I developed a number of good contacts and sources with local and state organizations, which were of great assistance with tracking down fugitives from justice.

I also knew I always had the assistance of my fugitive partner Herman Brewer and other deputies I came to rely on to assist with arrest operations. I was assigned a wonderful vehicle to drive, a black 1985 corvette with spoilers all around it, making it look a little like the bat mobile.

Herman Brewer, who served as the Northern District of Illinois Motor Vehicle Officer as a collateral duty, obtained me a free vanity plate. My license plate tag was "SLY BOY 1" which was pretty neat and the car blended in well with some of my undercover operations. The vehicle was seized from a drug dealer in St. Louis, Missouri. Herman located this vehicle and put in the paper work to put it into official use for me to use on the Organized Crime Drug Enforcement Task Force. I actually flew into St. Louis to get the car and drove it back to Chicago. Herman told me that some of the deputies in the Chicago office had a little envy of me having this vehicle and my license plate tag, "SLY BOY 1," saying Herman had wasted government money paying for the tag. Herman has always been a very sharp and savvy guy with excellent business sense. He let district management and concerned deputy marshals know that by adding the #1 to the tag, made the license plate not cost any money. I enjoyed my corvette work car. I still have the license plate "SLY BOY 1", and have it mounted on a plaque in my home office.

I was assigned a very interesting and complex case involving a number of dangerous drug fugitives who were indicted as part of the Northern District of Illinois most dangerous drug and murder case known as the Ghost Case. The Drug Enforcement Administration or DEA had indicted a number of individuals associated with this organized group. I received the case files on about five or six of these individuals who DEA could not locate when they made their sweeping arrests. DEA normally expends only a few days trying to locate those they had indicted on drug cases and then based on an agreement with the United States Marshals Service, the case files are turned over to the Marshals Service to work on. Unfortunately, many of these case files had very limited information on the individuals indicted.

The main individual DEA wanted was nicked named Slim. His real name and aliases were in the file. After receiving the file on Slim, my plans were to work relentlessly to find and arrest him. Slim also known as Future, who did not have a bright "Future" with my fugitive partners and I on his trail. This individual was the enforcer for a very dangerous organized criminal group. He was charged federally with murdering a DEA informant and at the time was the first federal fugitive indicted and charged with murder, which was usually a state or local charge. Slim had put out the word that he was not going back to prison and vowed not to be taken alive. There was one other individual who was wanted in this case with his name listed in the file. I will refer to this individual as Tom. Tom provided substantial cooperation to my investigation with the Ghost Case. The other individuals I had to track down were only listed by nicknames such as Baby-G, Little Joe, and Big Hands Man. My partner SB and I worked very closely with the Assistant United States Attorney assigned to prosecute the case.

As we worked on the case I had to prioritize my targets, review and analyze the limited information I had. I started obtaining additional information based on my research on Slim and the one individual I have listed as Tom. My partner and I started tracking Tom trying to find and arrest him. We did find Tom and arrested him. Tom was a street worker selling drugs at the street level for the organization. He was very cooperative when we interviewed him and asked if we could speak to the Assistant United States Attorney/Prosecutor on the case to get him out of jail and he informed us he could be very helpful with finding the other fugitives on the case including Slim. I decided to take a chance with Tom and used him as our Confidential Informant and went to the prosecutor on the case and asked that Tom be released to assist with the investigation as we had several individuals to locate and arrest and some of these individuals were only identified by their nicknames on the indictment. Tom was released from the Metropolitan Correctional Center also called the MCC to assist with the investigation. It proved to be a very good decision having Tom as a confidential informant during the investigation on this case. He provided substantial assistance, cooperation and information about this dangerous drug organization and those fugitives known by only nicknames. He did not know their real names but could draw and he drew very good pictures of the individuals with nicknames. There were no photos in the files of several of the fugitives, so this was excellent to have good hand drawn pictures. Tom also got out on the streets and helped look for these fugitives, obtaining additional leads and information. He always stayed in contact with me wherever he was as he called it "working the streets." I made it clear to Tom how important it was that I knew where and whenever he was assisting with the case for his safety. I was developing a good relationship with Tom.

The next fugitive in the Ghost Case I arrested was Baby-G. Tom had come across good information that Baby-G was still selling drugs and using a van to move his drug products. I was able to determine the true name of Baby-G and found a couple of addresses he used. It took me a few additional weeks, but I was able to find and arrest Baby-G. My partner SB was on vacation when I received word that Baby-G was on the lower south side of Chicago in his van selling drugs. I called my old fugitive partner Herman Brewer to assist me with the surveillance and arrest of Baby-G. Herman and I had excellent working relationships with several Chicago Police Department Gang Crimes Officers who we leaned on to assist us when we worked countless hours tracking federal fugitives. We contacted officers from the Chicago Police Department (CPD) to assist us and most importantly let them and their colleagues know we were taking down a high valued federal target indicted on a major DEA case. Herman and I arrested Baby-G as he was selling drugs out of his van. Chicago Police Department arrived to assist with the arrest and a small amount of drugs were seized. Baby-G was the second Ghost case organized crime member to be arrested by me with assistance from Herman Brewer.

Baby-G had a medical condition where he had a colostomy bag attached to him. However, he was still engaged in his illegal trade selling drugs. He told me he needed the drug money to help him provide the medical care he needed. I was very happy to have this second case closed and especially due to the fact that initially, I had only his nickname, no photo and no other information about him. Baby-G looked amazingly just like the picture Tom had drawn for me. The arrest of Baby-G occurred about three months after arresting Tom. This arrest proved to be the game changer on this major multi-defendant case.

Tom again provided very good information that led to the arrest of Little Joe. Again, I did not have much information on Little Joe other than his nickname and the hand drawn picture from Tom. One late afternoon in December 1989, I was at an event near downtown Chicago with several deputy marshals including Herman Brewer and our Chief Ed Scheu, when I received a call from Tom. Tom said that he knew where Little Joe was and provided me that information. I mentioned this good news to my Chief and the deputies who were with us at the event. Herman Brewer, another deputy marshal who I will name as Paul Smith, my partner SB, and I all jumped into our law enforcement vehicles and went to the location. I met with Tom, got a quick briefing from him, and he told me that Little Joe was still in the business establishment. I checked the hand drawn picture with Tom and he reassured me it was Little Joe. Our team took position and SB, Herman Brewer, Paul Smith, Chief Scheu, and I went into the business establishment. I observed Little Joe and we approached him announcing our office, the U.S. Marshals, and arrested him. My Chief placed the handcuffs on him and he was transported to the Metropolitan Correctional Center. We went back to the event and had a very nice time. This arrest was about two months after the arrest of Baby-G.

My investigation into this case continued with a major focus on finding and apprehending Slim. The fugitive known only as Big Hands Man was also still a target and SB and I, along with Tom, were still looking for him. SB and I located and interviewed Slim's Mother, ex-girlfriends and current girlfriends. We did not expect much cooperation, but had to make the contact and interviews. I especially made appeals to Slim's Mother telling her that it is known that he is armed and dangerous and that he has vowed not to be taken alive. I was trying to appeal to her as a mother and did not really expect her to turn her son in, but like most mothers I had encountered while hunting fugitives, I knew she did not want anything to happen to her son. As I interviewed ex and current girlfriends of Slim, I told them that Slim vowed not to be taken alive that he would rather die than go back to jail. I also told them that law enforcement knew Slim was listed as armed and dangerous and may shoot him with any furtive or strange moves that he may make and that I too was operating in the same mode as officer safety was paramount when dealing with dangerous drug fugitives. These ladies all spoke with me but did not provide any actionable intelligence or information as to Slim's whereabouts. Every now and then I interviewed these ladies to keep Slim off guard and on the run, hoping he would get tired of running and eventually slip up and SB and I would apprehend him. I often informed Slim's Mother, girlfriends, ex-girlfriends, and friends that other law enforcement officers and I were on high alert as we searched for him. I further informed these family and friends that I was prepared to shoot Slim in my efforts to locate and arrest him based on statements he had made of not being taken alive. I used Slim's own death wish statements in psychological efforts to get Slim's family and friends to get him to turn himself in to me without incident.

I used all of my available investigative tools to find Slim and Big Hands Man. I was pretty confident we would find Big Hands Man before we caught up with Slim. I found out that Slim had a brother in Milwaukee, Wisconsin, and SB and I made the short drive from Chicago to Milwaukee to meet with police detectives to ascertain information on Slim's brother. The detectives were very helpful providing information on the brother and told us that the brother was also wanted for a murder charge in Milwaukee.

I informed these detectives that if we had any information on the brother, we would contact them and forward that information. I asked the detectives to do the same if they developed information on either of the two brothers. It crossed my mind that these two brothers charged with separate murders, may be hiding out together combining resources to avoid being located and arrested. To further my investigation, I was constantly checking various phone records trying to determine if there were any calls made to numbers after my interviews with Slim's family members and other known friends and associates. I conducted numerous computer checks for any activity related to both Slim and Big Hands Man. I also met with and worked with my confidential informant Tom who was hard at work trying to help my partner SB and I catch both Big Hands Man and the so called 'Big Fish" known as Slim. I found out that Slim had used his brother's name on an arrest and this name was one of his several aliases used. This was the actual name of his brother who was wanted for murder in Milwaukee, Wisconsin. My investigation into the whereabouts of Slim led us to pool halls, night clubs, bars, and a number of surveillances of homes and relatives, girlfriends, friends and associates of Slim.

We finally got another break when Tom, my confidential informant, located some information on the location of Big Hands Man. Big Hands Man as I figured was still in the Chicago area not far from his known area of operation. Tom had bumped into a mutual friend with knowledge of Ghost Gang members and was able to obtain an address for Big Hands Man. I planned a takedown arrest of Big Hands Man at a house on the south side of Chicago with SB, Herman and a couple other district deputy marshals. We hit the house covering the front and rear of the house and arrested Big Hands Man without any incident. Again, the hand drawn picture of Big Hands Man by Tom was on point. Big Hands Man looked exactly like the drawing. Big Hands Man, Baby G, Little Joe, and Tom had been hunted and captured by SB and me, with assistance from Herman Brewer and other deputies I called on to work with us. It was around

March of 1990 when Big Hands Man was arrested and I was getting a little frustrated that Slim was still eluding me. I was beginning to wonder if I would ever catch this Ghost Gang Enforcer.

I continued to work on finding Slim with my partner SB and my confidential informant Tom and studied the case file and telephone records I had subpoenaed of various relatives and friends of Slim. I continued to also conduct interviews. After still being frustrated at Slim's ability to elude me, one night in May 1990, I was studying the Ghost Gang case file and a new subpoenaed telephone record of various telephone numbers. I noted a number I had not seen before. I was able to reach a contact I used in my investigations to obtain the address that belonged to this new telephone number. The address was on the far south side of Chicago in an area I was very familiar with. In my teenage years, I lived not too far from the address. I called my partner SB, gave him the address and requested he meet me at the residence around 7:30 in the morning. Our meeting point was a couple blocks away from the house.

We met around 7:30am and had a brief discussion about going to the house. I mentioned to SB that we had to be careful since it was just the two of us, and I would go to the front door and for him to go to the back door. Once we were in position, I knocked on the front door and rang the doorbell. A young teenager answered the door and I presented my identification, and introduced myself asking to speak to his parent or parents. The teenager informed me that his parents were not home and at work. I asked the teenager if I could come into the house to speak with him and he said his parents told him he could not let anyone in while they are away. I asked if he could call his parents as I wanted to come in and take a look around. The teenager said he could not nor would not call his parents. I then informed the teenager, that I was not going away and that my partner was at the rear of the house and I was calling for some backup assistance and would contact the United States Attorney's Office for a search warrant as my partner and I were looking for an organized drug criminal who was wanted for murder on a federal case. I also mentioned that once I had the search warrant, we would search the home completely and his parents may not appreciate how the search would be conducted. I again urged him to call his parents and he said he would. A short time later, I was surprised as the teenager came back to the front door and opened it and said I could come into the house.

I used my Marshals Service hand held radio to informed SB that I was entering the residence and would let him in once I was in the residence and could do so. Upon entering, I had a feeling that I needed to pull my service weapon which was a Sig Sauer P226, which I did when going into high alert or the red zone as my old Police Training Institute Firearms Instructor had trained us when I was in the Police Academy. The house had a front living room with stairs going to a lower level. I saw two men in the lower level and one of them, which I found out to be Slim, called my name as both men raised their arms. Slim stated to me "Please do not shoot us Mr. Jones." I ordered both men to lie face down while also monitoring the teenage kid who was still upstairs. Once both men were face down on the floor, I used my radio to contact SB and let him know I was opening the lower rear door for him to come in and I had two men face down and one of the men was Slim our fugitive. I opened the rear lower level door keeping an eye on the two men and my 9-millimeter pointed in their direction. Once SB was inside, I informed him to keep his weapon on the two men and to give me his handcuffs. I used SB's handcuffs and my handcuffs to handcuff both men and then called for assistance from our district office to assist with the arrestees' transport to our office in downtown Chicago. The second man was identified as Slim's brother who was wanted for a murder charge in Milwaukee.

I cannot explain the joy and relief I had after capturing not only my wanted fugitive Slim, the first federal fugitive to face the death penalty for murdering a DEA cooperating confidential informant, but arresting this fugitive's brother who was also wanted for murder. Not only one major federal arrest was made, but as a bonus, a second fugitive. I was very happy with the culmination of this major case, as all of the DEA wanted fugitives on this case were in custody. I called my chief deputy to report that Slim was in custody. The timing for my call could not have been better as my chief deputy and all of the district federal law enforcement leaders were at an executive federal law enforcement conference in Lake Geneva, Wisconsin. My chief told me he was going to go to the podium and give this excellent news to the executives at the conference. He called me back to thank me for a job well done and to let me know that when he made the announcement that DEA Ghost Case fugitive Slim was arrested, he got a standing ovation. This made me even more pleased with the work that resulted in the arrest of Slim. I received recognition not only from my local district leadership, but also from the U. S. Attorney at the time and the Chief of the United States Marshals Service Enforcement Division, Mr. Louie T. McKinney, who would later be my U. S. Marshal in the U.S. Virgin Islands, and then become Acting Deputy Director when I was Chief Deputy and my subsequent promotion to Assistant Director. I did not know at the time that Mr. McKinney would become a lifelong very good friend, mentor and tremendous supporter of my Marshals Service career.

My relationship with Tom ended and I called him to let him know that Slim had been located and arrested. I thanked him for all of his assistance with the wanted fugitives on the case and told him I would again let the case Assistant U. S. Attorney know how prevalent his assistance was to the Marshals Service with this very important case, which I did do. I did see Tom again when I realized we attended the same church. On one Sunday I went to church at the Apostolic Church of God under the leadership of the great late Bishop Arthur Brazier. I was running late and went thru a door I had never entered to get to my seat which was usually in the third row next to Bishop Brazier's lovely wife and my late mother-in-law, the late Elizabeth Brewer. I passed by the musicians and saw that my confidential informant Tom was a musician in the band. He saw me as well and we nodded at each other. I loved attending that church and taking in the late Bishop Brazier's enlightening and spiritually moving services. I called Tom to say I was happy to see that he served in the same church with me and that our law enforcement relationship would always be separate from the church. Tom agreed. I have never seen Tom again, but I hope he has lived and is living a good life.

CHAPTER FIVE

The Hunt: Working Fugitive Cases in Chicago and Military Deployment for Operations Desert Storm/Shield

After the Ghost Case arrests, I had a reputation for being a good fugitive investigator. Other federal agents working with DEA, Postal Inspection Service and the Bureau of Alcohol, Tobacco and Firearms (ATF) contacted me to help locate their wanted fugitives. I always coordinated these requests through the District Warrant Supervisor and was assigned to assist these agencies quite frequently. I was tasked to work with the Chicago Crime Commission and a program titled Chicago's Most Wanted named after the program, America's Most Wanted. FOX television partnered with the Chicago Crime Commission to produce the Chicago's Most Wanted Program. This program highlighted some of Chicago's Most Wanted fugitives by various Chicago area law enforcement agencies and the fugitives were aired on a news clip during the daily evening 6pm FOX News show. As a part of my participation in the Chicago's Most Wanted Program, I was often interviewed in my district office or at the location where I made arrests by FOX News personnel. I discussed my major cases, giving a short story about the case and how dangerous the fugitives were.

The first case highlighted on Chicago's Most Wanted Program was a high profile DEA drug case. I got to know the two DEA case agents who briefed me on the fugitive who was a major drug dealer in the Chicago area who had eluded the DEA arrests sweeps. The DEA case agents were two sharp agents and this was a major case resulting in a number of assets being seized. However the high profile major fugitive I will list by name only as Larry had eluded DEA and the DEA handed the case over to the Marshals Service to find and make the arrest. I was assigned the case and went to work on locating Larry.

I created a working file for Larry and started compiling information such as names of the usual family members, associates and lady friends. I interviewed these individuals who were spread out on the west side and south side of Chicago. As a part of my investigation, I highlighted Larry on the FOX News Chicago's Most Wanted program. I also went to the Chicago Crime Commission on the evening that FOX News aired the segment about Larry. I had a short clip that discussed Larry, showed his photo and listed that he was an armed and dangerous organized crime drug fugitive. In addition, I provided the audience with the telephone number for the Chicago Crime Commission's Hotline. While at the Chicago Crime Commission, I received a couple of calls but there was no solid information or leads as to Larry's whereabouts. I continued to investigate and interview, and tried to develop some solid leads. I located information about potential venues that Larry visited and started conducting surveillances with the assistance of the usual deputy marshals I enjoyed working with including Herman Brewer. I was working this case in the late summer of 1990. I did develop some good information about Larry from various sources including the husband of one of my closest cousins who knew Larry from a community they both had lived in before Larry became a prominent drug dealer. I was able to locate Larry in an apartment building on the south side of Chicago and organized a small arrest team to make the arrest. Larry was arrested without any incident and I called the two DEA case agents to give them the good news. The arrest of Larry added to my accomplishments, yet another high priority target drug fugitive arrested based on my relentless investigative pursuit along with the assistance of some top shelf deputy marshals working in the Chicago office. I was interviewed by FOX News both at the Marshals Service Chicago district office and on scene at the location of the arrest. FOX News showed one of the first cases highlighted and resolved under the Chicago's Most Wanted Crime Apprehension Program and I was on the news discussing the case and the arrest. I received a number of calls from friends and relatives who saw me on TV.

I continued to highlight several fugitive cases on FOX news Chicago's Most Wanted, and working with the Chicago Crime Commission. I made a couple of other arrests and was on the FOX News Program discussing the cases and the arrests. FOX News always showed a photo of the fugitive and had a video caption of a jail door slam closed with the photo behind bars, saying another of Chicago's Most Wanted was behind bars and off the streets. The FOX News Program was going well and the producers had a reception and invited John Walsh of the national America's Most Wanted Program. John Walsh did attend and I got a chance to meet and speak with him. I took a photo with him, but never received a copy of the photo from the reporter I was working with on FOX News who took the photo. I was able to obtain a couple of other photos from the reception. I was very proud to be associated with the Chicago's Most Wanted Program and still have some of the news clips from fugitives I highlighted on video.

While serving on the Organized Crime Drug Enforcement Task Force, I received a collateral lead from the U.S. District Court for the District of Columbia in Washington, DC, about a high profiled federal fugitive where there was information that this fugitive was hiding out somewhere in the Chicago area. This fugitive was described as a white male who was considered very dangerous and listed on the U. S. Marshals Service's Top 15 Most Wanted List. The collateral lead had some very good specific information and I assembled a couple of good deputy marshals to assist me. We located and arrested this fugitive in Wisconsin. This fugitive was obviously very important, as I was asked to fly to Washington, DC, with the fugitive that I will name as Rob in my care and custody. Our Enforcement Operations Division, working with the U.S. District Court for the District of Columbia arranged a charter flight from Chicago to the District of Columbia. I requested another Chicago District deputy marshal to accompany me on this very long trip.

The chartered plane was a small 8-seat propeller plane, which took nearly four hours to get from Chicago to the Nation's Capital. Upon arrival in DC, we were met by a team of deputy marshals who transported my partner, the Top 15 Most Wanted Fugitive, and me, to their office where they took control of the fugitive. They were very happy to have their hands on this guy and treated my partner and me very good. This Most Wanted Fugitive was wanted for his involvement in the murder of a doctor. We were introduced to the U.S. Marshal for the District of Columbia and his Chief Deputy. Several years later, I became good friends with this outstanding Marshals Service distinguished leader. My partner and I stayed the night in the District of Columbia and flew back to Chicago the next day on commercial airlines, which was nice as we were back in Chicago in an hour and forty minutes in lieu of the four hours propeller flight we took with the fugitive the day before to get to DC.

I was busy tracking and arresting fugitives and was also still busy with my Reserve military career as an officer. I was a senior First Lieutenant getting close to making Captain. I was in a Civil Affairs Army Reserve Unit with my close and lifetime friend Al Howard. During this time things were heating up with Iraq and their takeover of Kuwait. President George Herbert Walker Bush was leading a global effort to address the situation in the Middle East.

Military Deployment for Operations Desert Storm/Shield

I had a break with my Marshals work due to military action in the Middle East. Iraq had invaded Kuwait and was not responding to sanctions imposed by the United Nations and former 41st President George Bush was sending in U. S. troops to eradicate Iraq out of Kuwait. In late September 1990, I completed the Civil Affairs Officer Advance Course, a very good program that required me to travel twice to the U. S. Army John F. Kennedy Special Warfare Center and School. I drove to the September session with my good friend Al Howard. Members of my military unit were assigned in December to travel to Germany to conduct an operation with active duty units we supported in the Army's 5th Corps, which was located in the Abram's Complex in Frankfurt, Germany. It was during this assignment in Germany that we were told we would most likely be deployed in January 1991, and should start making plans to go on active duty early that month. I was elated to walk in the Abram's Complex as a First Lieutenant and be promoted a short while later to Captain. I was surprised to be promoted to Captain because I thought I would get that promotion when I returned to my unit back home in Illinois.

In January 1991 as expected I was activated for military duty for Operation Desert Storm and Desert Shield and placed on active duty for nearly six months. I was happy to be deployed as a Captain and not a First Lieutenant. The Marshals Service and my Chief Ed Scheu who served in the Marine Corps was very supportive of this deployment. My district, the Northern District of Illinois, sent three of its deputy marshals forward for this military engagement, me and two other district deputies who were in the Marine Reserve. Members from my Reserve Unit including my lifelong good friend Alvin Howard were sent to Green Bay, Wisconsin, to join a subordinate unit to the 308th Civil Affairs Group, the 432 Civil Affairs Battalion. My new unit, the 432nd Civil Affairs Battalion was sent to Ft. Bragg, North Carolina, for pre-mobilization, and readiness training for our deployment to the Middle East. For the next few weeks we received briefings and training, and then boarded fights to Saudi Arabia. Al Howard and I went out a night or two before we were to leave for the Middle East, as our unit was provided a mission number, and our number was coming up. We jumped in a cab to go out and had this interesting African American cab driver who figured out we were soldiers. He asked us in a southern draw "You boys getting ready to go to Saudi?" We responded "yes we are." The cab driver further stated, "Yall better get it all tonight." He was referring to getting some action with the ladies, as he knew it would be a while before anyone would be getting any action. Al and I got a good laugh at the comments from the cab driver as we were both married, and had our wives down to spend a little time with us before taking off on our mission

Preparing for deployment from Ft. Bragg to Saudi Arabia was a little intense. We received some good hands-on tactical refresher training, and briefings about customs and courtesies in the Middle East. The reassigned members of the 308 Civil Affairs Group were getting to know and bond with the members of our new unit the 432 Civil Affairs Battalion. Civil Affairs at the time was made up of primarily Army Reserve Units with one active duty unit, the 96th Civil Affairs Battalion. We received our mission numbers and our unit was moving out in a number of group flights. I flew out with a group, and was designated the Flight Mission Commander. As flight mission commander, I was in charge of all troops traveling for the on ground mission. This did not include the flight crew or the plane's Captain. We flew out on a C130 troop transport plane. I had packed my backpack with a number of cans of sardines and tuna not knowing exactly what the meal situation would be after we arrived in Saudi Arabia. As our plane was about to land into Saudi Arabia we saw a number of missiles being fired from American troops on Iraqi troops and their positions. It was like a scene from Star Wars with the missiles being fired in different directions.

Once we landed, we were met by members of our advance party, and transported to Al Jubayl with the rest of our unit members. I was happy to catch up with Al Howard, as we were located in the same building and room with a few other soldiers from our unit. The next few weeks we continued to prepare for our mission. We knew we would follow combat troops moving into Kuwait once the President gave the attack command. I had brought a small Sony hand television with me to try and obtain news on what was being discussed in the media about this conflict. I was not sure it would work, but it did and the small television picked up a couple of stations such as the Armed Forces Network and CNN. It was nice to receive some news about what was going on with the war and how it related to politics, as we anticipated the ground attack was going to be ordered soon. My unit was initially assigned to the 18th Airborne Division. We were subsequently assigned to the 7th Corps, which no longer exists due to deactivation. I liked the Army's 7th Corps. I have always liked the number 7, so I was happy to be switched to the 7th Corps.

When I retired many years later from the Marshals Service, I retired with the badge and credential number 0007 assigned to me. I could have chosen 0004 based on seniority, but 0007 to me was a better and cooler number. I always liked James Bond's number 007 and was happy to retire with badge and credential number 0007. While in Al Jubayl, we were all ordered to take anthrax shots to assist with any chemicals the Iraqi military fired at us using scud missiles. We often heard sirens on a number of nights as scud missiles were fired at us, and other American forces. We often had to put on our gas masks and leave the masks on until we received the all clear. This was almost a nightly occurrence, and got old quick. None of us wanted to take any chances by not putting on our protective gas masks. Your gas mask was a very important commodity.

Once we got the word when the ground attack was going to occur, we made plans to move out to Kuwait within a day of the ground attack. As history tells us, the ground attack occurred, it did not take long at all for the combat troops to do their work destroying the Iraqi Army, and chasing the Iraqi Army out of Kuwait back to Iraq. The United States Army which in my mind is the most powerful, lethal, and sophisticated military force in the world, was wiping out the Iraqi Army all the way back to Iraq. The Army's attack was called off to stop the devastating blows it was handing to the Iraqi forces. There was a Colonel who led our rather large convoy of vehicles and equipment into Kuwait as the Convoy Commander. A Convoy Commander is in charge of a convoy's movement. I was designated the Convoy Deputy Commander. I have never been the best land navigator, but wanted to make sure I had a good grasp of where we were suppose to go to enter Kuwait. The Colonel leading us got disoriented, contacted me by radio and directed me to take over as Convoy Commander. I had no choice in the matter, and was glad I was prepared to take over. I got us back on the right track, and we entered Kuwait. It was daybreak as we made it to Kuwait. Upon arriving in Kuwait was a sight to behold. There were dozens of Iraqi tanks and vehicles upside down and sideways. There were dead bodies all over the place.

The large convoy I led decided to take up a position at a warehouse in an industrial area. We used that location for our base of operations for all of our time in Kuwait. In Civil Affairs we have a number of specialty functions such as a Medical Team, Arts and Monument Team, Utility Team, Legal Team and Public Safety Team to name a few. Since our mission was largely a Reserve mission, unit members were assigned to a team based on their professions in their regular full time life. With a law enforcement background, I was assigned the Public Safety Team leader. My team was comprised of public safety personnel mainly firemen and police officers. I was introduced to a Kuwait Police General and he and I worked together conducting inspections of schools, police stations, fire stations, and the treatment of Iraqi prisoners. I was assigned a young Kuwaiti soldier who I will name as Haz to be my interpreter. On one of my first patrols, I saw Kuwaiti people who had been oppressed and had been hiding, who came out to greet us with great happiness, and joy. These good people were oppressed and under occupation by a brutal enemy. I remember a number of people repeatedly calling out the name "George Bush, we love George Bush." It was good to see the bakeries open and we looked forward to getting fresh baked bread. Kuwait was in bad condition, but started to get better with each day without oppression, or occupation by Iraqis. In my vehicle along with my Interpreter was my driver an older sergeant who I admired, and got to know well. As we drove by the Mercedes Benz dealership and other fancy car dealerships in Kuwait, the dealerships were empty. These exquisite car dealership show rooms had been cleaned out. The Iraqis had driven the vehicles north to Iraq. It was sad and hard to hear about the atrocities the Kuwaiti's endured during the occupation with murders and rapes. It felt good to be a part of the liberation and stabilization of Kuwait, which is a key mission of Civil Affairs.

The warehouse we took position in was our base of operation for the time we were operating in Kuwait. There were several good things about being in a Civil Affairs Unit. One very good point is that the Civil Affairs Units have all kinds of professional skills. In our warehouse base, there were no lights and no restroom facilities. Our generators provided us with lights and our carpenters prepared rest rooms. There were rooms on each side of our warehouse that were used as restrooms. On one end, a restroom was made for males, and on the other end a restroom was made for females. The guys skilled in carpentry took a large piece of wood and cut large circle holes in it. Buckets were placed under the holes to form a toilet. We used a little bleach to contain the odor until the next morning when there would be a "shit" burning detail of lower ranking enlisted individuals to get rid of the bucket's contents. As history tells us, and many of us observed, as the Iraqi forces left Kuwait, they burned a large number of oil fields. Our base of operations was near the oil fields. We lived under a dark cloud as equipment was brought in to try to put out the oil field fires, which took some time. Some of our patrols took us to locations out from underneath the oil clouds, which was nice. However, when we returned to base, it was under the thick dark oil clouds. Whenever I blew my nose, black particles came out. I enjoyed the patrols and the inspections of facilities. In inspecting the schools, we were looking for hazards and/or unexploded ordinance.

On one evening while back at our base in our sleeping quarters, a very curious Specialist or E-4 brought in an unexploded ordinance or bomb. As I saw him handling the unexploded shell, I told him in a very strong and firm voice to take that shell and immediately get it out of our quarters, and report the location where he placed it to the ordinance experts. When he returned, I gave him a good safety briefing, as he was one of my soldiers.

On another patrol, I met the Kuwaiti Police General at a Police station. This station had a large number of Iraqi prisoners in a large back room cell. My instructions were to make sure that the prisoners were treated humanely. I observed this large group of very dirty and smelly prisoners packed in the lock up. Some spoke to me in Arabic. I asked for an interpretation and was told they were complaining about their treatment in the Kuwaiti jail, complaining they were denied water and food. The General ordered his soldiers to give the prisoners basic rations and water. I inspected a number of police and fire facilities. Kuwait had been devastated and needed a major effort to rebuild. With the United States and other nations providing assistance, the effort to rebuild was starting to take place. I learned more and more about the culture of Kuwait noting that they were not as strict or prohibitive when it came to women. Unlike other very strict Islam countries, Kuwaiti women could attend schools, and religious gatherings with men. Women could wear jeans and did not have to cover up showing only their eyes. I still observed some women covering up. However, many women were more relaxed wearing jeans.

I went through a couple of sand storms where my goggles and scarf came in very handy. I saw tribal groups known as Bedouins and Nomads wandering from place to place, as they had no set home. They made temporary homes where they were. Before going to the Middle East I did not know what a Bedouin was. My unit and I, and other soldiers went through a Ramadan season where Muslims fast. Muslims did not eat during the day between sunrise and sunset. When I was with my Interpreter Haz, I joined him in fasting. I sometimes had a meal with Haz at his home, or his brother's home when eating was appropriate, taking my sergeant with me. Haz invited me a number of times to eat with him and his family, and friends. I had to take him up on his offer a few times. He was a sharp young man and a good person. We still keep in touch as he has visited the U. S. on business a few times. I had my 31st birthday in Kuwait, and had a couple of parties put together in my honor. Members of my unit had one birthday party for me, and Haz had another birthday salute for me at a dinner with his brother. I always tried to be very alert while on patrols remembering what my former Police Training Institute Instructor told me about the stage of readiness, 'White, Yellow, Orange and Red." I was operating in the Orange and Red stages pretty much all of the time with the exception of being in our sleeping quarters. On one patrol, my team and I saw some other military forces operating in the same area. One soldier appeared and approached us identifying himself as a United States Special Forces soldier. He told us he and other team members were operating in the area and we should leave the area. I told him, we were almost done with our assignment, and would leave when we were finished. He got a little testy saying the area was his area. I told him we were all on the same team, and we were going to continue with our mission and depart when we were done, which we did.

Another of my patrols took me to the southern edge of Iraq. My team and I entered Iraq and observed a large number of deceased Iraqi soldiers. While deployed, I received packages, and mail from family and friends. I always liked Gummy Bears and requested Gummy Bears as part of my care packages. I received a very nice letter from my Marshals Service Chief Ed Scheu showing me some support, and updating me on what was going on in the office. I still have that letter today. As a good military man himself,

Ed Scheu as I have mentioned earlier, was very supportive of his deputies who were serving in the Reserves as Soldiers.

As the days went on, it was good to see Kuwait rebuilding and getting power back on line. Someone had opened a grill nearby our base, cooking hamburgers and hotdogs. The smell of the grill food was appealing and a number of soldiers went to get in line to get a burger and hotdog, something we had not had in quite a while. After getting my hamburger and hotdog, I was interviewed by a news reporter with my burger and hotdog in hand. My photo was taken as a part of the interview, and I had no idea there was a UPN press article with my picture in it. I found out as I was responding to a letter mailed to "Any Soldier" to a supportive family in Houma, Louisiana, who had wrote me back asking me if I was the same Army Captain Sylvester Jones in a newspaper article being interviewed with a hamburger and hotdog. I wrote back to the very curious family acknowledging that I was interviewed by a reporter with a hamburger and hotdog in hand, and asked the family to mail me the newspaper article, which they did. I was surprised that my picture and the interview were in the newspaper. I have that newspaper article as it brings back memories of my time in Kuwait.

In the 5th month of my deployment, my grandmother who was ill, became very ill and the Red Cross at the request of family members, requested I return home. I went home with the expectation of returning to Kuwait after a visit with my Grandmother Rose. My unit's deployment to the Middle East was nearing its end. I spent my last 30 days on Active Duty at Ft. Sheridan Army base in Illinois that has since closed. I demobilized and returned to my family and job with the Marshals Service. The Marshals Service and the Military were my other two families I enjoyed and loved.

I went right back to hunting federal fugitives in the Chicago area to include another 10 week federal fugitive operation in Miami, Florida, led by the Enforcement Operations Division of the Marshals Service.

CHAPTER SIX

Operation Sunrise: Hunting, Finding and Arresting Fugitives In South Florida for the Second Time

In August 1991 I was again selected to work on a 10-week nationwide fugitive operation called Operation Sunrise. This fugitive operation targeted a number of major cities across the U. S. and I was selected for the second time in three years to go to Miami, Florida. Now I was a 4-year veteran of the Marshals Service and on my second major nationwide fugitive operation in three years. I was very excited at the opportunity to again display my fugitive tracking skills to the Marshals Service Enforcement Operations Division. I again left my family behind to go serve the agency I considered my extended family to find and locate very dangerous federal, state and local fugitives. This particular fugitive operation involved state and local most dangerous fugitives, some charged with murder along with dangerous federal fugitives many charged with dangerous drug crimes.

I met and became lifelong friends with Mr. Buz Brown who just like I was three years before, was relatively new with the agency and embarking on a long prosperous career. Buz Brown was assigned a female partner and so was I. He was assigned to work with another deputy marshal, while my partner was a police officer with the Hialeah, Florida Police Department. Buz and I hit it off well right from the beginning and always supported each other as we worked our assigned cases. Just as a senior deputy marshal took me under his wing in 1988 during Operation WANT II, I took a big brother or mentor role with Buz showing him tactics I learned in conducting fugitive operations back in Chicago and my first go around working in Miami three years earlier.

I was very comfortable working fugitive operations in South Florida and familiar with the City of Miami and surrounding cities and Broward County just North of Miami. As previously mentioned our fugitive apprehension team resided at the Embassy Suites the first time I was assigned to hunt fugitives in Miami. However, this second time in Miami, our team resided at a very nice Residence Inn off Highway (HWY) 836 just east of the Miami International Airport. I found the South Florida area pretty easy to navigate using HWY 836 going east and west, HWY 826 going north and south, and Interstate Highways I95 and I75 also going north and south.

Miami is a very pretty city with very good weather and plenty of nice scenery including beaches. I was eager to receive my assigned cases and get to work trying to hunt and find federal fugitives, which I had a tremendous passion for. It was a great feeling of accomplishment to track down and find a federal drug fugitive working off of very limited intelligence and other sources of information. Buz and his partner had a large fugitive warrant caseload and my partner and I did as well. Buz and I also teamed up without our partners to track down fugitives depending on the fugitive and known locations we discovered the fugitives frequented, especially those associated with the Jamaican Posse. We did leg work on these and other cases and when we were ready to execute a takedown or arrest, we called our partners in and if necessary, other fugitive teams and local law enforcement.

I remember working a fugitive case that Buz was assigned to. We had information or intelligence of a couple of fancy nightclubs that this fugitive frequented. Buz and I got our teams together along with another team and went to these clubs. Some clubs were expensive to get in. However, we were on the job and expensed the activity. We both enjoyed good music and nice scenery, so this was okay. We were serious about our business though and were looking to locate and arrest the fugitive. We did not find this fugitive at the clubs, but located him at another location. We discovered an address for the fugitive and arranged an early morning arrest. When we, along with our partners, went to the residence there was a Rottweiler chained to a pole and aggressively barking at us. I was familiar with Rottweilers as I had one. Buz and I decided to have our partners stand near the fence and gate. We decided if we could trick the dog to come after us in the gated area of the fence, our partners could shut the gate and the dog would be isolated in the gated area and still on the chain. Buz and I would jump out of the gated fence area where the dog was isolated. The dog fell for the trick and he was out of our way. We then proceeded to knock on the door and announced our office. There was no response. We heard a television on and thought we heard and observed some movement. We knocked on the door again and still there was no response. We tried one more time to get someone to respond by knocking on the door pretty loudly. The dog was barking but still secure.

We decided to force entry as we had our arrest warrant with good intelligence that the fugitive was living there and we were pretty certain he was home, based on the vehicle and movement we observed at one of the residence's windows. We forced the door down taking it off the hinges. As the senior guy, this was my call and I was fully responsible for this decision. After entering and clearing the house, we discovered a guy in a bedroom and checked his identity only to discover he was not our guy. He was a relative. We asked the guy why he did not answer the door and he responded that he did not want to.

I called our site supervisor to report the situation including the broken door. The supervisor informed me not to worry that the government would replace the door. He subsequently called me back as we had moved on to another case and he informed me that a lady had called complaining about us knocking down the door. The supervisor told me he told her that the next time she should tell the person to open the door and the door would not be knocked down. I was very happy that our site supervisor understood what we were doing and was very supportive. Buz and I were working on a major Jamaican Posse case trying to find a major fugitive. This fugitive was known to be very dangerous and reportedly had killed several people. Buz and I were working on several leads and one lead led us to a Reggae club frequented by a large number of Jamaicans. Again we knew that the guy we were looking for was very dangerous and we had coordinated with the police department prior to going in and my partner was teamed with Buz' partner.

My partner worked on the police department in the city where the club was located. We also had another team with us that included an Alcohol Tobacco and Firearms agent and his partner. When Buz and I tried to enter, the security guy or bouncer wanted us to go through a magnetometer to screen for weapons, which we refused. We reluctantly identified ourselves as U.S. Marshals and the guy still said everyone had to be screen. We noticed a couple of people go in around the magnetometers unscreened and asked why these guys were allowed to avoid screening. The security guy/bouncer said those guys were regulars. We went in also avoiding the screening and started looking for our guy and watching our backs. The manager of the establishment approached Buz and I after the Club Bouncer pointed us out. We again identified ourselves and the Club Manager told us he had called the police. I received a telephone call from my police partner who related the police were called and she again let her department know we were working on a major case. I told the manager, that we were the police and no other police would be coming. Our search of the club proved negative for our fugitive. We worked very hard on this case, but never located him. We came to the conclusion that he was not in the U. S. There were only a few of our cases that we could not find and arrest; the Jamaican Posse guy and a guy I will describe only as Budhoo.

Another case that I was assigned involved an elusive female fugitive with several aliases. This fugitive had been a fugitive for quite some time. I did my usual records checks and other inquiries trying to establish a location for her. After a couple of weeks, while working this case and a few others, I developed a lead for this fugitive's mother's home address. I coordinated with Buz and his partner, and my partner and one morning we went to the home address of the fugitive's mother. We introduced ourselves and showed our identification letting the mother know we had a warrant for her daughter. The mother stated her daughter was not there and that she had not seen her daughter in quite some time. We asked if we could look around the house and the mother said we could but that her daughter was not there. We looked around and could not locate the daughter and were about to leave the residence, when I saw a rather small cabinet we had not looked into. When we opened the cabinet, we saw our fugitive who was a very petite African American lady. She was shocked we found her in the cabinet and actually we were as well. When the mother saw that we found her daughter and was arresting her, she ran into the kitchen and I ran after her. The mother opened a kitchen drawer and reached in at which time I closed it with her hand still in the drawer and took control of the mother with my other hand. I asked one of the two female partners to take control of the mother. After the mother was secured, I opened the kitchen drawer and observed a fully loaded revolver in it. The mother was going to grab the pistol and there is no doubt in my mind she would have used it on us. We arrested both the fugitive and her mother, turning the mom over to the local police. We had done another good job and thank God no one was hurt.

This second 10-week fugitive task force was just as exciting and I would say even more exciting than the first 10-week fugitive task force assignment

I worked on as a rookie deputy marshal in 1988. Meeting Buz, his partner, my partner and many others on the task force and assigned to the Marshals Service Miami and Ft. Lauderdale offices, is a highlight of my 30 plus years in law enforcement. Buz and I went under cover in some very dangerous areas and clubs. We always had each other's back. Although we made a number of additional fugitive arrests, as previously mentioned, we never found and arrested the Jamaican Posse fugitive or the fugitive known as Budhoo, who we did not have any leads on. Together, Buz and I along with our partners had a very high level of dangerous fugitive arrests and were respected by our site supervisor and the other fugitive warrant teams working on the task force. My previous knowledge of the south Florida area proved to be an asset and afforded me tremendous confidence in my knowledge of the how south Florida worked and how to be an effective law enforcement agent working, hunting, finding, and arresting dangerous drug dealing fugitives who had made a mark with the drug trade that was booming at the time.

In 1991, I applied for two Witness Security Inspector positions, both in Chicago. I made the best-qualified list for both and traveled to be interviewed. I was excited about finally getting a Marshals Service interview for a job as I had applied for a number of promotional opportunities and was not making the best qualified list. I was most frustrated by not making the best-qualified list for several openings at our Training Academy at the Federal Law Enforcement Training Center in Glynco, Georgia. I often contacted the agency's Human Resources Division for information and guidance on what I could do better to compete. Our personnel in Human Resources were very professional and responsive. I think they grew tired of me reaching out to them but they were always responsive. One of the ladies working in our Human Resources Division (HRD) at the time, who was of tremendous assistance to me, did very well and ended up being a top boss for the Marshals Service's HRD. I did not get to be a Witness Security Inspector as others were selected. However, I took another path in my Marshals Service career continuing to track and find fugitives which I loved doing.

In November of 1991, my second fugitive task force operation in southern Florida ended with a job well done. I returned to my home district of Chicago and to my family. I was happy to return home to spend time with my wife, and children Sylvester Jr., Lawrence, Erika, Sean, and Justin. I was also happy to return to my job at the U.S. Marshals Service in Chicago and my Army Reserve Unit where I was a Captain and veteran of the Desert Shield Desert Storm war. I was still assigned to the Organized Crime Drug Enforcement Task Force and resumed working fugitive warrants until I was reassigned to the district Court Operations Section in 1992.

CHAPTER SEVEN

Closing Out My Chicago Marshals Service Career

In 1992, I rotated between the district warrant squad and the general operations squad where the usual court operations took place. I enjoyed working with our district judges and providing security for them in court or at the judges' conferences. I always learned something from working court operations, sitting in court with other deputy marshals securing prisoners and paying attention to court room decorum, listening to the lawyers jargon and trying to understand why judges made certain rulings.

The year 1992 was a very good year for me personally and with my Marshals Service career with one tragic exception, which I will discuss a little later. In April of 1992, my wife and I had my 6th child, a beautiful baby girl we named Ashley. Ashley has been a wonderful blessing and I now had four sons and two daughters. I was also still performing my Army Reserve duties as an officer with the 308th Civil Affairs Company hanging out with my good friend Al Howard who was selected to be the Headquarters Company Commander. I was very happy to spend time with my wife and all of my kids when I could.

In 1992 I joined the law enforcement organization known as NOBLE, the National Organization of Black Law Enforcement Executives. I was happy to join this organization and was selected by my District Chief Ed Scheu and the Marshals Service Equal Employment Opportunity Office to attend the NOBLE annual conference in New Orleans in July. I had been to New Orleans before and was looking forward to returning with my wife and my baby daughter. I drove there on Saturday July 18, 1992, with my wife and baby girl to save airfare. It was a nice but long drive and we arrived Saturday evening and checked into our hotel.

Earlier in the year I had the pleasure of meeting a new deputy marshal who sat next to me in our general operations or court operations squad room. This new deputy was a very good guy who was in good shape as he worked out a lot and was eager to learn fugitive operations. I worked with him, taking him out on his early fugitive operations and helping him with his fugitive cases. I showed him the ropes and he enjoyed trying to track and find fugitives. He asked really good questions about tracking fugitives. I remember taking him out to investigate a few leads and he was eager to learn. He was a good guy to work with as I could tell he was a people person as he could easily deal with people.

Going back to my first NOBLE conference in New Orleans, on Monday afternoon around 5pm on July 20, 1992, my partner and close friend Deputy Marshal Herman Brewer called me as I was getting dressed to attend conference sessions. He told me to turn on the news and informed me that the deputy marshal I was fond of and mentoring, had been shot and killed at the courthouse in Chicago along with a dedicated retired police officer and Court Security Officer. They were shot by a former police officer who turned bank robber along with his wife. This former bank robber and former police officer had lost his wife in a bank robbery in a gunfight with police officials. The robber was in federal custody in our district. He had planned and almost executed an escape, grabbing a relatively new district WAE or While Actually Employed Deputy Marshal's weapon and immediately shot the deputy I had befriended and was mentoring, also shooting a dedicated court security officer that provided security in the garage of the Dirksen Building Courthouse. The heroic court security officer, who I knew and talked to, was able to return fire before dying and seriously wounded the bank robber. The bank robber and former officer knew he was wounded very badly and finished himself off shooting himself. As I turned the news on that late afternoon on July 20, 1992, the news correspondents were covering the shooting in the Chicago Courthouse, reporting on what happened.

What I still remember today was the stretcher carrying the deputy marshal I knew and sat next to in our squad room that was located in the courthouse facility. I saw the brown shoes he wore which I knew it was the deputy I had mentored, and was very saddened by his death. The heroic court security officer, a retired Chicago Police Officer died from his gunshot wounds. I stayed for the conference but it was definitely an emotional time for me as I kept thinking of the deputy and the court security officer. I remember quite vividly prior to my road trip to New Orleans for the NOBLE conference, that a few very senior deputy marshals including myself, went to meet with the new chief deputy marshal and expressed our concerns that security was being jeopardized by not placing adequately trained deputy marshals together or at least having one senior deputy marshal with a guard when moving or handling dangerous federal prisoners in custody. We explained that we felt someone was going to get killed if a change was not made in how we were assigning personnel to handle prisoners in the courthouse. Ironically, this was Friday July 17, 1992. The chief told us at this meeting that he would take the matter and discuss it with the marshal when the marshal returned from being out of office. Unfortunately and tragically, the Chicago courthouse shooting occurred on the ensuing Monday creating a very sad time in the U. S. Marshals Service Northern District of Illinois and the agency as a whole. Having my wife and daughter with me was of tremendous assistance when dealing with the loss of these heroic colleagues. The chief and another supervisor were reassigned after this incident. As I previously mentioned,

1992 was a good year and time with the exception of this very sad occasion of losing two American heroes at the U. S. Courthouse on July 20, 1992. Around this same time, Presidential Candidate William Clinton came to Chicago and spoke in downtown Chicago not far from the federal courthouse. I along with several other deputy marshals went to the event and saw him speak. It was very crowded, but we could see Mr. Clinton speak and witnessed part of his rise to political stardom.

In the spring of 1992, my partner Herman and I were assigned to go to Dixon, Illinois, to a correctional facility to pick up a state prisoner who was being released from state custody but had pending federal charges. Herman had been assigned a new 1992 Ford Thunderbird Super Coupe. Herman and I drove to Dixon, which is known as the home of late President Ronald Reagan on a Saturday to pick up our federal prisoner. We picked up our prisoner and secured him in the backseat of the Thunderbird Super Coupe in handcuffs and waist chains. The route to Dixon from Chicago is west on Interstate 80. After securing our prisoner and heading back east on Interstate 80 approaching a tollbooth outside of Dixon, we observed an Illinois State Trooper also at the tollbooth. Herman and I drove passed the Illinois State Trooper. The speed limit was 55 miles per hour and we probably were driving about 60 miles per hour. Herman and I experienced what we both call profiling as this Trooper who observed three African American males in a new Ford Thunderbird passing him. The Trooper decided to stop us and after pulling over and stopping on the highway, I mentioned to Herman that I would approach the Trooper to let him know who we were and what we were doing with the prisoner. I got out of the vehicle as I was sitting in the driver's side, with my Marshals Service credentials in my hand and the Trooper got out of his car and immediately yelled to me to get back in the car.

I identified myself as a deputy marshal and let the Trooper know we were working and had a federal prisoner in the car. The Trooper yelled again to get back in the car. I told the Trooper I was on duty and would not get back in the car. The Trooper threatened to arrest me and I responded that he would not be arresting me. I further stated that if anyone was going to get arrested it would be him and I reached for my handcuffs. My handcuffs were on the prisoner in the backseat of our vehicle. At this point Herman got out of the car as he observed the behavior of the Trooper and he also displayed his Marshals Service Credentials. The Trooper demanded Herman's driver's license and Herman responded to the white Trooper that we had shown him our credentials and we will show him the court prisoner transport papers, which we did.

The Trooper said that our badges could be fake in which I asked him why he would take that assertion and asked him if it was because we were black. The Trooper responded that he did not appreciate me calling him racist. Herman then asked the Trooper to call for his supervisor. The Trooper who was a Corporal responded that he was the supervisor. Herman then responded to the Trooper, that he needed another supervisor as we were at a standstill and the Trooper would not get his driver's license. The Trooper reluctantly called for another Trooper and a second Trooper arrived. Herman and I asked this second Trooper if he was a supervisor and he said no, but he was assisting. The second Trooper who was also white was siding with the first Trooper. Herman and I both again requested a supervisor. The first Trooper finally requested a supervisor and a third Trooper arrived. This Trooper was a Sergeant and African American, but also backed the first Trooper in his actions but was more reasonable. After some further discussion, Herman agreed to accept a warning ticket to settle the matter and we continued on with our prisoner to the Bureau of Prisons' Chicago Metropolitan Correctional Center (MCC). On the ride back to Chicago with our prisoner who had been in jail for 20 years, the prisoner related to Herman and I, "regardless of whether you are a black and a prisoner or black and a law enforcement official, you still get profiled and disrespected." Herman and I documented the incident with the Illinois State Police Trooper and asked the prisoner to write a letter about his observations, which he did.

Herman and I attached the prisoner's letter to our memorandums, which we turned in to our superiors. The lesson we learned from this situation was that profiling by law enforcement was still an issue that our society had to deal with. Herman and I had been stopped and profiled before while working dangerous assignments tracking down federal fugitives by white officers working with the Chicago Police Department. Once we identified ourselves as federal law enforcement officers during stops by the Chicago Police Department, there were no further issues with the officers as they realized we were on duty and on official business. However, in Dixon, Illinois, with that State Trooper, it was a very serious and dangerous situation that I am glad did not escalate further and Herman and I completed our mission as we always did.

In September of 1992, I was blessed and very happy to be selected to be in charge of the first Just the Beginning Conference. This conference was very special to me as it focused on African American Article III judges and the initial conference was in honor of the previously mentioned historic late Honorable Judge James Parsons. I had the responsibility of picking my security team from our district and coordinating and writing the security plan for the entire event. I coordinated closely with Judge Ann Williams who was a coordinator of the conference. It was a pleasure to work with Judge Williams and her staff on this event. I coordinated and work with the Chicago Police Department District where the event was held and coordinated with hotel security, local hospitals and the Chicago Fire Department.

I drafted the entire security plan taking into consideration many factors as just about every African American judge in the country attended this event in my great home town including the late great actor Ossie Davis and his beautiful wife the late Ruby Dee who I had the pleasure of meeting and talking with and getting a photo with. I forwarded my draft security plan to my district management and the Marshals Service Court Security Division at our Headquarters. My plan was approved as a very good document addressing all of the needs for this very important and significant event. This conference was scheduled from September 18 to September 20. This conference proved to be historic and had some legendary federal judges in attendance and speaking such as the following late great federal Judges: the late Constance Baker Motley, late Leon Higginbotham, and Judge and Alpha Fraternity Brother Damon Keith. Justice Clarence Thomas was invited but did not attend. I recall a couple of the judges speaking criticizing Justice Thomas for his position on Affirmative Action and other sensitive issues affecting the black community.

I struggled for several years to be in charge of a major judicial function and now I had my chance with the Just the Beginning Judicial Conference. I truly believe my work on this event helped shaped my career ambitions and accomplishments with the Marshals Service to work in support of judicial security. When the Just the Beginning Conference started, I noticed the Marshals Service Court Security Division had sent a seasoned Court Security Inspector to make sure everything was handled professionally and well. This was a very important conference and the first of it's kind. I met the great late Julius Turner, an individual who was very instrumental in my life for years to come. Court Security Inspector and former Witness Security Inspector Julius Turner was dispatched by the Chief of the Court Security Division, Mr. Donald Horton to make sure that this very important conference was handled correctly and security was squared away. When the late Mr. Julius Turner arrived and met with me and asked me for my security plan for his review. I was thinking if my plan was not squared away, Senior Inspector Turner would have to step in and take care of business himself as the conference was too important for any shenanigans. Mr. Turner was very impressed with my plan and operations and told me so. He also attended the event but as an observer as he related he had nothing to do as my plan and the security operation was superb. The conference was a two-day event and went very well. I was very happy to meet the late actor Ossie Davis and his beautiful wife actress the late Ruby Dee. The photo taken with them is still one of my treasures to this date. There was another seasoned Court Security Inspector stationed in Chicago and I also met with him and briefed him on my planning for the conference. He was also impressed with my operational plan and how things were going with the conference as he also attended the conference. I had two Senior Court Security Inspectors checking out my work, and had no idea I would end up being very close to both of these guys and being the Chief of the Program and Senior Executive of the division supervising one of them before their retirement.

Senior Inspector Turner and the other Court Security Inspector reported to their Chief Donald Horton how well security was executed and the excellent security plan I had put together and that they had nothing to do but observe. Chief Horton was very happy with this report and wrote a very nice letter to my district management on my behalf. I also became very good friends with Don Horton as my Marshals Service career progressed. My security team and I received several letters of commendation from judges, the two Court Security Inspectors and attorneys on how well and professional the security for the initial Just the Beginning Judicial Conference was handled. I am quite certain my military and law enforcement training greatly assisted me with how I managed the security planning and operations for this wonderful judicial conference. I subsequently learned that Senior Inspector Julius Turner had mentioned to Chief Don Horton that I would be a great addition to the Court Security Division as a Court Security Inspector. Chief Don Horton and others on his staff would recruit me to join the Court Security Division as a Court Security Inspector. I would later on in my career lead both the Judicial Security Division and the Witness Security Division the two Marshals Service divisions with protective missions. Before 1992 ended, I went on a 3-week protective detail in the Southern District of New York. I was the senior deputy on the afternoon shift protecting an Assistant U. S. Attorney. I got in a little trouble on this detail as my partner, an older guy but less seasoned deputy marshal, complained that I spent too much time away from the detail, as he got too close to the family of the protectee doing things I would not have done such as carry grocery bags and changing light bulbs at the family vacation home in New England. I was always taught that on protection details or law enforcement assignments, you need to be very vigilant at least operating in the security zone "Orange" as my old firearms instructor taught me, and to keep my hands free and ready for action if needed.

CHAPTER EIGHT

United States Attorney's Task Force - United States Virgin Islands

In January 1993, a position was announced for a Criminal Investigator assigned to the U. S. Attorney as part of a Task Force in the United States Virgin Islands. My former chief who I had the utmost respect for had been reassigned to the Court Security Division, and there were new senior managers in my district, the Northern District of Illinois. I knew it was time for me to move on and leave my great City of Chicago. I applied for the vacancy in the Virgin Islands. The U. S. marshal there was a career deputy marshal who had accomplished much in his own rise to prominence in the agency, Mr. Louie McKinney. I was selected for the position, my first selection for movement in the agency. It was not a promotion, but a lateral move. I called and spoke with the U.S. Marshal McKinney and he gave me a choice of which island I wanted to be assigned, as a second position had been announced creating two vacancies in the district, as a deputy marshal assigned to St. Croix had died committing suicide. There was one position to be filled on St. Thomas and one position to be filled on St. Croix. I did a little research and chose St. Thomas. Another Deputy selected was assigned to St. Croix.

I believe it was late January or early February when the selection notice came out announcing that the other deputy and I would go to the Virgin Islands assigned to the U. S. Attorney with a reporting chain to the district marshal and chief deputy. I had a friend and colleague there who was the supervisory deputy marshal assigned to St. Thomas. I met this friend and colleague when I was assigned to work the fugitive operation WANT II in Miami in the late summer and fall of 1988. We kept in touch and now I was starting the process to relocate to the Virgin Islands. My wife and I started packing deciding what to take with us, and what to place in storage. The logistics were not much of a burden, as again my military training kicked in to assist my wife and me with the planning. We put our home up for rent, unfortunately had to sell our young one year old pet Rottweiler, and I contacted another deputy marshal I met while working fugitive hunting assignments in Miami for some assistance with a shipping company in Ft. Lauderdale, Florida, to ship our vehicle to St. Thomas. It was a very exciting time for me and my wife as we were making a family move in support of my Marshals Service career. Going to live on an island was interesting. I called and had conversations with the Virgin Islands District Marshal, Mr. Louie McKinney, a Marshals Service legend of his own with many tremendous accomplishments. I did not know that he would become one of my mentors and a lifelong friend and father figure.

After shipping what we could to the marshal's office in St. Thomas, my wife and I packed up our luggage and belongings we would take on the plane, and loaded it in our van and on March 1, 1993, we drove to Ft. Lauderdale, Florida. We stayed at a hotel in Ft. Lauderdale for one night, had dinner with a deputy marshal colleague who was assigned to the agency's Special Operations Group and who I worked with and got to know while working the fugitive operation WANT II in Miami. We enjoyed a nice dinner with this deputy who also had a very good Marshals Service career along his wife and kids.

We had a flight to St. Thomas the next day and dropped off our van and flew out to our new destination. We flew out to St. Thomas and was greeted by the supervisory deputy on St. Thomas, my old WANT II colleague. The supervisor helped me secure a condo to lease at Mahogany Run, a very nice condo complex with the islands only golf course located on it. Our two-bedroom condo over looked the golf course. I was not into golf much at the time, so having the golf course there was nice to just watch people golf sometimes. It was a blessing to have good friends and colleagues to help us get to the new assignment and get settled. Our condo was very nice with a great view. The supervisor drove us to a local market store so we could get groceries until I got a vehicle and could get around. That following Monday, the supervisor came to the condo complex and picked me up and took me to the Marshal's office where I met the Marshal's staff, and the marshal took me to meet the U. S. attorney where I was assigned. The U. S. Attorney Ms. Terri Halpern was very accommodating and a pleasure to work with. My time working for her was short lived as the new 42nd President of the United States Mr. William Clinton asked for all U.S. attorneys' resignations and Ms. Halpern was no longer the U.S. Attorney. An acting U.S. attorney was named from the existing staff. I received my equipment such as local cellular telephone, camera equipment and vehicle, a brand new Chevy blazer, and was ready for work.

Assimilation to the islands and culture was very easy. My wife, my daughter Ashley and I assimilated well. It was still cold in Chicago when we left there and it was nice and warm in the U.S. Virgin Islands. I was learning my job and learning the small island of St. Thomas. Some of the most beautiful beaches are in the Virgin Islands and on downtime or weekends we sometimes went to the beach enjoying the pretty water. On occasion we took a ferryboat ride to the Island of St. John, which had probably the most beautiful beach I had seen called Trunk Bay. We enjoyed the food and music as well as eating fish and some of the local dishes were quite tasty. Our timing was pretty good arriving in March as the next month there was the St. Thomas Annual Carnival where there were plenty of activities. A large parking lot adjacent to the local courthouse was used to construct a small village where a number of small structures were put together and served as food and drink booths.

I learned what a Carnival Jouvert is and watched the Jouvert, otherwise known as a large street party celebrated in Caribbean islands that started in the morning before dawn. Although I did not participate, I did observe some of the party people having a good time. I am not a big crowd person. My wife, daughter and I also observed the Carnival Parade where the various troops or groups passed by with their nice costumes and floats, dancing and having a good time. We enjoyed the culture and loved the weather especially in the winter where back home in Chicago it was freezing and we were a short distance from a beach and could always look out our windows and see the water and cruise ships moving in, docking, or moving out. We learned what the island prices were and what the off-island prices were when it came to shopping. If you lived on island, you would argue for the island price. Of course if you lived off-island, most likely you did not know there was a difference.

Getting back to work, I enjoyed a very good partnership with the U.S. Attorney's Office, Drug Enforcement Administration and Federal Bureau of Investigation. I was co-located with a DEA Special Agent and a FBI Special Agent. I worked closely with both agents, but was a little closer to the FBI agent. I was assigned major cases to work, some of which were cases initially investigated by the local police department. During my first year assigned there, the U. S. Attorney's Office investigated all major crimes committed on the island. The Virgin Islands Department of Justice prosecutors investigated and prosecuted all other crimes. There was one Virgin Islands Police Detective Sergeant that assisted us federal guys and I also worked pretty closely with him. I worked a few surveillances with him. I recall being assigned to travel to the Island of Montserrat for an extradition of a murder suspect who had fled St. Thomas and was apprehended in Montserrat. Montserrat is a British Island and territory. At the time the island was dealing with a volcanic eruption and some of its population had left the island while a good number of residents remained. I traveled to Montserrat with the detective sergeant I enjoyed working with and read the murder case file while on the plane heading to Montserrat. We changed planes in Anguilla, another British Island, and flew into Montserrat, which made for an interesting landing, as you could see the volcano erupting and the plane's approach to landing was near a mountain.

The local Montserrat police officials were very kind and supportive, picking us up at the airport and getting us squared away with customs and to the hotel. The officials picked us up and took us out to a nice restaurant for dinner followed by a nice bar for a few drinks. We were picked up the next day to come to the police station and claim our prisoner for the extradition. We secured our prisoner and the necessary paper work to move him from British authority to U. S. authority. As I spoke with the prisoner, he mentioned to me to make sure I had all of his property. I told him I had secured and inventoried the property that the Montserrat officials gave me. What was very interesting is I had noted in the case file of the murder, the description and clothing provided for the accused murderer who had fled the scene of the murder. I noticed and made an investigative report that the clothing I had inventoried and took possession of, including a very descriptive hat, was a part of the prisoner's belongings. I was certain, based on the clothing description, the descriptive hat and other identifiers, that the witnesses in the murder case were describing the prisoner I had now in my custody. I briefed the federal prosecutor working on the case of my conclusions and submitted to him my investigative report. The assistant U. S. attorney was very pleased with my investigative efforts and reports and used that information in the murder trial. The defendant was convicted of the murder.

To keep my Reserve military status going, I transferred from the Army Reserve to the Virgin Islands National Guard. I was assigned as an Operations Officers and reported to a senior officer I got to know well. This officer's name is Lieutenant Colonel (LTC) Clive McBean. I enjoyed working with LTC McBean and enjoyed my military assignment. I befriended and got to know other excellent soldiers serving in the Virgin Islands National Guard. There was a nice small mini Post Exchange for military personnel that I shopped at which was good as the island had only a few stores and groceries were expensive. LTC McBean was a good superior and military role model and ended up being the Commanding General before retiring. He was instrumental in my selection from Operations Officer to Company Commander of the 661 Military Police Company where I commanded two Military Police Platoons on St. Croix and the one Platoon on St. Thomas. It was good for me to keep my military service going as I have said before that both my military and law enforcement careers have made me who I am and attributed significantly to my success and understanding and love of people and culture.

I worked on several other major cases involving crime conducted in the Virgin Islands to include assisting the district deputy marshals with investigating the whereabouts of district fugitives, assisting with major court trials and hearings. The supervisory deputy marshal I previously mentioned working in St. Thomas had told me about an open case that was a triple homicide that involved his brother. His brother had been killed in St. Thomas the year before I arrived along with two other guys and it was widely suspected the triple murder involved drugs. I could tell this supervisor who was a friend was very bothered that the case was still open with no one identified or implicated for the shooting of the three people. I told the supervisor that I would certainly give the case a very good look and would work hard to see if I could crack the case, using an old law enforcement term. I worked on this case and found it interesting that there were no leads and no known witnesses. I interviewed every Virgin Islands police officer that was still employed with the police department who worked on the case. I developed a couple of leads of Virgin Islanders involved and convicted of crime but in custody in federal correctional institutes, one in Atlanta and the other in Pennsylvania. I traveled to both institutions and interviewed both of these prisoners trying to get them to provide some useful or actionable intelligence. One of the prisoners seemed to have some information and wanted to know what I could do for him as far as his prison sentence. I told him if he had any good information to provide I would certainly speak on his behalf to the U. S. attorney of the Virgin Islands. I told him I could make no promises as far as results other than approaching the U.S. Attorney. This prisoner said that was not good enough and did not provide any information. I continued to work the case. While working with my two partners who were with the FBI and the DEA, they both informed me that I should pursue obtaining Title 21 authority, allowing me to investigate and obtain subpoenas for drug crimes and investigations. This made sense to me in view of the kind of work we were doing.

I went to see Marshal Louie McKinney and let him know about the conversation I had with my Task Force partners about the Title 21 authority to investigate drug crimes. Marshal McKinney agreed and arranged a meeting with the DEA Resident Agent in Charge of the U.S. Virgin Islands to discuss the Title 21. This meeting was held in the Marshal's office. The DEA Resident Agent in Charge was a little protective of the Title 21 authority we were requesting her support for which meant her sending a letter to DEA Headquarters back in the DC area. The DEA Agent in Charge mentioned that one had to have a certain level training and skill in drug investigations. I told her that I had worked very closely with DEA on a number of drug cases over the years, would not be out there using bad judgment trying to buy drugs, and that I had very good common sense. The meeting ended with the DEA Agent in Charge saying she would consider the request.

I met again with my FBI partner and informed him of my meeting with the DEA RAC and he said if DEA would not support my Title 21 authority request, he would write his superiors at FBI Headquarters in the DC area and make the request, which he did. The FBI Title 21 authority arrived within days and a short time later, I received a letter with the DEA Title 21 authority to investigate drug crimes. I had desired to get one such letter with the Title 21 authority; now I had two such letters. I went back to work on the triple homicide case looking at every angle or aspect of the case. I developed a solid lead involving a potential witness to the case. This was a major breakthrough for me and I was very happy to get some kind of break with the case. I met with the witness who did have some very good information about the case. The witness was from the Island of St. Thomas and was living on island. After some deliberate but careful discussions, the witness was willing to cooperate but had some serious concerns about safety, which I understood as some of these groups I was now investigating were very dangerous. I had actually added a high power rifle to my weapons' arsenal on the island, as I was quite aware that some of the people I was investigating were well armed. One good thing about the federal law enforcement community on island is that we grew to be very close, socialized together and depended on each other for support.

I met again with the witness I had located who of course was very concerned for her safety and security for cooperating and asked me how safety could be guaranteed on such a small island. I asked the witness if he had family somewhere other than the U.S. Virgin Islands and was told that he had family in the states. I also mentioned the Marshals Service Witness Protection Program and the reputation of this program for security and let the witness know I would discuss the use of the Witness Security Program with the U. S. Attorney's Office to see if the U.S. attorney would sponsor this very important case for consideration of the witness entering the Witness Protection Program. This was a major breakthrough on the case and the U.S. attorney contacted the Department of Justice's Office of Enforcement Operations (OEO) to sponsor this witness. The witness was accepted into the Witness Security Program. I met with the witness again to inform the witness of the news of their acceptance into the Witness Security Program.

I was contacted by the Witness Security Program and provided some direction on when to move the witness. I started the planning process to move the witness off the island to a safer location. I received directions to move the witness to San Juan, Puerto Rico. I obtained the flight tickets and flew with the witness to San Juan. I met with two Marshals Service Witness Security Inspectors and turned my witness over to these two Inspectors to keep safe. I had worked on a major criminal case assisting with sponsoring a witness in the famed Witness Security Program, a program and division I came to lead in my 18th year of working for the Marshals Service. I found out a couple of months later that this witness did not want to live away from St. Thomas and most likely did not want to get further involved in the triple homicide case.

Another interesting case I was assigned to investigate was the Container Liquor Case. The owner of a major liquor distributor came to the U.S. Attorney's Office to complain about the theft of expensive cases of liquor from a shipping container that arrived in a container by sea to the island for the liquor distributor. The business owner was very upset about the theft of cases of Chivas Regal 18-year old Scotch and a case of Dom Perignon. The acting U.S. attorney escorted the liquor distributor owner to my office, introduced me to the business owner and informed me that he wanted me to investigate the complaint of stolen commerce. I met with the business owner who seemed to be a very nice man with some understandable frustration about his commerce being stolen. I took his statement and commenced my investigation.

I worked with the detective sergeant I had worked with before on this case and another good friend and colleague I got to know very well while assigned in St. Thomas, Tom Gordon, who was a Special Agent with Immigration. All deputy marshals assigned to the St. Thomas office had the opportunity if desired, to sign up to work out at Gold's Gym at government expense. This was also extended to me as well and I signed up and worked out three to four times a week at the gym. Plenty of people frequented Gold's Gym and I got to know a number of people who worked out there. I started asking questions about stolen liquor, asking if anyone heard of anyone selling Dom Perignon champagne and Chivas Regal scotch. The island is small and people know each other and hear things. Amazingly someone told me that they heard a guy was trying to sell expensive champagne and scotch and gave me a first name. I did not have a last name, but was happy to have a first name lead.

I decided to visit with some of the most popular night clubs and bars on island at the time including Club Z, the Old Mill and a couple of other locations. I wanted to interview business owners and managers to ascertain if anyone was offering to sell Chivas Regal and Dom Perignon champagne. I made several stops to interview businesses and had some success at one location. At the Old Mill the manager said someone did come by offering to sell Dom Perignon champagne and scotch. I mentioned the first name of a guy that someone told me at Gold's Gym and the manager recognized the first name and also knew the guy's last name. Now I had a first and last name and was soon working to close out this case. I soon had a description for this guy as he was somewhat well known. I was able to recover just about all of the Dom Perignon champagne and one case of the Chivas Regal scotch, discovering that there were two guys involved in the liquor container heist. I hunted, located and arrested both guys and they both cooperated in the recovery of the remaining liquor that was in their possession. I inventoried and returned the recovered liquor to the distributor who made the complaint.

The owner was very happy with my investigative work leading to the recovery of some of his stolen commerce and the arrest of the two guys who broke into the container and stole the cases of liquor. To the best of my memory, the liquor distributor did not wish to pursue criminal charges against the two perpetrators. The guys who I arrested seemed to be decent guys who were friends. According to one version of the situation, one of the two liquor thieves was passing by the dock area and observed the container open and decided, after discussing the situation with the other, that stealing the liquor would be a great opportunity to make money, and they came back to the liquor shipping container with a vehicle to take the liquor.

On another major case I investigated involved the murder of a Virgin Islands Police Officer on St. Thomas. I was actually relaxing off duty at the condo I was renting at Mahogany Run and observed a police officer who was towing a car. I like talking with people and went to speak with this officer. I introduced myself as a deputy marshal assigned to the U. S. Attorney's Task Force. The officer mentioned that he had heard of me and seemed very troubled. The officer asked if he could speak with me about a very sensitive matter. I responded back of course. The officer mentioned he was very concerned about some corrupt officers he was working with and that he had witnessed these officers take drugs and money from the evidence inventory. I asked the officer if he would like to give any names and cooperate against the officers with the U. S. attorney. He said he was thinking about it but also concerned for his safety. I gave the officer my card with my contact information and mentioned to him if he wanted to speak with me, or someone from the U.S. Attorney's Office to contact me and we could meet in a confidential manner. He took my card and said he would get back to me.

However, this officer who was obviously a professional and concerned about some problem officers would not get a chance to contact me or the U. S. attorney to discuss his concerns about drugs and cash being stolen from the police department's evidence room. The officer was murdered where he lived with his mother. He was shot numerous times by automatic gunfire, a day after I met him on a Sunday morning after he got home from his shift. This was in March 1994 as I started my second year serving on the Task Force living on the lovely small island. Once I heard about the murder, I contacted the U.S. attorney and informed him of my meeting with the officer and what the officer told me. I made a written report and the U.S. attorney authorized an investigation into the murder of this heroic officer who had served five years on the Virgin Islands Police Department and was only 26 years old. It was a very sad situation. I attended his funeral and felt a connection to the slain officer as the day before he was killed, the officer had provided me with information about the very serious crime and corruption in his department and was killed the next day.

I was assigned a lead role in investigating the officer's death, as it was clear that it was a calculated, pre-meditated murder. It was widely speculated that someone the officer knew and trusted very well killed him, or set him up to be killed by calling him out of his residence. As the officer came to the gate and he was killed in his pajamas. From my view and short time with the officer, I suspected he was killed by other Virgin Islands police officers or at the direction of officers. This fallen hero had information that could have put them in prison. My investigation entailed interviewing several officers who were suspected of being associated with organized criminal organizations. As we know, suspicion is not evidence and there was no known evidence to charge the officers I interviewed at the time with murder of the officer. The Virgin Islands Police Department had a Narcotics Strike Force and there was wide speculation that some of these officers were involved in criminal activity working with dangerous drug organizations. I also suspected officers from this group may have been involved in the death of the officer. I was focused on this case and trying to find and charge those involved with this young officer's murder. I interviewed the officers in question in my office at the U.S. Attorney's Office trying to obtain some leads as to who was involved with the officer's murder, also checking on the location of the officers in question. Some of the officers were very nervous during the interview, and a couple of others were not. I was unable to obtain any actionable leads. After I left, the investigation continued. To my knowledge no one was ever charged and convicted of the murder of this brave officer. I read a 2001 article where there was information that a Virgin Islands Narcotics Strike Force officer in a discussion while in prison stated that the slain officer in the 1994 case had to be killed because he was going to "snitch" on him and other officers who were taking drugs and cash from police evidence could not let him do that. However, it does not appear from any of my research that anyone was charged and held accountable for this very sad and horrible murder of an honest policeman.

The Marshal for the Virgin Islands, Mr. Louie McKinney, who I had come to know well was being considered for the Director's position for our agency late in 1993, and left the island with his family, returning to his home in the DC area to prepare to become the Director. I remember that we had a very nice farewell for him and his family and we were very proud and excited for him. Soon after Marshal McKinney got to Washington DC, the designated Attorney General who Mr. McKinney would work for, had issues with an undocumented worker in her home and removed herself or was asked to step aside from consideration and a new Attorney General candidate was revealed, Ms. Janet Reno, who was confirmed as the United States Attorney General. With this change came a new person to be nominated and appointed as the Director of the United States Marshals Service, Mr. Eduardo Gonzalez. I knew Louie McKinney but did not know the new Director. Director Gonzalez had been an outstanding local law enforcement executive with the Metro Dade Police Department in Miami and as Chief of Police in Tampa, Florida, prior to his Presidential Appointment as our Director by President Clinton in 1993. I was blessed to know and serve under both Director Gonzalez and Acting Director McKinney as Mr. McKinney was appointed by President George W. Bush to act as Director for a while when he was elected President in 2001.

In July 1994, the Marshals Service announced seven Supervisory Deputy Marshal positions in various districts. There are 94 federal judicial districts where the Marshals Service has offices including the

Superior Court in Washington, DC. The Superior Court Deputy Marshals essentially act as Sheriffs Deputies as this district secures and produces those charged with crimes in Washington, DC, that are not federal charges and also conducts civil evictions. With seven opportunities for promotion to supervisory deputy marshal, I figured my chances to finally get promoted above journeyman level was pretty good and applied for all of the positions knowing if selected I would take the job. I was thinking I would most likely get a selection to a position out West, as I applied for the following districts as a supervisory deputy marshal: U.S. Virgin Islands, St. Croix which would keep me and my family in the Virgin Islands; District of Puerto Rico, San Juan, another very nice but much larger island; Southern District of Texas, McAllen; District of Maryland, in the DC area; Central District of California, Los Angeles; and the District of Kansas, Wichita. The selections came out in July 1994 and Director Eduardo Gonzalez selected me for the Supervisory Deputy Marshal position in San Juan, Puerto Rico. I would be in charge of the Seized Assets Squad a job in my opinion, helped shape my successful law enforcement career.

I met Director Gonzalez for the first time in late July 1994 at a law enforcement conference in Richmond, Virginia. I was in my third year as a member with the National Organization of Black Law Enforcement Executives and attended my third conference with the organization in Richmond. Director Gonzalez was a keynote speaker and I met him at the agency meeting during the conference. A new U.S. marshal was selected for the Virgin Islands and he also attended the conference. After meeting Director Gonzalez, I thanked him for his selection as a supervisor in Puerto Rico. The Director told me what he has told me after promoting me two more times making me one of the agencies youngest Chief Executives, that I earned each promotion by being the best qualified candidate and a hard worker.

Director Gonzalez asked me if I was going to be in the DC area before heading back to the Virgin Islands and if so, he wanted to meet with me.

He let me know if I was going to be in the DC area, I should stop by his office. The Director informed me to call his secretary and make an appointment and I did just that and made an appointment. I drove up to Washington, DC, from Richmond, Virginia, in a rental car with the new Marshal for the Virgin Islands, and met with Director Gonzalez. The marshal met with the Director first for a few minutes and I met with Director Gonzalez afterward for a nice visit. I could not believe I was meeting with the agency Director and we were discussing the job, family and my new assignment. The Director's secretary, who I also have come to know very well over the years, came into the Director's office to let him know he had a couple of people waiting to see him and we ended our meeting. I must admit I was on a natural high during and after meeting this great leader. I went back to Richmond and flew back to St. Thomas and resumed my work there until my move to Puerto Rico. My good friend and colleague Deputy Marshal Buz had transferred to the District of the Virgin Islands in September 1994 and was assigned to St. Thomas. It was very good to see him as we had kept in touch since meeting in 1991 in Miami. I got to work with Buz again, but only for a month and a half or so, as I was moving to Puerto Rico.

During this time I received a call from my good friend who I have spoken of a number of times, Bill Walker. I had lost contact with Bill as he was doing his business with the Drug Enforcement Administration. He had left Chicago after taking a job with DEA and his first assignment was in New York. Bill Walker had kept up with where I was by contacting mutual military colleagues we both had in Chicago. Bill obtained my phone number from one of the military mutual colleagues and called to let me know he was up for a new assignment and was coming to St. Thomas because there was an opening and he had put his name in for the job. I told Bill that I was closing out my assignment as a deputy marshal on the U.S. Attorney's Task Force and had been promoted to Supervisory Deputy Marshal, a GS-13 position. Bill related he had been the Resident

Agent-in-Charge in the Bahamas and was now stationed in Miami. He further gladly mentioned that he was ahead of me in grade and that he was a GS-14. Bill Walker told me he would call me right back as he had to call DEA Headquarters and pull his name out from the St. Thomas job since I was moving on to San Juan and that he would put his name in for DEA openings in San Juan. He related there seemed to always be openings there. Bill called me right back and related he was now going to San Juan. I was very happy to know my longtime friend would also be living and working in Puerto Rico and moving his family there. I had one other friend who I was getting to know who was a Federal Bureau of Investigation Group Supervisor and stationed in San Juan with the FBI. I met this fellow when he came over to St. Thomas to check on my partner on the Task Force who reported to him. Cary Thornton and I also became very good longtime friends and neighbors living in the same community in Rio Piedras, Puerto Rico.

CHAPTER NINE

Puerto Rico-Supervising the
Seized Assets Squad

On October 14, 1994, I reported to San Juan, Puerto Rico, moving with my wife and two year old daughter. Just as with the U.S. Virgin Islands, I had never been to Puerto Rico. This was another good opportunity and assignment for me that allowed me to continue to serve, learn and grow in my career. Now I was a frontline supervisor and used my military experience and leadership to assist me with this assignment. However, I had to use balance and judgment. My employees were not my soldiers; they were a combination of operational, administrative federal employees and contractors. My wife, daughter and I flew from St. Thomas to San Juan on a Saturday and took a week of administrative leave allowing some time for us to transition doing such things as obtaining drivers' licenses, picking up our car we had shipped, grocery shopping and learning a little about the area. We spent the next three months in temporary lodging. I shipped some boxes to the Marshals Office in Puerto Rico and I stopped by the office and picked up the boxes and obtained my building access identification.

When I reported to work, I met the U.S. marshal who welcomed me but told me in a kind way that he had recommended someone else for the position. I told the marshal that he would be very happy with my work and accomplishments serving in his district. I had a nice little office near the employees I supervised. This was my first office that I had all to myself as I shared a rather large office suite while assigned to the Virgin Islands with my two colleagues from the FBI and DEA. I met individually, one by one, with my small team of five people. I was in charge of the district's seized assets squad, which at the time in October 1994 had either the Marshals Service second or third largest inventory of items seized, mostly from organized drug dealers. The Southern District of Florida and the Southern District of New York rounded out the top three districts with seized assets waiting to be disposed of and forfeited by court order to the United States. These assets were managed and sold and the proceeds deposited into the seized assets deposit fund. This funding was eventually returned to the U.S. Treasury minus any portions of the assets that were considered to be equitable shared. Equitable Sharing is a term used by seized assets whereby the proceeds from seized assets sold was shared with state, county and local law enforcement working jointly on an investigation where assets are seized from criminals and their organizations.

I had never been assigned to the seized assets squad in my five plus years assigned to the Chicago office as it was difficult to get assigned to work on that team back then. I was always interested in learning the various aspects of the job. However, this was one unit I was not be able to join as a deputy marshal in Chicago. I was assigned as earlier mentioned to go on asset seizures in the Northern District of Illinois or the Chicago region, and the seizures were sometimes complex, targeting multiple assets and criminals at the same time. Now I was the supervisor of a district's seized assets squad and had plenty to learn about the full operation. I was eager to learn and get the job done. I set up meetings with various property managers of the district's seized assets, meeting with the real property management company, the vehicle property management and the vessel property management company. I had periodical meetings with all three of the property management organizations including coordinating vehicle and boat auctions. I enjoyed the boat and vehicle auctions as there were numerous very nice cars and boats to be auctioned and the business process was very interesting to learn and be a part of.

My wife and I found a nice home in Rio Piedras, Puerto Rico, right about the time our temporary quarters allowable funding expired. This house was an exit away from a small shopping center and not too far from the office. My friend and FBI colleague, Cary Thornton, and his wife lived less than a block away. A couple of other colleagues from my office lived in the development to include an employee I supervised. The one problem I did not like with the housing in Puerto Rico, especially the San Juan metropolitan area was that no matter how nice your housing development was, there was always a low-income housing area close by and the housing area was a high rise. I asked a couple of people from Puerto Rico why the low income housing area was so close to other nicer housing areas in San Juan and was told that a former Governor decided that he wanted those people who could not afford nicer housing to not feel that they are too far from living a better life. This made some sense to me but my issue with that concept was that those that were involved with crime were too close and could look down over the residential homes. I did enjoy the fact that Cary and his wife, and my wife and daughter, could walk to each other's homes for dinner or just to visit.

During my first year on the island, I was very busy with operations, but also continued to focus on learning all I could about seized assets and took business courses to assist me with my knowledge of business and procurement. I enrolled in and completed the Contracting Officer's Technical Representative or COTR class in the spring of 1995. This course was offered in the DC area in Mclean, Virginia, and lasted a week. I always enjoyed visiting the Washington, DC, area and looked forward to any classes I could take in that area. Later in the spring of 1995, I also completed a course titled Small Purchasing, which was also in Mclean, Virginia, bringing me to DC for another week. I was also enrolled and completed a Berlitz Spanish training course, attending classes in the evening after my regular duty hours in early 1995.

Additionally during my first year in San Juan, I teamed up with federal law enforcement colleagues and friends to create the Caribbean Chapter of the National Organization of Black Law Enforcement Executives. My longtime good friend Bill Walker, and FBI Group Supervisor Cary Thornton, Author of the book "Oath of Office," and several other federal and local law enforcement officers and I, decided to establish a Chapter of NOBLE for the Caribbean region. Our plan was to target law enforcement officers in Puerto Rico, the U.S. Virgin Islands and other islands where there were law enforcement officers with an interest in joining the organization. Chapter members had to be members with the National Organization in the DC area and then be members of the Chapter. We held monthly meetings and voted on the Chapter officers. I was elected Chapter President, Cary Thornton elected Vice President and Bill Walker held another Chapter officer position along with a few others. We had good support from the National office, but found it very challenging to build the Chapter and recruit members from Puerto Rico. We gave it a good try to recruit members from Puerto Rico to join the organization, but were not that successful, only able to get a small number to join. Cary, Bill and I said that when we left Puerto Rico, the Chapter would most likely fold which it did not too long after I got promoted and moved to the Washington DC area in October 1996.

Puerto Rico is a large island much larger than the three U.S. Virgin Islands. I worked closely with the U. S. Attorney's Office, the Drug Enforcement Administration, the Federal Bureau of Investigation and the Internal Revenue Service on various operational and administrative seizures. Anytime there was a pending major seizure of assets, I met with the assistant U. S. attorney working on the case and the investigative agency or agencies, as sometimes there were more than one investigative agency working on the case. For example, the DEA could be investigating a case where a business was involved and the Internal Revenue Service (IRS) would also have a special agent working the case as the criminal organization usually selling drugs not only purchased vehicles, boats, and houses, but purchased a business and there may be some tax implications that the IRS was investigating. I worked one such seized assets case that involved the seizure of vehicles, houses, a boat and a boating business. This case involved DEA and the IRS and we seized plenty of assets. Seizing the boating business was interesting. I had to hire an accounting firm to inventory all items in stock at the business, which was a process that took all day. We seized several nice vehicles including a beautiful Porsche that I took a photo in.

On another DEA seizure, we traveled from San Juan to the western side of the island to the Mayaguez area. We seized a farm and had to inventory livestock and other animals. I procured a company or organization that could help us with this seizure and maintain the farm. On this farm there were several pigs and alligators that were a part of the seizure. This was definitely different than any seizure I participated on in my home district of Northern Illinois in the Chicago area. Another seizure I participated in was in Santurce, Puerto Rico, in an area called Barrio Figueroa, which we were briefed was a very dangerous area. This was a seizure and arrest operation of some of the islands most dangerous drug dealers. The Federal Bureau of Investigation took the lead on this case and had a FBI Special Weapons and Tactics team make the initial entry due to the threat level. No arrests were made at the location. There were other locations on the island also being targeted where arrests were made.

What resonates with me most from this operation was that after we secured the apartments we went in and seized several items. When several of us were walking to our vehicles and it was now light outside, I remember little children walking happily to school stepping on hundreds of pill cases and other drug paraphernalia. To see the kids going to school walking over this stuff really touched my heart. As previously discussed in this book, I grew up on the south side of Chicago. I had seen gangs in the neighborhood, crimes committed including a young man get shot running with a basketball behind the house my family and I lived in. I heard this young man running and observed two men or older teenage men when one of the men shot the younger boy, and like a movie I had seen, the basketball was rolling in the alley. The younger guy laid shot right where I saw him get shot and we heard he died. My Mother told me to get away from the window and asked me what I saw and I told her. The police interviewed residents in the area and I told the officers what I observed. I also lost a young female friend to a drug overdose. The girl and I were classmates in the same grade and she lived about three houses from where my family and I lived at another apartment. We were both 12 years old. My point to these stories is crime can be anywhere. The Barrio Figueroa housing area bothered me because kids should be able to walk to school in any area anywhere and not be subject to walking over drug paraphernalia and countless pill casings.

Other than Barrio Figueroa, I was thoroughly enjoying my assignment and working in Puerto Rico. I got along great with my chief deputy who I reported to and also got along well with the other two district supervisory deputy marshals. The marshal and I developed a very nice working relationship and friendship. He told me that he was very happy I was working in the district. I also got along well with everyone else working in the district and enjoyed outings at Marshals Service colleague's homes and on occasion, a pig was be roasted. I am a cultured person and appreciate different cultures. I enjoyed the food, music and dance of the island. On Thursdays, people got dressed up very sharp and went out after work. The women dressed to impress. I went out with some of the guys in the office and enjoy the scenery and at times some good dancing. I also spent time with DEA Group Supervisor Bill Walker and FBI Group Supervisor Cary Thornton. Cary and I spent time and a little money at the island's nice casinos, especially the casinos nearby San Juan and Old San

Juan. We did okay at the tables playing craps. As I mentioned, Cary and his wife lived less than one block away from my house.

In September of 1995, Hurricane Marilyn made its appearance in the Caribbean. This hurricane was threatening Puerto Rico, and the U. S. Virgin Islands and most likely other nearby islands. My home had shutters to cover windows and I went on the roof to obtain the shutters and put them in place. My home was secure. I received a call from Cary Thornton who told me his wife was cooking dinner and asked if I wanted to come over and deal with the hurricane at their home. This sounded good to me and I packed up a few items to include a bottle and joined Cary and his wife to endure the storm. We had no idea how bad the hurricane would be and where it would hit as our region was reported as a major target for the "eye" of the hurricane. We were sitting at the Thornton's home when the weather got bad with very strong winds. Cary had secured his home as best as possible and we had a nice meal and listened to the radio trying to hear storm/hurricane related information. I became use to these storms and hurricanes from living in St. Thomas. I had endured another hurricane watch and storm losing power and water while living on St. Thomas.

As we now know the hurricane did not inflict much damage to Puerto Rico, although it was reported that one man lost his life trying to move an antenna and was electrocuted in Puerto Rico. I got a little sleep at the Thornton's residence and we woke up to see the damage. The Thornton residence was fine. I walked to my house to see how things were and everything was fine with the exception of power being lost which I believe was the case in many areas of metropolitan San Juan. I was very concerned about my friends and colleagues in the U.S. Virgin Islands and used my Marshals Service radio to communicate with Marshals Service personnel in St. Thomas. I communicated with the supervisory deputy marshal on St. Thomas who was my good friend and he told me the island was devastated with many homes damaged or destroyed and power was gone as the island used power lines on poles above the ground. I knew this to be the case as I had seen first hand how the storms take down the power lines.

The next eight weeks was very memorable to me as I assisted with the public safety response in St. Thomas. On the day after the hurricane hit St. Thomas, and after checking my home, I went back to the Thornton residence and told them I needed to go to St. Thomas and got on an aircraft to get there a little later in the day. I asked them to check on my home and let them know I was keeping my shutters in place for now and would take them off later. I contacted my marshal using my marshal's radio. I knew my marshal also had a military background and he was well connected on the island. I let him know I would be activated as the Military Police Company Commander for the Virgin Islands' National Guard in response to the hurricane and he agreed with my thoughts on the matter. I asked him if he knew of any support aircraft going to St. Thomas and he told me he would check and contact me back.

He did contact me and told me about a flight going to St. Thomas and gave me the time. I did not have much time before the flight left but told him I wanted to get on it and asked him to come pick me up and take me to the airfield which he did. I was use to deploying for the military and packed my military backpack with some uniforms and a few can goods and left with the marshal to the airfield. I thanked the Marshal and told him I would be in touch and flew to St. Thomas not knowing what to expect. I contacted the supervisory deputy marshal and told him I was on a flight and asked him to come and get me at the St. Thomas airport, as I needed to locate my military unit and get to work. As I arrived, my friend the supervisor along with the district marshal picked me up. What I saw was pure devastation with damage homes, power lines down, and trees down all over the place. As we approached the downtown area, there were a number of small boats that were tossed from the water into shops and buildings along the main street. There was an 80-foot Coast Guard Cutter ship lifted out of the water and sitting on the sidewalk. Unlike the smaller boats, the Cutter was heavy enough that it was not be tossed into the shops and buildings. St. Thomas was very badly damaged by Hurricane Marylyn. I did not link up with my military unit until the next day.

As nightfall approached, I decided to stay the night with the district chief deputy and her family. I knew the chief deputy from my assignments working fugitive operations in South Florida when she was a supervisory deputy. On the next morning I got up early and located my military unit. My two Military Police Platoons had arrived from St. Croix, as the island of St. Croix did not obtain devastation although there was damage from the hurricane. My higher military headquarters was located at an old St. Thomas government building near the east side of the Island. I led our Military Police operations out of this building for the next two months. The initial public safety response was from my two platoons from St. Croix as we patroled the island assisting with law and order and handling law enforcement calls for assistance from citizens on the island. The Virgin Islands Police Force was not online as the police officers were taking care of their family needs from the devastating hurricane. I was the Incident Commander for this disaster until the Virgin Island Police came back online which was about two days later. My driver and I responded to several calls for assistance helping restore order and resolving disputes, thefts of property and burglaries.

The patrol responsibilities and responding to calls for assistance, reminded me of my patrol duties as a police officer back home in the Chicago area on the Markham Police Department. I was doing what I knew how to do. Once the police were back online, my units' functions were moved to a supportive public safety function assigning Military Police teams to food and water distribution centers and ice storage centers. Food, water and ice were critical needs and had to be protected from those who would take it and limit the organized distribution. Around the same time as the Virgin Islands Police regained operational control of law and order, my third platoon personnel from St. Thomas was just about all reported in. I already had assigned my two platoons from St. Croix to various duties around St. Thomas. I also had a large number of Virgin Island National Guard military personnel assigned to my unit, the 661st Military Police Company, to augment our operational requirements, and my platoon leaders who were First Lieutenants and one senior non-commissioned officer were busy putting the augmented personnel to work as there was plenty to do.

As days passed on, more resources came to the island; military units arrived, volunteer Fire and Police Departments arrived providing assistance. I attended high-level meetings with the Virgin Islands Police Commissioner, Commanders from the Virgin Islands Police Department and other federal law enforcement officials including the Marshals Service. This was neat to me, as I worked in one capacity wearing my military uniform while working with my law enforcement colleagues and partners. The Marshals Service sent an Incident Management Team to the island to also assist with the disaster response. Deputy marshals and a U. S. marshal arrived to assist with the security of the federal courthouse, also assisting the local Marshals office with other judicial security responsibilities. The U.S. marshal assigned as the Incident Commander for the Marshals Service response also attended the daily high-level meetings for coordination of resources. This marshal later in my career selected me as an Assistant Director, which I will discuss in more detail later. It was a very busy time on the island as there was no power and the use of generators provided power.

However, the generators were initially limited. My unit had generators as a part of our equipment list. Some residents had generators they procured from knowing that these devastating storms can leave one without power and telephone capacity for weeks and months. I estimated from the severe damage that it would be a couple of months before power and telephone service would be restored. As was reported in September 1995, many homes were destroyed and six or seven people on or near St. Thomas died as a result of this hurricane. The majority of these fatal casualties resulted from people being in the water on their boats. As previously mentioned, boats in the harbor near the water front of downtown were tossed out of the water and landed upside down, some of which were on buildings.

During the first week or two in the aftermath of Hurricane Marilyn, my company command group stayed in the government building with my platoons and those augmented to assist us with the Virgin Islands National Guard response. After two weeks, my unit command team moved to vacant furnished condos as the owners of the condo complex offered the condos for use to the military. The condos did not have power. We had battery-powered lights and used beach water to flush the toilet. This move by the Command Team to the condos worked out fine as the troops had their space and did not worry about the leaders being with them when they were off duty and resting. Portable Johns or toilets were shipped in as the island only had so many of the portable toilets. These portable toilets were needed, with all of the resources coming from various parts of the U. S. to assist with the disaster response. I saw military units putting up their tents at various locations mainly near the airport. At one meeting I bumped into a former Reserve Officer Training Corps (ROTC) colleague. He was now a Major on Active Duty with the Army. During our ROTC days back in college, I outranked him. Now years later he outranked me as active duty officers normally get promoted quicker from Second Lieutenant to Major. It was good to see him as we spoke about old times and friends from our ROTC days.

As the days progressed into weeks, the island was improving as expected. Debris was being moved off the roads and people were getting generators and roof tarps that they needed to keep further rain from entering their homes. I periodically checked on people I knew fairly well to see how they were and to see if they needed supplies. One lady I knew pretty well and had lived in one of her apartments at her Villa needed a tarp for the roof of one of her apartment units. I told her I would locate a tarp for her and return and put the tarp on, which I did. She was very happy that I checked on her and assisted her. I became close to her and her family especially her husband who had died recently. I enjoyed talking to her husband after work and he was a great guy who adored and loved his wife and kids tremendously. He was a retired successful businessman from my hometown of Chicago and retired with his wife in St. Thomas.

After about a month after the hurricane, there was substantial improvement and progress with the infrastructure of the island. Power was restored in many parts of the island. Some areas were worse than others and it took a lot of time to get back to normal. Some homes and structures had to be rebuilt. Some of the residents of the island left the island walking away from their homes. My military unit and those military members from the Virgin Islands National Guard continued to perform our assignments of providing security for the distribution centers. My time on duty for this assignment was very rewarding and meaningful to me. I developed many close relationships from the eight weeks that I served assisting with public safety and security of St. Thomas and its residents after Hurricane Marilyn.

During my eighth week, I received a call from my marshal back in Puerto Rico. He mentioned that he had heard there was vast improvement on the island and that he needed me back at work to run the seized assets unit. I responded to him, that things were much better and I was still on the orders and that the orders should be ending soon. I told him I would report back to work on San Juan the following week as I had to take care of a few last things and leave my most senior First Lieutenant in charge of my unit. That weekend, I boarded a military aircraft and flew back to San Juan. I returned to my office and rejoined my team and got back to work catching up on what had transpired the past two months and what the unit was currently working on. Later I was recognized by my Battalion Commander for my service and leadership with the Army Meritorious Service Medal and Certificate, my second such award as I received that medal and certificate from my service in the Middle East for Operation Desert Shield and Desert Storm. I also received the Virgin Islands Meritorious Service Medal and the Virgin Islands Commendation Medal for my efforts during Hurricane Marilyn. The rest of 1995 was pretty much business as usual for me with a few property seizures and property auctions, and the sale of a few homes.

In 1996 I was well into my second year of working and living in Puerto Rico. In early 1996 I noticed that the Marshals Service had announced a Chief Inspector position in what was then known as the Prisoner Services Division. This would be a promotional opportunity for me and would be a paid move back across the ocean to the Washington DC area. I was very interested in this position and applied. I made the short list or best-qualified list and was invited to travel to Headquarters for an interview. My chief called me into his office and informed me that he was notified of my upcoming interview. I was also registered for yet another business course in support of my efforts managing the seized assets unit. The course was titled, Basic Contract Administration, and was in Chicago. It just happened to work out that my interview for the promotional opportunity was the week before the aforementioned course in Chicago. I was able to get a late week interview date to allow me to travel from Washington DC to Chicago where I spent a weekend in Chicago and started the Basic Contract Administration course the following Monday. My good friend and former fugitive partner Deputy Marshal Herman Brewer was also enrolled in this class. I had a great opportunity to spend time with my family including my children in Chicago. I also got a chance to get together with Herman after class and we spent a little time with some of our former colleagues in the Chicago Marshal's office for drinks and catch up on things with our former office. The interview was held in the office suite of the Prisoner Service's Division at our Headquarters, which I thought was very strange as the Human Resources Division normally coordinated the Merit Promotion process to include conducting interviews. I found out in the next few weeks what was going on, as there was a plan by the assistant director of the division to promote someone else. The interview panel was comprised of the acting chief of the division and two other chief deputies from field offices. The acting chief was also a field chief deputy who was on detail to act as the second in charge of the division under the assistant director.

I traveled to the Washington, DC area the night before the interview and checked into my hotel. I had made plans to go out to dinner with a friend and colleague that was assigned to the Seized Assets Division at Headquarters. We went out to eat and went to a local Maryland nightspot to hear a nice musical band. I did not stay out too late as I had the interview in the afternoon the next day. I was interviewed and told my score was a total of 66 out of 100. I had done my best during the interview and just accepted the score realizing that I would not get the job. I called my chief deputy, my boss, back in Puerto Rico and told him about my interview and score of 66. He told me he had talked to the Chair of the interview panel, a good friend of his, and was told I most likely would not be getting the job. This discussion with my chief confirmed my thoughts that I would not get the position and I mentally moved on thinking maybe the next time.

I traveled to Chicago my favorite town the next day and that cheered me up from the prospective that I had missed this opportunity to get promoted and be moved back to the main land. I arrived in Chicago on a Friday and checked in a hotel close by my family for the weekend. On Sunday I moved to a hotel in downtown Chicago for the weeklong training session. It was good to see my family including my children and others. On Monday I saw Herman Brewer and greeted him as class started. We all made our introductions in the class as to our names and what agency we worked for and where we worked. Herman had been promoted to a supervisory deputy position a little over two years prior and was assigned to the Eastern District of Louisiana in New Orleans.

While attending this training session on a break, Herman and I met a young African American guy who told us he was glad we were with the

Marshal Service and also mentioned that it must be very hard to get on board with the Marshals Service. I told him it is hard to get on board and asked him why he was saying it was hard to get on board. The guy related he had taken a test and received a score of 100% and had not heard anything from the Marshals Service. Herman and I looked at each other in amazement and could not believe what the guy was saying. I asked the guy to give me his personal information and I would check on his situation with our Human Resources Division when I got back to Puerto Rico, as I knew some of the staff in the Human Resources Division. This was a very good visit and it was good to be home. I also spent time with my grandfather during the visit, the patriarch of our family who at the time was approaching his 77th birthday.

During this training course I received a telephone call from my office in Puerto Rico. The lady on the line told me that I had a call from another lady from Headquarters regarding the chief inspector position in the Prisoner Services Division. I responded to my colleague that I had already interviewed for the position and did not do that well and had mentally moved forward not thinking I had any kind of chance for the position. The lady in my office back in Puerto Rico responded back to me that all she knew was that I needed to call the lady back at Headquarters as soon as possible. I thanked her and told her I would immediately call the lady back to see what was going on.

I called the lady back from the Human Resources Division and was told that I had an interview scheduled for the Prisoner Services Division's Chief Inspector position. I was astonished and mentioned to the lady that I already interviewed for the position and received my score. The Human Resources lady told me that the Director found out that the Assistant Director of the Prisoner Services Division held interviews outside of the Human Resources Division purview and disallowed that entire process because it was outside of established policy and directed that the Human Resources Division conduct interviews and manage the process as they normally did. The lady asked me if I wanted to be interviewed again for the position and told me they were holding the interviews in St. Louis in about two weeks. I responded resoundingly with yes. I knew I had new life with this opportunity to get promoted for the job and said to myself that I would study much harder and be strongly prepared for the upcoming interview.

Upon returning to Puerto Rico, I did contact the agency's Human Resources Division to inquire about the guy who related he had received a 100 on the entrance exam. The lady I spoke with related she would look into the matter and call me back. A short time later the lady called me back and told me it was true that the guy scored a 100 on the exam. I asked her what happened to the guy and was told that his name was accidentally deleted. I asked her what could be done to get the matter corrected and she told me that if I could find a U. S. marshal that would take the guy, the guy would be enrolled in the next Marshals Service training class in our Training Academy. By attending the National Organization of Black Law Enforcement Executives annual training conferences I got to know a number of marshals who also attended that conference. I called and emailed a few of the marshals and one marshal got back to me right away saying he would take the guy. I closed the loop on this matter right away, contacting the lady at Headquarters in our Human Resources Division and sealed the deal and the guy was in fact enrolled in the next Marshals Training Academy session.

I called the guy back and let him know the good news. This guy was working for the Federal Bureau of Prisons and would soon be a deputy marshal. He is still working in the agency as a supervisory deputy marshal. I also called Herman to let him know the status and good news for this guy who ran into the right guys at the right time at the Basic Contract Administration course. During the summer of 1996, I coordinated the movement and deployment of my Military Police Company from the Virgin Islands to Camp Blanding, Florida, for our 2-week annual training which is a requirement each year to assist with maintaining operational readiness and equipment operability. We had a very successful 2-week training session as we flew over and back on military transport planes. I also continued my monthly drills with my units making sometimes two to three trips from San Juan, Puerto Rico, to either St. Croix or St. Thomas, U.S. Virgin Islands.

I received a call in my office from another colleague who worked for Seized Assets at Headquarters, shortly after I returned to Puerto Rico from Chicago for the Basic Contract Administration course. This colleague seemed frustrated and very upset that the interviews held in the Prisoner Services Division were tossed and disallowed. He said that the deputy director cancelled that process and asked me if I were going to interview again. I told him that I was as it was an opportunity. I responded back asking him if he were going to be interviewed and he said yes. This colleague who I knew and had talked to a number of times started providing some information about possible interview questions and some supposedly factual data about the Prisoner Programs. I found this very strange that a competitor for a promotion opportunity would be helping me by providing useful information about the program. However, as a good detective and investigator, I decided to check on this supposedly helpful information as I had already made my mind up that I was going to work very hard to prepare myself for the second chance interview. It just so happened that I had received another employee in my unit that was downgraded one grade to get back to Puerto Rico for family reasons. She was a very sharp lady with a strong financial background. I asked her to check on the information my friend and colleague provided me for accuracy. She told me she would and got back to me in a day or two. Not to any surprise to me, the information provided to help me by my friend and competitive colleague was totally wrong. This information as one of my subordinate senior chiefs said sometimes was "Flim Flam or Shenanigans or Tomfoolery." Now my mission was on and I was preparing myself for the next interview. I traveled to St. Louis and had my interview, being very confident with excellent responses to interview questions and multiple options to show demonstrated decisiveness, strong policy knowledge and flexibility. My score was a 95. I was elated and very proud of my preparation and the results. I was thinking to myself I cannot be denied, with this kind of score I had obtained. I found out that the colleague who gave me the "Flim Flam" information did not do that well on the interview.

I was selected for this job by the late and Honorable Director Eduardo Gonzalez. This was to the displeasure of my new assistant director who wanted someone else for the position. The story with this promotion was not over. I had been selected by the Virgin Islands Army National Guard to attend the Army Command Arms and Services Staff School at Fort Leavenworth, Kansas. This was a 10-week resident course, which at the time was needed for Captains to be promoted to Major. It was very hard for a Reservist or National Guard Officer to get selected to attend this resident course. Additionally, this course was the last 10-week course to be offered. The course was later changed and reduced to 6 weeks. My new assistant director used a subordinate manager, actually a peer of mine once I reported, to call me and put pressure on me to report to my new assignment in the Prisoner Services Division. This peer called me a couple of times in Puerto Rico and told me that the assistant director needed me to report right away. I responded back to this soon to be peer that I had my orders and that I would report as soon as I am done with my military assignment in 10 weeks and would multi-task while at Fort Leavenworth to facilitate my move to my new position. I had been in the military at the time for 16 years and had been deployed to a war zone and knew first hand that I did not have to report for my civilian promotion neglecting military orders for service. My Marshal in Puerto Rico was very supportive of the 10-week assignment and wished me well. I went to Fort Leavenworth for the 10 weeks and completed this excellent course and I have always been very glad I did.

Upon the completion of my 10-week assignment, I had the movers come in my home, pack and move my furniture and belongings. I was a little late getting back to Puerto Rico and asked my friends and neighbors Cary and his wife to let the movers in my home as they had keys to my house. When I arrived home from my travel, Cary's wife was at my home with the movers and they were half done getting my items packed and loaded on the truck for the boat ride to the main land. That night I had dinner with Cary and his wife and checked into my hotel. The next week I closed out my office in Puerto Rico, said my goodbyes to my bosses and other colleagues and flew to Washington, DC, to assume my assignment as a new Chief Inspector.

I remember a telephone call I had with my good friend Bill Walker after I found out that I was promoted. I called Bill and told him I had caught up with him and was promoted to GS14. Bill Walker, responded to me by saying "you have not quite caught up with me yet," and then asked me what I was, a GS14 Step 1 or 2? Bill related he was a GS14 Step 6 or 7. I responded that he was right that I had not quite caught up with him. We both laughed. I further told Bill that I would never see GS14 Step 6 or 7. He asked me why not and I told him I would make GS15 first. We both laughed again as I told him when my last day in Puerto Rico was which was October 14, 1996. My date leaving Puerto Rico was strangely the same day I arrived, October 14th. I was assigned to the District of Puerto Rico for exactly two years and was moving on, headed to the Washington, DC, area to put in some Headquarters time and continue to learn about the Marshals Service. I learned plenty about Puerto Rico and enjoyed my time there very much, making several good friends, some of which I still communicate with. This assignment with the business courses I had completed made me a very competitive operational employee compared to my peers who did not have all of that business training and experience with seized assets.

CHAPTER TEN

Leading National Prisoner Programs in the Prisoner Services Division USMS Headquarters

I arrived in Washington, DC, on October 15, 1996 for my new assignment as Chief Inspector of the Prisoner Services Division. This was a tough assignment, but a perfect assignment for my leadership skills, and the business and procurement courses I completed. I soon found out I had an initial hurdle or barrier to get past. My new Assistant Director did not want me to get selected for the position, and my assignment and promotion stopped her from getting the candidate of her choice. When I arrived and reported for duty, I had to deal with some "Shenanigans." The assistant director had my new peer tell me that my office was not ready, and that I had to share an office with a subordinate employee, one grade lower than me. I knew exactly what this was about, and did not let it bother me as they had two desks in the one office. I knew I would be spending the first week or so just learning my way around my new environment and meeting plenty of colleagues at Headquarters. However, after one week, I told the subordinate employee that the following week he had to move out of the office, and I was taking his office for my use. There was not enough room for the both of us. I told him it was not personal but a business decision. I could not supervise employees and have a subordinate near me with no privacy for matters involving my other employees.

I made it known to other managers why I was taking this position. All of a sudden, I was told my office was ready and I moved in. One thing that some people may not know about military people is that some of us have training in psychological operations. While in my Civil Affairs Reserve unit back in the Chicago area, my unit and other Civil Affairs units were under the Special Operations Command Headquartered at Fort Bragg, North Carolina. The Psychological Operations Units were also under the Special Operations Command. I spent time talking to the soldiers and officers assigned to Psychological Operations or as we call the units "PsyOps" trying to understand their doctrine and strategy. I also learned from Army Drill Sergeants who were also good with using "PsyOps" tactics and who placed pressure on new soldiers and military members. I did well understanding and dealing with these tactics. The tactics employed by my new assistant director were nothing but "PsyOps" designed to place pressure on me. However, thank God for the United States Army and the training I received from this great organization that prepares leaders and soldiers to deal with all kinds of issues, problems and situations. I was ready and prepared to be a good Chief Inspector.

After getting past my first hurdle the office issue, my next hurdle or challenge was to understand and learn everything I could about how our agency Headquarters operated. I learned as much as I could about our Human Resources Division, as I had plenty of contact with this division as I was advancing my career. I got to know people who I spoke with or emailed often while in the Chicago office. I also learned more about how policy was developed and implemented. I volunteered for various committees and was selected for some of those committees.

I recall that my new assistant director called me into her office and gave me an early tasking. She made me aware of a major program area that was severely back up with performance and work. The Inter-Government Agreement (IGA) Program was backed up with hundreds of state and local per diem requests to house federal pre-trial detainees. The IGA Program is a major prisoner detention program in the Marshals Service that negotiates prison detention space with state, county and local jails. This was a large standing problem that needed solutions. The assistant director informed me that she could not get the staff assigned to that section to make any progress on the backlog, and that it was my assignment to try and motivate my new team to get them to reduce and control the backlog. I was told that it would most likely be a futile effort for me, but they worked for me, and I needed to try and turn the situation around. The assistant director related that it may take an act of Congress to fire any of the employees, as they all had 25 to 30 years of federal service. I told my assistant director that I was going to develop a plan of action and go to work on this project, and we would change directions and get the backlog reduced.

As I noted in the last chapter, I had completed the Army's 10-week Combined Arms Services School held at Fort Leavenworth, Kansas. This course focused on staff development, problem solving, conducting briefings, and working together to get the job done. My military skills from this training would be a huge asset to me in dealing with this staff's productivity problem. I used the military decision making process to address the problem, and got my staff on track, and resolved the huge backlog of IGAs. My staff was comprised of two senior inspectors and eight administrative personnel including my administrative assistant. I took a little time to think about the problem and developed courses of action, and prioritized the courses of action. I came up with a strategy to get the IGA backload under control. I decided that we would use a task force effort using all of my team's efforts at one time to reduce one IGA specialist's backlog, using one week at a time. We all worked in the large conference room and set up telephones and reviewed the files of the IGA Specialist. I picked the IGA specialist with the heaviest backlog to start with using the taskforce efforts. During a meeting with my team, I briefed the plan and concept of the operation to get each of the IGA specialist's backlog reduced and manageable. On the coming Monday, the project was set to begin.

On Monday we all reported to work and everyone was in the conference room with the exception of the IGA specialist who was to bring his cartload of files. The IGA specialist came to the conference room with an empty cart. I asked him where his files were. He told me this project was not going to work right in front of my entire team. I was furious but maintained my composure. I told my staff that we were not starting the project today but would start the project the next day at the same time and place. I told the IGA specialist who came with an empty cart to meet with me in my office. At this meeting I asked him again why he came with no files knowing what the strategy was - to get the backlog of work reduced. Again I was told the strategy was not going to work. I informed the IGA specialist that I thought it would work, and that by working together as a total team we would get the backlogs of each IGA specialist reduced and manageable going forward. I mentioned to him that he should not come empty handed the next day and if he did, I would have his files moved down and proceed without him, and I would address his insubordination afterward. On the next morning we were all in the conference room and we heard a cart rolling in the hallway. The IGA specialist was on his way with a cart full of files. We all went to work that day and the rest of the days that week. Several of us were making telephone calls addressing various issues, while the IGA specialists were negotiating per diem rates. We were documenting and updating files and by the end of the week, we made a major reduction in the IGA specialist's file caseload. This specialist was amazed at the progress that the team effort made. His caseload was reduced to a manageable number. Everyone was impressed with the process, and the following week we moved on to the next IGA specialist. The success was repeated a total of six or seven times, and the total backlog for all IGA specialists was brought under control and manageable. The progress was recorded in a report. I was very proud to present the report of this major accomplishment to my assistant director. She was astonished at the progress we made, and asked me how I was able to get that IGA situation turned around. I gave her a synopsis of how we got the job done. She congratulated me saying I moved a mountain. I was beginning to win the support and admiration of my new assistant director.

As the operational Chief Inspector in the Prisoner Services Division, I had supervisory responsibility for several key national Marshals Service Programs. I was responsible for the leadership and management of the nationwide Jail Inspection Program. This program was responsible for the oversight and training of deputy marshals who were assigned collateral positions by their district offices as Jail Inspectors. The jail inspectors have the responsibility of inspecting the operations and administration of state and local jails the Marshals Service had agreements with to house federal pretrial detained prisoners or detainees. I also attended the Jail Inspector Training Course. I wanted to fully understand what was taught to the jail inspectors and learn what they were being taught. It was a very good course as the Marshals Service adapted and used the policies and guidelines for prisoner detention as set by the American Correctional Association. I joined the American Correctional Association and attended a couple of their annual conferences.

Regarding the IGA Program, it is a very interesting program and the business and procurement courses I took while assigned and working in Puerto Rico benefited me. The IGA Program had several Contracting Officers and Grants Analysts who negotiated with approximately 2,000 state, local and county jails to house federal detainees in their facilities for a per diem rate which covered lodging, meals and medical needs. The rates were negotiated based on procurement guidelines that took in consideration the jails actual costs, location and other data to establish a per diem rate. Some jails or government agencies that were over the jails sometimes contested the proposed per diem rate. I got involved with the rate negotiations at times to assist with the process to agree on an acceptable per diem rate for both the facility and the federal government. On numerous occasions I spoke with sheriffs, county leaders or other executives to resolve disputes over the per diem rates.

During this time period I met and got to know L.B. Clinton (LBC) who I will refer to hereafter as LBC. LBC became another very good lifetime friend. He worked for the Marshals Service but for another division at headquarters. He was also a NCAA Division I basketball referee. I always enjoyed college basketball and was a huge DePaul University Basketball supporter and fan. I also enjoyed the Georgetown Basketball Program largely because of their legendary coach known as Big John Thompson II. Because of my friend, and mentor Don Horton, I was now becoming a big Georgetown fan and started attending Georgetown men's basketball games. On occasion, I saw LBC on the court refereeing a Georgetown basketball game or on television refereeing other college basketball games.

As a part of my Chief Inspector duties in the Prisoner Services Division, I also led the Cooperative Agreement Program or CAP. The CAP Program consisted of Contract Specialists and Grants Analysts. The purpose of this program was to offer funding or grants from the federal Office of Justice Programs to renovate, expand, or enhance a jail that the Marshals Service utilized or was working towards establishing an Inter-Government Agreement with. In return for this grant funding, the Marshals Service was guaranteed a certain number of detention beds and agreed to a high level of use of the prisoner beds, paying a negotiated per diem rate. The CAP Program, during my time leading these programs, was very much sought after by several local governments including my former district where I worked, the Virgin Islands. I assisted with a $1 million dollar grant to renovate a facility in St. Thomas in order that federal pretrial detainees could be detained on the island. I traveled back to St. Thomas to work on and complete this project as the Marshals Service leaders in the Virgin Islands and the U. S. Attorney's office said it was a critical need. I met with officials from the Virgin Islands Department of Justice to seal the deal for this project. I was promoted before the project was completed. To the best of my knowledge the Virgin Islands received the money for this project, but never completed or even started it.

I traveled to Los Angeles, in the Central District of California; San Diego, in the Southern District of California; Phoenix in the District of Arizona; Houston in the Southern District of Texas; and San Antonio, in the Western District of San Antonio working on various prisoner detention housing projects. I enjoyed working with our Marshals Service district offices, and the local officials addressing and trying to resolve various detention issues. We called it detention management. The Southwest Border area experienced a huge increase in border crossing arrests and available detention bed space was becoming a problem.

Additionally, I also managed the agency federal Prisoner Tracking Program and Federal Excess Property Program. The Prisoner Tracking or PTS program was critical to track and account for the large number of pretrial detainees who were in state, local and county jail space throughout the United States. The Federal Bureau of Prisons or BOP allocated some detention bed space to the Marshals Service. However, they had their own detention needs for prisoner bed space for sentenced prisoners, and the Marshals Service needed more pretrial detainee bed space. In my estimate it was during this time that the surge in private jail space took off and is still a booming billion-dollar business today. I remember thinking I should have bought stock in Corrections Corporation of America (CCA) back in the day. However, procurement rules limited those thoughts as my division did business with CCA to house pretrial detainees.

The Federal Excess Property (FEP) Program was a small program that provided guidelines for transferring federal property that was still in good condition to other federal agencies or offices and local jurisdictions. I later used the FEP to transfer a number of computers in good condition to my new military National Guard Unit, the 260th Military Police Command. I eventually transferred my military status from the Virgin Islands National Guard to the District of Columbia National Guard. I was again assigned as an Operations Officer. Before my military unit transfer request, I traveled when I could back to St. Croix for my military weekend drills staying five or six days to make up for days missed while being in the DC area. I finished my Company Command time and was assigned to work for another Lieutenant Colonel on St. Croix. This Lieutenant Colonel was a very good superior, and understood my duty status situation. He was very supportive knowing I had been promoted with the Marshals Service and assigned to the agency Headquarters in the DC area. Prior to transferring from the Virgin Islands National Guard to the District of Columbia, I was promoted from Captain to Major.

The Commanding General of the Virgin Islands National Guard, the late Major General Jean A. Romney was attending an Adjutant General's meeting at the National Guard Bureau in Arlington, Virginia. The General's Chief of Staff who I developed a good relationship with called me to see if my promotion could occur at Marshals Service Headquarters. I thought it was a good idea and asked Director Gonzalez if he would participate in my promotion to Major and assist with pinning my rank on with Major General Romney. Director Gonzalez agreed to participate. My promotion to the rank of Major was conducted in the Director's conference room at Marshals Service Headquarters. I was pinned with my rank by the late Director Gonzalez and the late General Romney with pictures taken. I look at those photos every now and then and reflect on how my life was touched and influenced by these two great American leaders of justice and service. General Romney passed on a few years after he promoted me to the rank of Major. He was truly a great man of vision and wisdom and cared about family, friends and all of his soldiers.

In 1997, I purchased my first home in Maryland. I also received a new boss, as the Prisoner Services Division received a new assistant director. The former assistant director moved to another agency. The new Assistant

Director, Mr. Al Solis, was a career deputy marshal who worked his way up through the ranks in the Marshals Service as a deputy marshal, to the position of assistant director as a senior executive. I met the new assistant director while assigned as a deputy marshal in Chicago. I attended a Hispanic Law Enforcement Conference in Chicago and met my new boss there. My former assistant director was an attorney and came to the agency from the Department of Justice and was a Charter Senior Executive Member. I was happy and felt lucky to work for my new assistant director who also served in the Army and we shared that and other commonalities. He certainly challenged me with interesting assignments including, as I will discuss later, serving on the Marshals Service Committee for law enforcement accreditation to meet the requirements of the Commission on Law Enforcement Accreditation (CALEA). I was called to brief him on various issues and projects in his office or during our division staff meetings. My preference was to give some good background on an issue and then brief the issue or results. He sometime said to me during meetings "Sylvester, I do not want to know how to build a clock. Just tell me what time it is." The assistant director said that to me a few times, in which I knew at that point, I needed to get right to the point.

One assignment I had was very interesting. In this assignment, I learned about aircraft safety. The Prisoner Services Division at the time also had the Marshals Service air and ground transportation system or Justice Airline and Prisoner Transportation System, also referred to as JPATS, under the assistant director's leadership. My Assistant Director had received a number of complaints from union and non-union members working for JPATS about safety issues such as pilots not getting enough sleep, safety inspections not being properly done and general management issues. I did not know hardly anything about airline safety procedures and polices other than what we learn as airline passengers. I was eager to take the assignment to learn new things. I started reading the complaints doing my best to understand and learn about airline safety terminology. One complaint was that JPATS managers were not timely with the required C Check inspections. The complaint stated in part that the managers did not want to have an aircraft out of service while the C Check is being conducted. The C Check lasts one to two weeks and the entire aircraft was to be inspected. The complainant stated that managers had a schedule to move prisoners and did not want to fall behind creating a serious safety violation. For my investigative work into the complaints, I found out about the various inspections checks, listed as A Check, B Check, C Check and D Check. Each have requirements and the A and B checks are considered lighter checks while the C and D checks are considered heavier checks.

As a part of my preparation for the assignment, I contacted a special agent working with the Drug Enforcement Administration who was also a pilot. I obtained his name from another law enforcement colleague. I called the DEA Special Agent/Pilot and spoke with him. I met with him in Dallas when I traveled to the JPATS Oklahoma headquarters to conduct my interviews and fact finding for my report. The meeting with the agent/pilot was very insightful as he provided me with good information about aircraft safety and the C Check process. I thanked the agent and boarded my flight to Oklahoma. I had limited experience flying on a JPATS aircraft for one week, providing prisoner security while working in the Chicago's Marshals office that I discussed earlier. I also provided ground security support for JPATS aircraft while working in the Chicago's Marshals office. Other than that I did not have much knowledge or experience understanding aircraft safety. I landed in Oklahoma, checked into my hotel and went out to dinner to grab a good Oklahoma steak. I went to work the next day at the JPATS hanger meeting first with the top two executives for an entrance overview of the scope of my investigation. I met again with them when I ended my work and gave them a synopsis of my findings. I interviewed pilots, managers and safety officers as part of my assignment. I spent several days there to complete my inquiry and making my notes for my written report. I returned to the Washington, DC, area and went back to work in my office completing my written report, documenting the interviews and findings.

There were some issues in the complaints that were confirmed. However, there were several issues that I found to not be confirmed or true. From the list of flight operations and safety issues confirmed, I did find that one pilot in command who also served as a maintenance supervisor failed to display proper decision-making and this pilot did not follow some of the Federal Aviation Regulations, lacked some common sense in the use of repair parts, maintenance operations and did not provide the safest aircraft possible for the Marshals Service. I wrote up about nine issues regarding this pilot's actions regarding JPATS aircraft and flight operations. These violations were turned over to the Marshals Service's Office of Internal Affairs to be investigated. The Office of Internal Affairs contracted with an aircraft flight operations specialist to assist with the investigation. This assignment was very interesting and rewarding as I did learn about aircraft safety to include actually going through a C Check with JPATS employees of one of the JPATS aircraft that was due for such a check.

I always valued the input of field chief deputies and supervisors and found it useful to establish a committee or sounding board to run situations and matters by. I knew of some very good chiefs and supervisors and invited them to be on the committee. Herman was a supervisor and I asked him to join the Prisoner Services Committee and he agreed. The committee came to Headquarters a few times a year to meet and work on national prisoner detention issues. The committee was a very good diverse group and we came out with a number of solid policies and initiatives. We created a very good District Security Officer Policy that is still being used in district offices. We met to re-write the entire prisoner services agency-wide policy and it was an excellent product. This was an exhaustive process and we used sub-committees to work on sub-sections of the policy. The policy almost got published, but was held up as Director Gonzalez was making changes to policy format and the agency was going through law enforcement accreditation. The Commission on Law Enforcement Accreditation or CALEA was something local law enforcement agencies complied with. It was not a usual process for federal law enforcement. Director Gonzalez was definitely rocking the boat with the decision to have our agency comply with the complex policies of accreditation. This was a major change for the Marshals Service and required a lot of work. I was assigned to be on the Accreditation Committee and received accreditation training from CALEA. I was always eager to learn to be a better deputy marshal/criminal investigator and this was a good process to be involved with. After a couple of years of dedicated hard work led by our esteemed Director Mr. Gonzalez, we received our accreditation. I attended and enjoyed the accreditation ceremony. I believe the U. S. Marshals Service is the first federal law enforcement agency to go through the Accreditation Process and be accredited. This huge accomplishment was due to the great leadership of late Director Gonzalez.

In early 1998 there were two GS15 promotional opportunities both in the DC area. One was the Chief Deputy for the Superior Court in Washington DC with responsibility for the courthouse in downtown Washington, DC, which houses Superior Court judges and federal prosecutors prosecuting local cases with arrests made by the Metropolitan Police Department. The Marshals managing Superior Court were essentially sheriffs as they produced prisoners in court and secured the prisoners while not in court at detention facilities in the DC area. The deputy marshals also tracked down those that absconded from the court's jurisdiction and conducted civil seizures and evictions.

The other GS15 position was the National Program Manager for Court Security reporting to the Assistant Director for Judicial Security. This position was responsible for coordinating national security policies and protocols for all federal judges, federal prosecutors, and courthouses and court facilities. Additional responsibility included providing protection for Supreme Court Justices, working closely with the Supreme Court Marshal and staff. I applied for both positions and made the best-qualified list for both jobs. I was interviewed by a panel of three very seasoned chief deputies who were tough with their questions and follow on questions. These three guys were in my opinion the guardians of the GS15 rank - the highest career position managed through the agency Career Board process. In district field offices, the GS15 grade is the highest ranked non-political chief executive. A U.S. Marshal position in our agency is a Presidential political appointment with confirmation by the U. S. Senate. Director Gonzalez was involved with an effort to change the top position from political to career, but in my view, the Senators did not want to give up those appointments. I did a good job on my interview score with this tough board scoring a score of 80. I knew that was a very competitive score and I was selected by Director Gonzalez in April 1998 as a GS15 young Chief Executive. I was 38 and on the move doing great work and learning as much as I could, both on the job with the Marshals Service and with the military. In this position I succeeded another good friend and mentor, Donald Horton, who took a lateral move to the U.S. District Court for the District of Columbia where he served the federal judges, prosecutors and the public visiting the federal courthouse as Chief Deputy and then the U. S. Marshal. I consulted with Don Horton often, as I knew Don had plenty of experience leading security programs for judges and courthouses. He was an excellent resource and good friend for years to come.

CHAPTER ELEVEN

Leading the National Court Security Program
In the Judicial Security Division

I was very happy and proud to be a national program manager for Court Security and called my longtime good friend Bill Walker to let him know I made GS15. He was still a senior level GS14. Bill was very happy for me and told me he would now have to try hard for his GS15 with DEA and started applying for GS15 opportunities in the Washington, DC area to catch back up with me. As I mentioned earlier, Bill Walker and I had a good-natured friendly orientated competitive drive between us both in our civilian careers and our military careers. I always outranked Bill in the military as I received my military commission to Second Lieutenant about a year and a half prior to him receiving his commission. Bill was ahead of me in our federal careers as he started his federal career about 4 years before me. Now I had actually passed him in grade in our federal careers. So I knew he would be very happy for me, and that my promotion to GS15 would push him to obtain his GS15. Additionally, I kept my word of getting promoted to GS15, not staying too long as a GS14. As I mentioned to Bill, I was not going to see GS14 Step 6 and I did not.

My assignment as Chief of Court Security was very demanding. However, I really enjoyed the work. I focused on developing and enhancing court and judicial security policies and got to know as many judges as I could. I worked very closely with the Administrative Office of the United States Courts or AOUSC. The AOUSC is the administrative office for all federal judges and federal courthouses. I also worked very closely with the Judicial Conference Committee on Security and Facilities. This committee focused on security issues for judges and courthouses to include the Court Security Officer Program. As the Chief of Court Security, the Court Security Officer Program or CSO Program was under my leadership from a national perspective. The CSO Program when I led it had approximately 5,500 court security officers providing security for 450 courthouses and buildings where federal judges were located. These officers are mostly retired police officers or former military personnel who assist the Marshals Service with providing security at courthouses. These individuals are outstanding law enforcement professionals who provide an excellent service for the courts. I had a Contracting Officers Team and a Technical Security Team under my leadership. The Contracting Officer Team administered the contracts for the CSOs and technical security equipment required to provide security enhancements for courthouses. The Technical Security Team had the responsibility of staying on top of the latest security equipment for courthouses such as magnetometers, hand metal detectors, closed circuit cameras and alarms.

I also had a core group of senior inspectors called Court Security Inspectors working for me. These inspectors reported to two chief inspectors that reported directly to me. I had direct contact with them as they had direct contact with judges and Supreme Court Justices. These women and men were dedicated hardworking security specialists who led protective details for judges and the Supreme Court Justices, and federal prosecutors who required protection. They also conducted physical security surveys of federal courthouses and by special request for state and local court jurisdictions. I developed very good relationships with these individuals. All but one of the core group or legacy Court Security Inspectors have retired. I still maintain contact with about six or seven of them.

I also had a Duty Desk function reporting to me. The Duty Desk had four senior inspectors who worked with various judicial districts by region, handling requests from Marshals Service district offices for Special Assignments for major trials. A special assignment is normally a major court trial or protective detail requiring funding for added deputy marshals to come to the assistance of another district office to augment that district's staffing to adequately handle the security requirements of the trial or protective detail. The district is required to submit a staffing plan to request the desired added resources. The Duty Desk Senior Inspectors reviewed the plan and presented it to me to authorize. They worked closely with me monitoring threats against judges and prosecutors, developing the response to any such threats, and working with the district offices.

During this time, I was selected by Director Gonzalez to serve on the Marshals Service Career Board with the responsibility of meeting periodically with other Career Board members to review and rank Marshals Service promotional candidates for career advancement to Supervisory, Assistant Chief, and Chief and Chief Deputy vacant positions. The U. S. marshals and assistant directors also ranked the candidates in the order of their preference. The Career Board serves as an independent group of career professionals that assist with identifying conflicts with those being considered for promotion, taking the agency views into consideration over a particular promotional candidate or position. The agency's Human Resources Division selected me to work on the committee to work on enhancing our promotional exam and reviewing exam questions that operational employees challenged or had issues with. I enjoyed working with the Human Resources Division personnel and always appreciated and respected their expertise and diligence to take care of employees.

As the Chief of Court Security, I worked very closely with Director Gonzalez when it came to key judicial security issues, as he was very focused on the importance of judicial security. The Judicial Conference Committee on Security and Facilities held two meetings a year where we addressed critical court security and courthouse security issues. The issues discussed at these meetings focused on new courthouses, security of courthouses, budget, and court security officer staffing and other relevant security issues. My office and staff worked with the Court Security Office at the Administrative Office of the United States Courts on the agenda for the committee meetings and other relevant security issues developed. I worked very closely with the Chief of the Office of Security at the AOUSC. He and I are still friends and colleagues although he has retired. I worked closely with his successor until I was reassigned to another division.

One of the first major tasks during my first year as Chief of Court Security from my Assistant Director was to get on a plane and travel to Alabama to meet with a federal judge and let the judge know the Marshals Service would be removing his long-term protective 24-hour detail. The Assistant Director who was my immediate boss informed me that it would be a difficult task as the judge was a very seasoned no-nonsense judge and would not be happy to see me. I did my homework on the case involving the threat against the judge reading the threat assessment and quite clearly making my notes as to what I would say to the judge. I periodically met with any judge under long term 24-hour protection and there were two other judges with long term protection details in place in response to threats related to the prosecution and conviction of terrorists involved with terrorism attacks against the United States. I called the judge in Alabama and made an appointment to meet with him.

I also consulted with my predecessor Don Horton who had done and exceptional job directing the activities of the Court Security Division prior to the reorganization making the division the Court Security Program. I asked Don if he knew the judge and for any insight and advice. Don

Horton did know the judge and provided some very useful advice to me. I flew to Atlanta, Georgia and was met by one of my Court Security Inspectors. After I was picked up at the airport, we immediately drove from Atlanta, Georgia to Alabama for my meeting with the judge. I first met with the United States Marshal for the district as I called the Marshal to let the Marshal know I was coming to the district and the purpose of my trip.

I met with the judge after meeting with the Marshal. It was a one on one meeting. The judge was prepared and anticipated the purpose of my meeting. I met with the judge and introduced myself and informed him of the purpose for the visit. I let him know that due to the threat assessment along with other information, there was no reason to maintain the 24-hour protective detail. The judge had at his desk a box full of letters from various people communicating with him. He handed me some of the letters and I read them. I advised the judge that if he receives letters that concern him and are inappropriate, he should turn those letters over to the Marshals Service to review as we list troubling letters to our judicial family as inappropriate communications and want to take a good look at those letters. I informed the judge that the protective detail would not be removed immediately, but would be removed in a reasonable time period allowing for a methodical transition and that after the time period, some form of reduced protective detail would be in place for another reasonable period of time. The judge was not happy with this decision, but understood it and was appreciative of the plan to transition the protective detail using a solid methodical plan. I completed this difficult task with the respect of the judge.

It was very important to me to understand all aspects of Judicial and Court Security. I made it my business to understand the duties of all of my employees, in particular those working in support of any security function. I also made it my business to know what was important to federal judges, Supreme Court Justices and the Administrative Office of the United States Courts. I had the responsibility of conducting information and security briefings to all new federal judges and all elevated federal judges promoted to Chief Judge and Appellate or Circuit Judge. I did my best to make sure my schedule was clear to conduct these briefings as the judges had a series of meetings and briefings and meeting with the Chief of Court Security was one of the meetings scheduled. I conducted these meetings along with the Chief of Security for the AOUSC.

The Marshals Service had several good security programs in place to protect judges and courthouses. My job was to keep the programs in place, obtain the most from the programs and staff, enhance existing policies, develop additional policies as needed, and develop good external relationships with law enforcement partners. I also worked closely with the Executive Office for United States Attorneys or EOUSA. This office had a similar role as that of the Administrative Office of the United States Courts has for judges as the EOUSA provides coordination and leadership for the 94 United States Attorneys and their Assistant United States Attorneys and other staff. I worked closely with the EOUSA security office addressing any security concerns the office had for federal prosecutors. During my tenure as the Chief of Court Security there were a number of federal prosecutors across the country that had significant threats against them and had short or long term protective details provided by district offices and/or my staff to ensure their safety. I had a rewarding job and was doing meaningful work using all of my skill sets to lead and get the job done.

My new division the Judicial Security Division had two major operational programs. The two programs were my program, the Court Security Program and the other program was the Witness Security Program, which had a GS15 Chief managing and directing its operations. My new boss the Assistant Director convinced Director Gonzalez that these two programs could work more efficiently conjoined or married to each other with the Witness Security field Chief Inspectors directing the activities of the Witness Security Inspectors and the Court Security Inspectors. I found out years later that Director Gonzalez had done some good research on this joining of the Marshals Service protective missions and resources before signing off on the proposal as a good Director should. Director Gonzalez contacted the founder of the Witness Security Program retired organized crime Department of Justice federal prosecutor, the Honorable Mr. Gerald Shur and asked Mr. Shur what he thought of this merger of protective programs.

I learned that Mr. Shur responded to Director by saying that it was not a good mix and provided his rationale for his thoughts on the matter. Director Gonzalez thanked Mr. Shur and decided to sign off on the merger of having both the Court Security Program and the Witness Security Program conjoined. This would mean that on Court Security matters, the Witness Security field Chiefs would report to me and for Witness Security related matters that they would continue to report to their normal Chief, the Witness Security Program Manager. If the Witness Security Program Manager was out of office, I handled Witness Security matters for his attention and he did the same for me if I were out of office. This was my first executive level experience working with Witness Security.

The Witness Security Case Management function was also co-located in our division office space. My Assistant Director prior to his promotion to the Senior Executive Service was the Chief of the old Witness Security Division. The marriage of these two very important protection programs did not last long as it was problematic. The Court Security Inspectors had the benefit of the freedom to communicate with their customers the federal judges. The Witness Security Chief Inspectors were more hands on with their management style and wanted the Court Security Inspectors to not communicate with the federal judges without using the chain of command contacting them first. This slowed down the established contacts and protocols these security professionals had with federal judges and Supreme Court Justices. This was not well received by the judges and Supreme Court Justices and Director Gonzalez heard about these issues from the customers themselves. Director Gonzalez took corrective action after further evaluating the situation.

Director Gonzalez again contacted Mr. Gerald Shur, Founder of the American Witness Protection Program. The Director asked Mr. Shur to conduct a senior level management review of the merger of the Court Security and Witness Security Programs. Mr. Shur agreed and conducted a senior level management review of the afore-mentioned merger. I soon met Mr. Shur as he interviewed me as well to get my thoughts and experience with this joint venture of having the programs conjoined. I enjoyed meeting Mr. Shur when he interviewed me in my office. I had no idea I would eventually come full circle and later for many years direct the activities of the Witness Security Program and Division and become very good friends with Gerald Shur an incredible, extremely intelligent and humble public servant.

During my interview with Mr. Shur I told him what I thought of the merger and some of the problems associated with it. I let Mr. Shur know that there were some positives with having the programs work together. However, I listed some powerful reasons why the merger was not in the best interest of either program. I related that the programs should be separate and operate separately due to nature and differences of the two protective missions and differences between the customers. After Mr. Shur completed his senior level management review and turned it in to Director Gonzalez, Director Gonzalez reorganized the Judicial Security Division leaving the Court Security Program and all related programs in the Judicial Security Division. The Director moved the Witness Security Division to the Investigative Services Division. The Witness Security Program reported to the Assistant Director of the Investigative Services Division for six years until I eventually had the Program under my leadership as a Senior Executive as I will discuss in later chapters. I continued to do my job leading the Court Security Program and my colleague who led the Witness Security Program moved out of our office suite to the new division.

During this time I also enrolled in a Master's of Science Program at the University of Maryland University College or UMUC. I wanted to obtain my Master's Degree and enrolled in a Master's of Public Administration Program while assigned to the District of the United States Virgin Islands. I completed one course prior to my promotion and reassignment to the District of Puerto Rico. I deliberated a while about trying to complete my Master's Degree in Puerto Rico. However, I decided I to wait until I returned to the stateside to enroll in a college and obtain my Master's Degree. Education and training has always been very important to me, and I was committed to this endeavor. I took a couple of classroom courses at a UMUC satellite office not too far from my home. I was very busy with my Master's courses, Court Security work, and military duty as I was now assigned to the 260th Military Police Command in the District of Columbia National Guard.

One of the benefits of being the Chief of the Court Security Program was I could attend any judicial conference in any of the federal circuits that I wanted to. I usually was invited to participate and speak at several different circuit conferences. I was briefed by one of my Senior Inspectors in my Chicago office that Appellate Judge Ann Williams and the Just the Beginning Foundation, was having another conference that was scheduled to be held in Detroit. As I discussed earlier during my time as a Deputy Marshal in Chicago, Illinois, I was in charge of security for the first Just the Beginning Conference where the judges celebrated the great career of the great late Judge James Parsons. Now I would attend the conference in Detroit, Michigan as the Chief Executive of the Court Security Program, the program responsible for providing security for all federal judges and all federal courthouses.

I was excited at the opportunity to participate and attend the conference. I also looked forward to seeing Judge Ann Williams and many other federal judges and federal prosecutors I knew from my travels and experiences while working with the Marshals Service. I saw and greeted

Judge Williams at the opening reception for the conference at the Mayor's mansion. Judge Williams was very happy to see me and I was very happy to see her. As I noted earlier, Judge Williams and I worked together on the security for the first Just the Beginning Conference and I produced detained prisoners and provided security in her courtroom numerous times when she was a district judge. It was absolutely wonderful to see all of the federal judges, prosecutors and other dignitaries in attendance at the conference.

I always enjoyed the Eleventh Circuit Conference as the Eleventh Circuit conference includes the states of Florida, Georgia and Alabama. These states were good venues for conferences as the weather is usually milder in these areas. Additionally, Alabama and Florida offer nice beaches. One particular very nice conference I was invited to attend and participate in was in Point Clear, Alabama at a very nice resort. I had a very nice room with a view over the beach. My Director Eddie Gonzalez attended this conference and we really enjoyed it. I remember the Director, his lovely wife, and I took morning walks around the hotel area. We also got together for dinner during the conference. This was Director Gonzalez last conference with me before he stepped down as Director and returned to Florida where he did consulting work and worked on several projects for the Commission on Law Enforcement Accreditation or CALEA.

In May 1999, I worked on a security initiative with my friend and colleague serving as the Chief of Court Security for the Administrative Office of the United States Courts. The initiative was a publication titled Offsite Security Booklet for Judicial Officers. This booklet was a joint project and focused on security initiatives for judicial officers while they were offsite from the courthouse and was well received by the Administrative Office of the United States Courts and federal judges. In June 1999 with one year of experience under my belt as the Chief of Court Security, Director Gonzalez retired from the everyday life of the demands of working fulltime. His Deputy Director became the Acting

Director. The Deputy Director was very close to my boss who was the Assistant Director for Judicial Security and asked my boss to become the Acting Deputy Director. I was asked to act as the Assistant Director of the Judicial Security Division and gladly accepted. I certainly missed the leadership of Director Gonzalez and seeing him around the Marshals Service headquarters. I received three promotions under his stewardship as Director and was very fond of him and his wife.

The good thing is that we maintained contact after he retired. Director Gonzalez usually stayed busy after leaving the Marshals Service working as a consultant and assisting with consent decrees for police departments such as the Prince George's County, Maryland Police Department and the Detroit Michigan Police Department under federal court involvement based on litigation and community issues that negatively affected both departments. I acted as the Assistant Director until November of 1999, when President William J. Clinton selected and appointed John Marshall as Director of the Marshals Service. The Acting Director retired, the Acting Deputy Director returned to his position as Assistant Director, and I returned to my regular position as Chief of Court Security. I had a good run as Acting Assistant Director and during the 6 months, I worked on a number of excellent security initiatives for the federal judiciary.

Within a year of receiving my promotion to GS15, I received a call from Bill Walker letting me know he was moving to the Washington DC to compete for a GS15 position with his employer DEA. Bill arrived in the Washington DC area soon afterwards. I was happy to have him in the area. We were both from Chicago, both worked in Puerto Rico and now we were both in the Washington DC area. Our time together in the Washington DC this time around would be short lived as I was considering taking a lateral assignment to be the Chief Deputy in the Northern District of Georgia, with the main office in Atlanta. The district had a Chief Deputy vacancy as the incumbent had retired. I called the Marshal, Robert McMichael and had a brief conversation with him about an Assistant Chief position that was open a couple of years before, and he was looking at another one of his employees for that job who was a Supervisory Deputy. Now I was calling this Marshal again about another position. I called Marshal McMichael to express my interest in his Chief Deputy position, which was his deputy and second in command next to him. I briefed the Marshal on what I would bring to his district highlighting my significant Marshals Service headquarters experience. The Marshal was actually looking at trying to elevate his Assistant Chief to the position. This is the same person he wanted and got as his Assistant Chief.

I made a contrast between myself and his current Assistant Chief who the Marshal was considering for promotion, and told the Marshal I appreciated his time and would call another Marshal who I knew was interested in me serving as his Chief Deputy in a nearby district in the Northern District of Florida. I called that Marshal and he said he would love to have me as his Chief Deputy. Within a few minutes of hanging up with the Northern District of Florida Marshal, I received a call from the Northern District of Georgia Marshal in Atlanta letting me know he wanted me as his Chief Deputy. I let the Marshal McMichael know that I needed to call the other Marshal back right away to let him know I want to be the Chief Deputy in Atlanta as I had my two youngest sons living in the area and I liked the Atlanta area. I called the Northern District of Florida Marshal back and let him know I had to back off being his Chief Deputy and had received a call back from his colleague in Atlanta letting me know he wanted me to be his Chief Deputy and I had family in the area. The Northern District of Florida Marshal who was an outstanding United States Marshal and leader, told me he reluctantly understood, but wished me well.

I called my pending new boss back the Marshal in Atlanta and let him know that he needed to call the Director who he had known when the Director was his colleague as Marshal in the Eastern District of Virginia, and let the Director know of our agreement for a lateral transfer to the

Northern District of Georgia to initiate the process and we worked out a date for my move to Atlanta. The Marshal contacted Director John Marshall and my lateral transfer was approved. I reported to my new job as Chief Deputy in the Northern District of Georgia the following month in December 1999 leaving my position as Chief of Court Security. I was hoping to return back to the Washington DC area as an Assistant Director preferably for the Judicial Security Division, an office and job I knew well. I also knew I could live well and enjoy being a field Chief Deputy especially in the Northern District of Georgia. Prior to leaving the Washington DC area to go to Atlanta, I received a very nice letter of commendation from the Director of the Administrative Office of the United Courts. The very nice letter praised my many positive contributions I made during my tenure as Acting Assistant Director for the Judicial Security Division, implementing security policies for judges, enhancing communications between deputy marshals and judges and bringing new court security officers on board and wishing me the best of luck as Chief Deputy for the Northern District of Georgia.

CHAPTER TWELVE

Transfer to the Northern District of Georgia as Chief Deputy

In December 1999, I reported to Atlanta as Chief Deputy of the Northern District of Georgia. I kept my home in Maryland and located a nice 2-bedroom apartment near downtown Atlanta. I had a 10-minute drive to my new office. On my first day in my new position as Chief Deputy, I had a nice meeting with the Marshal of the District Mr. Robert McMichael, followed by meetings with my Assistant Chief, 4 Supervisory Deputy Marshals, and my Administrative Officer. I wanted to hear the concerns of my new boss the Marshal and of my subordinate district managers. In each new leadership position I took, I spent some time preparing for the job before arrival by reading any known management reports of the performance of the office or district. In this case I was moving from a Marshals Service Headquarters position to a senior district leadership position.

I contacted the various headquarters divisions that worked in support of district offices to determine if there were any substantial issues with my new district. The Northern District of Georgia was in pretty good shape with only minor issues obtaining pre-trial jail space from local jails. As previously mentioned, while serving as the Chief of the Court

Security Program, I performed security work for the Judicial Conference Committee on Security and Facilities. One of the judges I worked with on the Committee, Judge Orinda Evans was the Chief Judge in my new district. I established a good relationship with just about all of the judges on the Security Committee and had a very good relationship with this judge who I was going to work with more closely as the Chief Deputy Marshal of the Northern District of Georgia.

After finding out I was going to be the Chief Deputy Marshal in her district, the Chief Judge met with me and gave me one major task. The Chief Judge told me that the district had been trying for years to develop a 24-hour perimeter security presence using Court Security Officers, and not the limited contracted security guard force that the Federal Protective Service had in place. The Chief Judge related that the contracted security guard force was not in place for 24 hours, and was only on duty to a certain time in the evening. The Chief Judge let me know that others in the Marshals office had worked on an initiative to remove the contracted guard force and expand the perimeter security to 24-hourss using Court Security Officers without success. The Chief Judge then gave me the task to get the 24-hour Court Security Officer perimeter project in place. The Chief Judge further stating she had full confidence in my leadership abilities, and that she was aware that I had worked on a project successfully to implement a 24-hour Court Security Officer perimeter security project for one of the New York Districts.

As the Chief of Court Security for the Marshals Service, I worked on and provided focused leadership to obtain the funding and implement a 24-hour perimeter security project for one of the New York district offices. The Chief Judge and other district court officials further let me know that the General Services Administration had been reluctant to give up responsibility for perimeter security for the Atlanta district court house. I had a major tasking from my new Chief Judge, which was also strongly supported by my Marshal and the District Court Security Committee. I fully understood the project, and the context of what I had to do to be successful. I enjoyed challenges and tough tasks in difficult environments. I was good at team building and developing solutions to get the job done. I looked forward to completing this difficult assignment and task.

From my experience leading the Court Security Program, I was keenly aware that good proactive district courts have either a District Court Security Committee (DCSC) or a Building Security Committee (BSC) to address courthouse or federal building security issues. The District Court Security Committee was chaired by another federal judge and had other court family members and the Marshals Service participating on the Committee. This Committee met on a regular basis to address or follow up on security issues and projects. I was continuing to conduct my district assessment, which normally takes me between 60 and 90 days to complete. I immediately addressed any urgent matters discovered during my new office or position assessment, raising these issues to my boss with some courses of actions for solutions. I completed my assessment and developed my district management plan that included a few changes in staffing assignments, a plan to implement the 24 hour perimeter security project, addressing detentions issues with local jails, and a Marshals Service policy compliance review. The Marshal was pleased with the plan and I went to work.

In January 2000, Bill Walker called me to announce that he was promoted to GS15. I was very happy for my good friend and congratulated him. I let him know I was looking forward to having him on the east coast as he was relocating from Puerto Rico to the Washington DC area. Bill let me know that since he was a high level GS14 that he was going to be a GS15 Step 4, and a GS15 Step 5 the next year. Bill asked me for my within-grade, step level. He further asked was I a step 2 or 3. I confirmed I was a GS15 step 3. Bill let me know he was a higher GS15 than I was. I responded to my good friend Bill Walker that I was never going to see GS15 step 5 or 6. Bill asked me why. I mentioned to him that I did not plan on staying a GS15 that long. I told Bill I planned to be promoted to the Senior Executive Service, which is the next step in the promotion process for career executives working in the Executive Branch of government. We both had a good laugh and ended the call after discussing our families.

My new district had three other courthouses for a total of 4 courthouses counting the Atlanta courthouse. The Eleventh Circuit of Appeals Court was nearby by the Atlanta courthouse. As the Chief Deputy, I visited the Appeals Court often. As the Chief of Court Security, I knew several of the Eleventh Circuit Judges, and the Circuit Executive. I met the Circuit Executive at the Circuit Executive's annual meeting. The Eleventh Circuit Executive and I called each other number of times while I was Chief of Court Security discussing various security issues. I saw more of him in my new position. I established weekly meetings with all district employees and worked very closely with my district Warrant Squad, which was very active conducting fugitive investigations and making arrests. The district also had Deputy Marshals assigned to a local fugitive task force that conducted major fugitive investigations and made a number of arrests. The district had a good group of professional Court Security Officers. I enjoyed working with them.

The Northern District of Georgia or specifically, the Atlanta area has a very close-knit local and federal law enforcement community. The law enforcement community in the Atlanta area has an organization called Metropol. Metropol is an organization comprised of the law enforcement community that focuses on and addresses crime issues in the metropolitan area. The organization had meetings to discuss ways to jointly fight crime, also discussing the best use of each agency's resources to protect the community. The Metropol meetings had a focused agenda, and sometimes speakers were invited to include community leaders. The community leaders shared their concerns about the community, discussing specific crime areas and their desire for increased law enforcement presence in high crime areas. Metropol is a very good organization. I enjoyed attending the meetings with my Marshal. It was a excellent venue to get to know the law enforcement executives from the various agencies, and to work jointly focusing on the needs of the community.

Former Marshal McMichael is very well known in the Atlanta area. He is known for his excellent work as a District Attorney Investigator, for having served as the Sheriff of Fulton County, Georgia and for his eight years as the U.S. Marshal for the district. I formed a very good relationship with the Drug Enforcement Administration Assistant Special Agent in Charge as my district fugitive guys and DEA Special Agents worked on several major cases together. On occasions I went out on some of the major law enforcement operations with my Deputies and DEA Special Agents. These operations reminded me of my days hunting and finding fugitives.

While working and living in Atlanta, I was also able to spend plenty of time on weekends with my two teenage sons Sean and Justin who lived in the area. I had purchased three season tickets for the Atlanta Falcons football team for seats at the Georgia Dome. The Georgia Dome is very close to the federal courthouse. The proximity of the courthouse to the Georgia Dome was so close and I could park my vehicle at the courthouse where I parked for work, and my sons and I walked to the stadium. This was the same situation when we took in a basketball game, or went to see the Atlanta Hawks. My sons and I also went to a couple of Atlanta Braves games. Like Chicago, Atlanta is a very good sports town, and I certainly enjoyed the town to include some of the nightlife when I did not have my sons with me.

I worked out in the courthouse gym three or four times a week with my Information Technology Specialist. The Information Technology Specialist and I and on occasions, one of my Supervisory Deputy Marshals went out on Fridays after work. We enjoyed locating the venues each month for the First Friday's parties. Those parties were very nice. That summer my second oldest son Larry came to live with me for the summer before going to college. I spent some nice time with him along with my two youngest sons. My daughter Ashley visited that summer as well. My apartment was full, however, we were all family and had a good time doing things together in Atlanta. My oldest son Sylvester Jr. was close by as he had enrolled in and was attending college at Alabama State University. On a few occasions, I made the short drive from Atlanta to visit my oldest son at Alabama State. I was beginning to think I could live and work in Atlanta long term. I had a good job I liked, and my two youngest sons were there. I considered purchasing a home there, and started to look around for nice areas to live.

The Marshal and I developed a very good working relationship and friendship. Early on in our relationship, I implemented a change of assignment for a major project from a subordinate Supervisory Deputy Marshal, and the Supervisor went to the Marshal complaining about the assignment change. The Marshal overturned my decision. The Marshal and I had a meeting on that matter, and the Marshal made it clear that he was not a part of that decision and did not support it. We agreed to meet on major changes so that we both concurred with the move. After that our relationship was rock solid. The Marshal and I had lunch once or twice a week dining at various venues returning to some venues several times, as we liked the restaurants. The Marshal introduced me to former Atlanta Mayor, Civil Rights Activist and Ambassador Andrew Young. The Marshal and I attended an event at the Martin Luther King Jr. Center, and he introduced me to the late Coretta Scott King who he had known for years. The Marshal introduced me to other important people and officials in Atlanta including Atlanta Police Chief Beverly Harvard. Beverly Harvard is an outstanding lady and public safety official who was the Police Chief at the time. I worked with Beverly Harvard again as President Obama appointed her as U.S. Marshal for the Northern District of Georgia. According to my knowledge, Beverly Harvard is the first and only African American woman to receive a Presidential appointment as U.S. Marshal. I developed a great partnership with my Marshal, and we worked very well together.

While working on various district matters such as the status and accountability of the districts prisoners, the courthouse closed circuit television system and card reader access system, I worked on my task from the Chief Judge to obtain 24-hour perimeter security for the courthouse. From my headquarters experience in the Judicial and Court Security arena, I made many contacts with the General Services Administration (GSA) and the Federal Protective Service. I started making calls to get the 24-hour perimeter security project going. I also obtained support for the project from the Marshals Service Central Courthouse Management Group. The Central Courthouse Management Group coordinated all Marshals Service Office space renovation and expansion projects including new courthouse construction projects. The Central Courthouse Management Group had excellent contacts and working relationships with the General Service Administration. I could find out what roadblocks were ahead of me for the perimeter security project, which I did. I was able to obtain support for this project from the General Services Administration Headquarters in Washington DC. After several telephone calls to GSA executives and the executive heading the Federal Protective Service, I made a breakthrough. The GSA relented and pledged support for the project.

I evaluated the funding level for the contracted security force that was going to be replaced. I recognized the project could not move forward without extra funding. Now I had to obtain extra funding from the Administrative Office of the United States Courts to accomplish the project. I did not think that was going to be a problem, as I had worked on the project and formulated a good business plan. My experience working with the Administrative Office of the United States Courts Office of Security, showed that if you had a good business plan that was focused, justified, and tied to required security, you had a good chance of having your proposal approved. Additionally, I had a good working relationship with the Chief of Security for the AOUSC. I worked on a staffing formula with my staff, and submitted the proposal to the Chief of the AOUSC

Office of Security. Shortly thereafter, I received a call that the project was approved along with the date we could implement the initiative. I immediately let my Marshal know that the initiative was a go and we could move forward. The Marshal was very happy and impressed at how quickly I got the project approved. The Marshal was very much aware that this project was very important as a security enhancement for the courthouse to the Chief Judge and the District Court Security Committee.

The Marshal told me to let the Chief Judge know the good news. I called the judge's chambers and asked her assistant if the Chief Judge was available, which she was. I went to the judge's chambers and gave her the good news about the 24-hour Court Security Officer project approval. I let the Chief Judge know the details of the plan to get everything in place. The Chief Judge was very happy the project was finally approved and put into place. It took only a couple of months to bring the additional Court Security Officers on board to add to the existing force, which made the courthouse a 24-hour perimeter security facility.

In August 2000, my former Assistant Director in the Judicial Security Division retired, and the position was announced for backfill. I applied for this position knowing I was a good fit for the job. I had the confidence of, and tremendous support from various federal judges, and a number of people from the Administrative office of the United States Courts. My Executive Core Qualifications (ECQ) experience was excellent from my vast array of significant national Marshals Service program exposure and accomplishments. Executive Core Qualifications are carefully evaluated by the federal Office of Personnel Management and include the following criteria; Leading Change, Leading People, Results Driven, Business Acumen, and Building Coalitions. I anticipated my experience and accomplishments made me a top candidate for any Senior Executive position. All applicants for the vacant Judicial Security Assistant Director position had to submit an application including their ECQs to be considered for the job. I submitted my application package to the Marshals

Service Human Resources Division. I let my Marshal know I was applying for the job, which was no surprise to him. The Marshals Service did not have an African American Deputy Marshal rise through the ranks to make Assistant Director. I was certainly looking to change that. I did make the interview list and had my interview late in September. I was very happy to go back to the Washington DC area for the interview and to check on my home and visit close friends. I was prepared for my interview, and did well.

Sometime in mid to late October while having lunch with one of my former Court Security Inspectors who was stationed in Atlanta, I received a call from my Marshal. My Marshal told me I had a call from the Director of the Marshal Service. John W. Marshall was the Director. As I mentioned at the end of the last Chapter, Director Marshall succeeded Director Gonzalez receiving his Presidential Appointment as Director of the U.S. Marshals Service in November 1999. For further context on Director Marshall, his father is the late great Thurgood Marshall Sr., the first African American Associate Justice of the U.S. Supreme Court appointed in 1967. Getting back to the telephone call I received, my Marshal kidding with me, asked me if I was too busy to come back to the office to speak with the Director. I told the Marshal of course not, that I would be back in the office soon, and wrapped up lunch. I felt good news was coming about the Assistant Director for Judicial Security position. I reported back to the district and went right to the Marshal's office. Marshal McMichael called the Acting Deputy Director Louie McKinney. Director Marshall appointed Mr. McKinney as Acting Director after his appointed Deputy Director was reassigned. Louie McKinney who was retired and doing some other work was available to assist Director Marshall as Acting Deputy Director. The Marshal got Acting Deputy Director McKinney on the telephone and the Acting Deputy Director had us hold on while he went to get the Director.

I was very excited as I anticipated that this was going to be a great day for me. Director Marshall got on the telephone and greeted us all stating, "that today is a historic day." He further added that he was selecting me to be the first African American Deputy Marshal to be promoted to the Senior Executive Service as an Assistant Director. I was overcome with joy, but kept my emotions somewhat in check, and responded by saying I was very happy with my selection, and appreciated the Director's confidence in me. I let the Director and Acting Deputy Director know that I would do my very best in my new position. The Director left the call and the Deputy Director let me know they needed me to report to the vacant Assistant Director's position as soon as I could. Acting Deputy Director McKinney further told me that I should contact the Human Resources Division to coordinate a reporting date for my new position, also coordinating the reporting date with my Marshal.

As the Marshal and I got off the phone we sat in his office and just talked a while. The Marshal related to me that he was very proud of me and my accomplishments including the work I did in his district for about a year. The Marshal and I agreed on a reporting date for me to leave my position as Chief Deputy the following month in November 2000. The district held a very nice going away party from me a week before I left. The party was well attended with leaders and staff from various law enforcement agencies, the court family, the Court Security Officers, and district Marshals Service employees.

I got on the telephone to call my good friend William "Bill" Walker who was promoted by the Drug Enforcement Administration the past January to GS 15, and proudly told me he was a GS15 step 4, and soon would be a GS15 Step 5. I greeted my good friend and asked him what in-grade step he was. He told me he had recently got his Step 5. I congratulated him. I again told him what I had said before, that I would never see GS15 Step 5. I let him know I was selected to become a member of the Senior Executive Service and that I was soon to report back to the Washington DC area as the Assistant Director for Judicial Security for the Marshals Service. He was very happy for me and told me I was right about never seeing GS15 step 5. We talked some more about family and the military. We ended the call knowing we would be living and working in the same area again.

CHAPTER THIRTEEN

My Historic Selection and Promotion to the Senior Executive Service As Assistant Director for the Judicial Security Division

In November 2000, I reported back to the Washington DC area to Marshals Service Headquarters as the Acting Assistant Director for Judicial Security while my paper work was processed to complete my appointment to the Senior Executive Service. The appointment process normally takes a couple of months or more to get done after being selected. The Department or agency that selects a person for a Senior Executive Service position, has to work with the Office of Personnel Management to get the process finalized. I met with the Acting Deputy Director Louie McKinney to discuss various matters related to my job, and an extra task he and Director Marshall wanted me to do. Acting Deputy Director McKinney informed me that he and Director Marshall wanted me to fill the agency vacancy as Deciding Official for Agency Discipline. As the Deciding Official for Agency Discipline, I decided agency discipline cases for all Marshals Service personnel facing a suspension of 14 days to removal from position.

I let Acting Deputy Director McKinney know that I will accept any assignment or task from him or the Director and do my very best to complete the assignment. In the next few days a memorandum came out from the Director's office announcing that I was selected be the deciding official for all agency discipline. This was a collateral duty I had from November 2000 to June 2004. The normal deciding official assignment was for a period of 2 years. Not only was I very busy with my duties as the Assistant Director for Judicial Security, I also had the responsibility as Agency Deciding Official for Discipline. I was also performing my part-time military duties as an officer, along with working on my Master's Degree. I decided to make the best of my time by taking courses at the University of Maryland University College (UMUC) online. UMUC had a very good worldwide online program. I could do my course work at anytime, anywhere, and also work on other priorities.

After getting situated in my office and getting reacquainted with my Court Security Program staff, and attending meetings with other programs in the Judicial Security Division, I went to work continuing to build on previous Judicial and Court Security relationships. I re-connected with the Administrative Office of the United States Courts Office of Security and other AOUSC senior level staff. There were a few security programs I wanted to enhance. The Chief of the AOUSC Office of Security and I had some new initiatives we wanted to work on. I needed to make an assessment of the Judicial Security Division, as I had been out of the division for a year serving as Chief Deputy Marshal in Atlanta. My old position as Chief of Court Security was filled. My direct reports included the Chief of Court Security, Chief of the Court Security Officer Program, Chief of Contracts, Chief of Technical Security, and the Chief of Courthouse Management, all GS15 employees. I decided to announce and fill a GS14 operational Chief Inspector position to head up a small oversight office I established to help me manage and track major division issues. The Court Security Officer Program was formerly under the Court Security Program. The former

Assistant Director elevated the Court Security Officer Program making it independent of the Court Security Program, a good thing to do. I had a good senior level division management team. We had plenty of security work to do on behalf of federal judges, Supreme Court Justices, federal courthouses, and court facilities. To accomplish our work, my division and I had to work closely with the Marshals Service district offices and the AOUSC Office of Security.

As the Deciding Official for Agency Discipline I started receiving dozens of discipline cases to read and work on. I had to make decisions on the appropriate discipline penalties. I worked closely with the Human Resources Division Employee Relations Branch on the cases I received. A new Chair of the Marshals Service Discipline Proposing Panel was selected. The Chair of the Discipline Proposing Panel and I were to attend the Department of Justice National Advocacy Center (NAC) in Columbia, South Carolina for a one-week training session on managing the discipline process. The NAC is a very nice complex and professional learning center on the campus of the University of South Carolina. The Chair of the Proposing Panel, and I along with other Department of Justice officials attended the NAC course. The facility has lodging, meeting and training rooms, and a very nice cafeteria. The week training session was very helpful to me as over the following 3½ years, I made discipline decisions for over 100 cases.

The courses I took in my Master's Program in Human Resources Management also assisted me with deciding discipline cases. I reviewed and decided a vast array of discipline cases and suspended many employees after careful consideration of all facts including the employee's written and personal responses with their attorneys or other representatives present in my office. Some of the cases I decided involved employees socializing or having close relationships with non-immediate family members who were felons who were convicted of a felony. Other cases I decided involved miss-use of government vehicle or government credit card, improper use of office or law enforcement credentials, an inebriated employee urinating on his Chief Deputies desk, and sustained romantic relationships between supervisors and employees. Unfortunately, I had to terminate some employees for more serious violations. I imagine these cases are probably the same type discipline matters decided at other agencies.

Focusing on the improvement of security policies and procedures for judges and courthouses, and working closely with the Judicial Conference Committee on Security and Facilities and collaboration with law enforcement partners were my priorities as the senior executive of the Judicial Security Division. My Chief Inspector for Oversight along with other senior Court Security Inspectors were tasked to work with me on overhauling and enhancing various security policies and procedures. We did some good work completing the overhaul and enhancement of a number of judicial security policies. My staff and I continued to work closely with the Judicial Conference Committee on Security and Facilities, and the Chair of the Committee at the time Appellate Judge Jane R. Roth. Judge Roth and the other judges on the Committee were very dedicated to all security issues involving judges and facilities. The next couple of years, my division, the AOUSC Office of Security and the Judicial Conference Committee for Security and Facilities worked jointly to accomplish many initiatives. It was certainly a pleasure to get to know the judges on the Committee who worked in various federal judicial districts, especially Judge Roth. I enjoyed meeting and spending some time with Judge Roth's late husband the outstanding Senator from Delaware. Senator William V. Roth Jr. was a true gentleman, a great man, a great legislator, and a sponsor for legislation that led to the creation of the Roth IRA.

In June 2001, I took a weekend trip home to Chicago to attend my Grandfather's 82nd birthday party. I visited with a few good friends including Al Howard. I usually got a hotel room when I returned to Chicago, but on occasion I stayed a night with one of my Aunts or Al Howard and his family. This time I called Al before my trip to Chicago to coordinate my stay at his house on Sunday night with him and his family in my usual basement bedroom. On my way to Al's house, I called him to let him know I was stopping by one of my favorite barbecue restaurants to purchase us some ribs. Our plan was to eat some ribs and watch a National Basketball Association basketball game. I think it was either the playoffs or the finals.

Back in the office I worked very hard on judicial security matters, handling discipline cases, continuing with my monthly military obligation, and taking courses in my Master's Program. My good friend, mentor, and a father figure Julius Turner had been battling an illness and was hospitalized in Maryland. I visited him often while he was in the hospital. We always had some interesting conversations. One of our conversations occurred during the November 2000 Presidential election between Vice President Al Gore and Texas Governor George W. Bush. We were watching Cable News Network (CNN) on the news on the night of November 7, 2000. Julius was resting and sleeping during my visit. He woke up at 8pm eastern-time to see CNN make a projection that Al Gore was going to win the election and be the next President of the United States. Gore was winning in Florida at the time. As we now know the state of Florida was the state that was going to swing the election to one of the candidates based on the election projection results of other states, and the number of college electoral votes in a very close election. During that evening as Julius went to sleep and woke up again, we both saw CNN retract their earlier projection about 2 hours later saying the election was too close to call. The last words I heard from Julius Turner was "don't tell me George Bush won the election." I responded back to Julius that according to CNN George Bush was most likely going to win the state of Florida. That same night or early morning CNN projected that George Bush had won the election.

The events of that historic election as we now know were very contentious as the final vote count was held up for about one month based on a number of factors including absentee voters and more specifically punch card ballots that were reportedly not counted by the vote tabulating machines creating "chads". I had not heard of that vote term before, but now just about anyone who was of age to understand voting at the time, is familiar with the term "chad." Interesting enough at least in my mind, as the 2000 election was being finalized with lawyers and court rulings, the election results were appealed to the 11th Circuit Court of Appeals. The 11th Circuit Court of Appeals panel made a ruling on the matter and I received a call from my immediate superior the agency Deputy Director who gave me directions to have one of my Court Security Inspectors go to the 11th Circuit Court and obtain a copy of the panel of judge's ruling and take it to U.S. Supreme Court Justice Anton Scalia who was on vacation on the east coast. I contacted a Court Security Inspector as directed and had the Inspector obtain the sealed ruling and hand deliver it to Justice Scalia. The 2000 Presidential election was headed for a ruling at the United States Supreme Court. The U.S. Supreme Court decided the case December 12, 2000, allowing the earlier certification of George W. Bush as President by the Florida Secretary of State to stand, and the rest is history. During this time my good friend, mentor, golfing partner, and father figure Julius Turner passed away in that hospital where I visited him.

In January 2001, as we know President George W. Bush became the 43rd President of the United States. Right before President Bush took office, his new Administration immediately dismissed just about all of President Clinton's Appointees who were leading federal government departments and agencies including my Director John W. Marshall. I was saddened to see John Marshall leave an agency he had worked for over 8 years. He provided critical and outstanding leadership as a U.S. Marshal and Director. The Bush Administration apparently looking to have some Executive Branch continuity selected a number of officials as Acting Directors or Administrators of agencies. Louie McKinney was the Acting Deputy Director, appointed to that position by Director John Marshall. Mr. McKinney was selected by the Bush Administration to be the Acting Director of the Marshals Service effective January 21, 2001. I was pleased that Mr. McKinney was going to be the Acting Director, as he had served in a number of leadership positions during his career with the Marshals Service. Acting Director McKinney appointed a Chief Deputy as his Acting Deputy Director. The Chief Deputy, a female was going to be the second in command as Acting Deputy Director, and my immediate boss along with supervising all of the other Assistant Directors while serving in that position.

At least one Assistant Director that I am aware of took issue with Acting Director McKinney's Acting Deputy Director selection. I had known the Acting Deputy Director for many years. She was my class Counselor when I was a new Deputy in recruit class. She also briefly worked for me when I was Chief of the Court Security Program. She left the agency and returned, coming back on board in my program. This career Deputy Marshal was subsequently selected as Assistant Director and served as the Detention Trustee, and had her own historic selection as the first female Director of the Marshals Service in 2011.

As 2001 was moving along, my division and I were busy handling a number of judicial security related matters, I was waiting on the finalization of my selection process to the Senior Executive Service. I strongly believe there were a few people in the Marshal Service at the senior executive level, who were hoping my selection to the Senior Executive Service was not going to be finalized. A few good friends of mine told me they were aware of at least two of my new colleagues who were not happy with my selection and promotion. These friends told me they overheard discussions between two of my new peers about how to block my promotions. My promotion finalization process slowed down with the new Administration in place. I was told the new Administration placed all positions on hold as they were reviewing all position. I knew my new position was not political, but a career position. I was concerned with the process because there was a new Administration in place, and in my view, politics can be good and bad. I remembered a conversation I had with a distinguished federal judge I got to know in Atlanta. He told me when I get to Washington DC for my new position, "if they messed with you and give you any 'shit' give me a call." The judge with his knowledge and experience, anticipated things may not go smoothly for me with my transition to a very high career government position. The judge related that he would assist me with addressing any unnecessary roadblocks.

In early August 2001, I was getting fed up with the delay in finalizing my selection and promotion to the Senior Executive Service. I decided to call the judge and let him know of my concerns with the delay in finalization of my SES selection. The judge told me he was going to check into the matter with his own Department of Justice contacts. I received some good news, as within a few days of my call to the judge, the judge called me back and told me he coordinated a meeting for me at the Department of Justice. Within a few days my selection to the Senior Executive Service was finalized. I was very happy that the process was finally complete. I contacted two former Directors; Eduardo Gonzalez, and John Marshall to let them know my SES appointment was finalized, and again express my sincere appreciation for their leadership, trust, and support. I contacted family members and friends to share the good news. Now I could continue to focus on the many tasks and things I had to accomplish. I also completed the Army's Command and General Staff College in August of 2001 making me eligible to be promoted in the Military to Lieutenant Colonel. This was a tough correspondence course with plenty of writing assignments.

During this same time period, I received a call from a senior Department of Justice career prosecutor who was assigned to work for DOJ in Colombia, South America. This attorney asked to meet with me to discuss a project he was working on, also letting me know the DOJ and his office in Colombia needed assistance from the Marshals Service with training in protective operations for law enforcement personnel protecting judges and prosecutors. Colombia had a problem with Cartels and other criminals assassinating judges and prosecutors. The U.S. Department of Justice and the U.S. Department of State had funding to support training and assistance for the country of Colombia to assist the country with its fight against in-country terrorism groups and dangerous and violent Drug Cartels. I met with the attorney from DOJ and he briefed me on what he had been working on in Colombia. The attorney related senior officials in the DOJ supported the training plans to assist Colombia with changing how they hold court and charge dangerous criminals with crimes. The country was going from a non-accusatory judicial system to an accusatory judicial system. As a part of the new judicial system witnesses had to come to court and face those they were testifying against, which did not occur before the change in their judicial system.

The attorney let me know that the country of Colombia needed the Marshals Service assistance with a plan to conduct protective operations training and provide other assistance. He also added that Colombia needed my office to develop a plan to conduct protective operations training and provide other assistance to strengthen the protective operations for the country's judicial family. The attorney also wanted to see if the Marshals Service Witness Security Division could also participate in a comprehensive and collaborative training program helping Colombia protect witnesses. I responded that I could not speak for the Witness Security Program, however, I could speak for my division, and worked with some of my team members to develop a good plan to assist Colombia strengthen its response to protecting judges and prosecutors. I mentioned to the attorney that I was going to put a core team together to work on our plan. I further mentioned our plan included an in-country assessment. I referred him to my colleagues directing the activities of the Witness Security Program so he could meet with them to address the need for Witness Security related assistance. I had no idea of knowing at the time that I was going to be involved with training programs in Colombia for the next 12 years. I was also unaware I would make numerous trips to Colombia to support programs, direct training for thousands of Colombia law enforcement operations along with other U.S. agencies including the U.S. Military.

I researched Plan Colombia and the need for such a program as it relates to regional and worldwide security. I found out the program was very important and started working on putting together a strategic leadership team to work on our strategy to formulate a very good plan. I appointed one of my Chief Inspectors as the Program Chief reporting directly to me for operational and tactical command. I then selected one of my most tactical Senior Inspectors as the in-country team chief. I had both team chiefs coordinate an assessment visit to meet with the DOJ attorney I had met with, and Colombian government leaders involved with their prosecutions and law enforcement programs. In September 2001, I sent another team to Colombia from my division to meet with officials about facilities and technical security requirements. The operational protective training mission was going well, and I was waiting on my other administrative team to return from Colombia with their assessment. The administrative team was held up and remained in Colombia for a few extra days after the terrorist attacks against the United States. As we know terrorist airplane hijackers on suicide missions attacked the U.S. causing a tremendous loss of life on American soil killing nearly 3000 people at multiple locations including hundreds of first responders.

On the morning of September 11, 2001, I was driving to work on Interstate 395 South on a highway in Washington DC and observed Senior Inspector Buz Brown who was assigned to work the Court Security Program Duty Desk in my division after being promoted from the District of the Virgin Islands. Buz was also on the same highway driving to work. Buz called me on my cellular telephone and told me to turn my radio on as it was just reported that an airplane had hit one of the twin towers in New York. I turned my radio on and heard the report of the airplane crashing into the tower. Buz and I expedited our drive to our headquarters offices to find out what was going on with the airplane crash. We arrived and hurried to our office suite and turned on the television in my office to see the news. It was at that point that the second plane hit the second tower. We both knew the deliberate plane crashes were acts of terrorism.

That day and the days to follow were very long days for me, my staff, and law enforcement agencies across the country. From the Marshals Service perspective, our priorities were to account for all of our employees and the court family and we staffed our Emergency Operations Center. As I mentioned, I knew I had two employees stuck out of country in Colombia. I knew the employees were safe and contact with them. I attended a number of high-level meetings with my agency as we addressed the Marshals Service response to assist in the protection of our homeland. As was published in the media, the Marshals Service had an important security role as Deputy Marshals were assigned to provide security at airports around the country. We also enhanced security protocols for all court facilities. Louie McKinney was still Acting Director. However, a new agency Deputy Director was appointed by the Bush Administration to work with him a couple of months before the September 11, 2001 devastating cowardly terrorist attack. My two employees who were trapped in Colombia conducting the facilities security and technical security assessments, made it back safely home after limited airplane traffic was allowed. All airplane traffic had been stopped until the United States government was certain the attacks were contained and no further planes were in jeopardy of being hijacked.

In response to the September 11, 2001 attacks, and the killing of Americans in New York, Pennsylvania, and Virginia at the Pentagon, I worked on a major security initiative with the Chief of Security for the Administrative Office of the United States Courts. He and I had several meetings on this critical initiative that brought 106 Judicial Security Inspector positions to the Marshals Service. After the Chief of Security for the AOUSC and I developed the concept of this new plan, we involved our respective key staff to assist us with implementation of the plan. The Chief of Security for the AOUSC and I had our respective financial experts work on everything needed to implement this new initiative. We wanted to formulate the best budget proposal possible for the Committee on Security and Facilities to approve, as this funding would come from the federal judicial security budget and not the Marshals Service budget. The Marshals Service did not have the funding to add 106 GS13 operational positions. The addition of these positions to the Marshals Service amounted to an increase of 25% of the agencies GS13 existing staffing levels. The Chief of Security for the AOUSC and I wanted to make sure that we had everything in place to execute our plan and make this program increase a success. We were significantly enhancing judicial and facility security in response to the terrorist attacks, but also as a part of many serious discussions we had (prior to September 11, 2001) about enhancing judicial security in case of a terrorist attack of any kind. As a part of our budget formulation, we needed 106 new government vehicles, weapons, computers, cellular telephones and related office space. This program increase was a huge initiative for Marshals Service operational employees. We had 106 law enforcement people get promoted. We obtained approval from the Judicial Conference Committee on Security and Facilities to fund this very important initiative. I briefed my agency senior executives and the Director on various phases of the initiative including the success of the funding. I worked with my agency Human Resources Division and Finance Division to bring the 106 positions on board.

The Chief of Security, and other executives for the AOUSC, and members of the Committee on Security and Facilities had a concern that senior level Marshals Service officials may try and take some of the 106 allocated positions to work for other Marshals Service missions other than for Judicial Security. These officials desired that I maintain all of the 106 positions under my leadership and control, as they were aware of my dedication and focus on security for judges and courthouses. I had another thought about how to deploy the 106 positions. My plan was to keep 12 of the new Judicial Security Inspectors to add to my core group of Court Security Inspectors, adding one of the Inspector positions to each of the 11 federal judicial circuits, and one for the Washington DC Court of Appeals. The remaining 94 positions were to be allocated to each of the 94 judicial districts to focus on all court security related requirements, including the Court Security Officers in each district, and the districts technical security needs such as closed circuit television, and alarm systems.

I made a case to the decision makers at the AOUSC that I did not need my division to grow by 106 positions. I emphasized that it was better for each district to have one of the new positions, and my division be enhanced by 12 positions. I further added that in the new policy I was working on with my staff that any future Assistant Director of Judicial Security would have oversight and some control over all of the positions, including annual professional development training. With this approach and plan, I won the support of deploying one Judicial Security Inspector to each of our district offices. For the next couple of months, my staff and I worked on the new initiative, which included the development of the position description for the positions.

In November 2001 Acting Louie Director McKinney was replaced as our agency leader. President George W. Bush appointed a new Director for the Marshals Service. I was not happy to see Mr. McKinney leave the Marshals Service as his veteran leadership during the September 11, terrorist attacks was needed as we addressed a number of security issues including a proposal to take on the duties of the Air Marshals program providing air security for airplanes. As I recall, the new Deputy Director opposed the Marshals Service taking on the Air Marshals security responsibility. At the request of the U.S. Attorney General the Marshals Service assisted with security for numerous medium and high volume airports. Mr. McKinney who a few years ago, authored a book, One Marshals Badge, continue to be a good mentor and friend to me.

I provided several briefings to the new Director on the status of Judicial Security matters, including the Judicial Conference of the United States Committee on Security and Facilities, Administrative Office of the United States Courts, judges, courthouses and court facilities. The next Judicial Conference Committee meeting was scheduled in a little over a month in January 2002, and the new Director needed to be prepared to attend the meeting.

As 2002 arrived, my division was very busy working on various judicial security matters including the new Judicial Security Inspector initiative for the new 106 Judicial Security Inspector positions. I shared our draft policy for the 106 Judicial Security Inspectors with the Chief of Security for the AOUSC. The Chief provided a few comments on the policy, and the policy was completed. I asked our Human Resources Division to announce the 106 positions for the agency Career Board to convene and consider for their recommendations to the Director. The Director makes all selections for operational employee promotions. A number of U.S. Marshals contacted me informing me of their choice for Judicial Security Inspector positions. I also provided input on those being selected for the positions. I concurred with just about all but a few of the U.S. Marshal's recommendations that were sent to the Director. The 106 positions were announced and selected, and my core team and I put together a one-week training curriculum for the new initiative. I scheduled 4 training sessions bringing the new Judicial Security Inspectors in for training dividing the group by 25%. I selected the training locations. The budget formulation for the initiative included a training session for each year. This initiative is an ongoing program and has been a total success enhancing judicial security.

During this time, I met Joseph Alexander, a very interesting and very intelligent gentleman. I met Joe through Don Horton as Don moved from the Court Security Division to the U.S. District Court in Washington DC as the Chief Deputy. Chief Horton subsequently received a Presidential appointment to be the U.S. Marshal for the District of Columbia by

President Clinton. Joe Alexander worked for the Chief Judge for the U.S. District Court in Washington DC as an Executive and impressed me with his intellect. I asked Joe If he would consider working with me in the Judicial Security Division to work on a number of projects and he agreed. My division was lucky to have someone like Joe assist us with various judicial projects. During this time I was also able to get LBC to transfer from the division he was working in to work for the Court Security Officer Program in my division. I had a number of very good people working with me in support of security for federal judges and court facilities. I became very good lifetime friends with both LBC an Alpha Phi Alpha Fraternity Brother, and Joe Alexander.

Along with the implementation of the Judicial Security Inspector Program, I was working with my Plan Colombia training team on the new training program in Colombia, South America, which was started in 2002. I made a few trips to Colombia in 2002 to meet with my team conducting training, Colombia officials such as the Attorney General and his staff, the Department of Justice program coordinator, and to speak at course graduations. Our training program was very successful and was sought after by various Colombia law enforcement officials. As I mentioned, the focus of the training was protective operations, and protecting judges and prosecutors.

My Chief Inspector, in-country team leader, and the training teams were doing an outstanding job with the training. It was a pleasure to travel and visit the training and spend time with my training team and the various Colombian law enforcement officers. The Colombian law enforcement officers were very happy with the new skills they were receiving from the training team. These officers are very proud officers who wanted to make a difference in their homeland's fight to uphold justice. Along with the close working relationship my team established with the Colombian law enforcement organizations, we developed a close working relationship with some members of the Colombian military. We partnered with the military procuring the use of some of their facilities to assist with training.

On my 3rd or 4th trip to Bogota, my in-country team leader arranged a military helicopter ride as they inserted my arrival into one of the training scenarios. I got a chance to have a nice view of the beautiful city of Bogota. I was okay with the scenario, but was not okay with the second helicopter that followed the chopper I was in. I expressed this to my in-country team leader, but he related that the Colombian military would not have it any other way. My in-country team leader told me the Colombian military did not want anything to happen to me. I enjoyed participating in the training scenario, which went very well. I am very proud of this training initiative, my training team, and the thousands of law enforcement officers that went through the training.

I married again in 2002. This was my 4th time exchanging wedding vows. We had a destination wedding in St. Thomas U.S. Virgin Islands. We had another larger ceremony back home in Chicago. My new wife relocated to the Washington DC area in June 2002. We purchased a house in Maryland, which was my second Maryland home. I kept my other home for a few years before eventually selling it. My duties as the Assistant Director of Judicial Security kept me busy. I was also working very closely with the Executive Office of the United States Attorney's Security Office focusing on security issues for federal prosecutors, and working on various protective details around the country for prosecutors under serious threat.

As 2002 closed and 2003 arrived, I was still focused on leading my division with innovative and creative ways to do a better job at protecting courthouses and federal judges. The Judicial Security Inspector Program and related training support programs were going well. I invited United States Supreme Court Justice Stephen Breyer to participate in our training programs and be a guest speaker at our dinner program, which he agreed to do. The Judicial Security Inspectors, Judicial Security Division managers and I were very happy Justice Breyer participated in our training. His speeches were encouraging and motivational. Justice Breyer became my favorite U.S. Supreme Court Justice. I was also concentrating on two long-term 24-hour protection details on federal judges who presided over terrorism cases. I visited and met with these judges at least twice a year to hear any concerns they had with the protective details. The protective details were in place when I arrived in the division the first time as the Chief of Court Security. My staff and I were reviewing the continued need for the details, and working on a successful strategy to reduce the details, which we accomplished. When it comes to protection, I was taught by one of my mentors, Don Horton who as I previously mentioned served in the position of Chief of Court Security before me, that you have to be very detailed, and error only on the side of caution, when it comes to protection details. I have tried diligently to use that wise counsel when working on protection details and protection strategies.

While serving as Chief of Court Security, one of my most seasoned Court Security Inspectors who was at the top of his trade in security vulnerability countermeasures, met with me and discussed a concept that was very important with protection details. The concept of Counter Surveillance Detection was not a new concept as some security conscious organizations including the military use it. I immediately liked the idea and worked on a strategy with this Court Security Inspector and another Court Security Inspector. We partnered with the United States Army for training, and started training our division personnel in Counter Surveillance Detection. The training was superb and we decided to approach the Witness Security Program and invite their personnel to join us in the training to assist that division with their protective mission. At the time, I had no idea I would be assigned to lead that program as a division. The Witness Security Program was more than happy to get in on this good training. A number of Witness Security Inspectors received the training. In my division, we started to use this new concept as a part of our protective operations.

In 2003, I continued to work diligently in support of security for Marshals Services protectees with the exception of protected witnesses. I continued to meet with the Judicial Conference Committee on Security and Facilities, the Executive Office for United States Attorney's Security Office, give security and update briefings to new federal judges, promoted judges to the Appellate Court, and District Chief Judges, and continued with the professional development of the Judicial Security Inspector Program. There were a number of protective details placed on judges and Assistant United States Attorney's while the threat against these officials were investigated and resolved. I had another beautiful daughter that we named Morgan. I enjoyed being a father again, and spending time with my new little girl. Morgan and her mother often accompanied me on some of my Marshals Service travel requirements.

I continued to visit my division protective operations training in Colombia, South America and met with Colombian officials as a part of my visit. In November 2003, I received a Director's Award from the Director of the Executive Office for United States Attorneys. I was very proud to be recognized at the Executive Office for United States Attorneys Annual Director's Award ceremony along with 166 other Director's Award recipients. My award citation was meaningful to me as it recognized me for providing timely and effective security support to employees of the United States Attorneys' Offices. My Maryland family attended the nice ceremony held at the Ronald Reagan Building in Washington DC.

In 2004, it was much of the same as it was in 2003. My division was going in the right direction and we had the support and respect of our protectees and other supporting organizations. The division worked on and completed the Occupant Emergency Plan for all district offices, the National Security Survey, refresher training for the Judicial Security Inspectors, Security Orientation for nearly 1,000 Court Security Officers, the Division Annual Activity Report, Division Customer Satisfaction Survey, a Joint Integrated Security Construction Conference with the

General Services Administration in Miami, Florida, and trained an additional 250 Colombian law enforcement Officers in protective operations with a total of 451 officers trained for both 2003 and 2004. We nearly completed the Study on the Security Relationship between the Marshals Service, the Federal Protective Service and the Judiciary as mandated by Congress. This security study was 85% complete when I was reassigned to lead another division.

I was administering the last session of the annual Judicial Security Inspector's refresher training in Philadelphia in May 2004, when I received a call to return to our Headquarters to meet with my boss the Deputy Director. I planned to join many of the Inspectors for a Philadelphia Phillies baseball game on a Thursday evening, but drove back to the Washington DC area for a Friday morning meeting with my boss. The Deputy Director obtained the Director's approval to reassign me to a newly formed division labeled the Witness Security and Prisoner Operations Division. The Director and Deputy Director reorganized some of the agency divisions, and moved the Witness Security Program to the Prisoner Services Division creating the new titled division. This new division title was out of sync with all of the other divisions which all had only three words and three abbreviated letters.

I was not happy about this reassignment. I worked my behind off leading the Judicial Security Division, developing new policies and security procedures for judges and courthouses. I led the development of several critical and successful security initiatives, working with some of the best and most intelligent security professionals. I worked long hours each day getting home each night around 8pm, working nearly 12 hours a day, and then working some more before I retired for the night. I somewhat anticipated the move as a couple of judges on the Judicial Conference Committee on Security and Facilities mentioned to me that they were concerned that the Deputy Director and the Director (both appointed under the Bush Administration), may move me from my position as head of Judicial Security because I was working very hard on their behalf protecting their interest, and in some instances in direct conflict of my superiors the Deputy Director and Director. These judges knew I did my best not to let the Deputy Director misalign any resources or efforts that supported their security programs. The Deputy Director at the time did not get his wishes of taking 42 positions from the 106 new Judicial Security Inspector positions that the Courts obtained funding for to enhance court and judicial security 2 years prior. It is my belief that he had malice for me, as he knew he lost in that effort primarily to my strategy to make sure it did not happen.

Additionally, the Deputy Attorney General at the time, the Honorable Larry Thompson left his position to return to private practice, leaving a void at that position. In June I was reassigned from my position as the Assistant Director of Judicial Security Division, to take on my new assignment as Assistant Director of the Witness Security and Prisoner Operations Division. One evening I received a telephone call from the wife of one of my most senior and trusted Court Security Inspectors. She told me she received a spiritual message to call me and encourage me, letting me know that God had another plan for me with my new assignment. She told me that I worked very hard in support of federal judges and the courts putting in long hours, and that I will find a silver lining with my new assignment. Her words were very encouraging and it made me look at the reassignment differently. I received a very nice note from U.S. Supreme Court Justice Stephen Breyer. The note which I have placed a copy of in this book, essentially thanked me for my service to the judiciary, acknowledging that I was taking on a new difficult assignment, and wishing me well. I was happy to receive the note as it also encouraged me. I soon understood the meaning of the call that I received from the Court Security Inspector's wife about the silver lining after starting my new assignment.

CHAPTER FOURTEEN

Reassignment to the Witness Security and Prisoner Operations Division

After taking my new assignment as the Assistant Director of the Witness Security and Prisoner Operations Division, I soon found out my Director and Deputy Director were not aware of the procedure to make a major organizational change moving a major program or division. They did not make the required Congressional notification and obtain Congressional approval. After learning of their mistake, they did submit the required notification and approval request. I moved into my new office in the Prisoner Operations Division formerly named the Prisoner Services Division. As I mentioned, I served as a Chief Inspector in this division, leading several major programs. Many of the career staff I worked with before, were still working in the division.

As the Assistant Director of the division, all of the division's programs were under my leadership, including the prisoner medical program. The Prisoner Medical program is a large and significant program responsible for providing medical services for all Marshals Service pre-trial detainees except those housed in the Federal Bureau of Prisons (BOP). The BOP has its own medical staff. However, if there were any significant issues with Marshals Service Pretrial prisoners detained in BOP facilities, the BOP and the Marshals Service worked together to resolve the issues. I received briefings on the division from the division leadership, and went to work. I worked with the Office of the Federal Detention Trustee (OFDT), which had been created to provide oversight of the one billion dollar Federal Detention Appropriation. The OFDT also had the responsibility to facilitate detention issues and conflicts between my agency and Immigration Customs Enforcement (ICE). The Immigration part of ICE was formerly under the Immigration Naturalization Service (INS). The INS was at the time an agency within the U.S. Department of Justice. U.S. Customs and INS were moved to what is now known as the Department of Homeland Security (DHS) in a major federal re-organization in response to September 11, 2001.

While under the Department of Justice, both the Marshals Service and Immigration Service worked together for needed pre-trial jail space. With the new federal law enforcement re-organization, both the Marshals Service and ICE were in fierce competition for needed jail space. The OFDT assisted with de-conflicting issues related to outbidding for jail space. As I recall, there were areas where there were some major issues related to detention management involving available jail space. There were detention problems with jails and correctional institutions including prisoner assaults, sexual contact between jail officials and prisoners, and reports of prisoner sexual assaults.

My prior experience leading the operational jail programs assisted me with dealing with these issues. It was good to work with the professionals I worked with before in the division. These civil servants were still compassionate about their work involving prisoner security, accountability and jail space management. I was briefed on some Marshals Service district offices including Southwest Border districts that still had critical detention bed space issues. There was still a need for more federal pretrial detention bed space. I mentioned to a few of my division managers working on these issues, that the same detention issues existed when I was working in the division six years ago. Immigration arrests mostly in states in the Southwest Border were still keeping the pre-trial detention numbers up. I recognized that detention management and incarceration was thriving and was growing into a huge multi-billion dollar business.

I met with the Acting Federal Detention Trustee to work jointly on critical detention issues such as jail space and the rates negotiated for jail space. The Office of Federal Detention Trustee is a U.S. Department of Justice component. I worked on a number of national detention matters involving various Marshals Service district offices. I had numerous meetings and conference calls with Marshals Service district leaders and officials from many counties across the country. My staff and I met in person with the Sheriff from New Orleans Parrish, executives including a judge from Mansfield, Texas, local and federal officials from Cleveland, Ohio, and Nevada regarding detention issues. Many of these meetings were held in my office, and focused on proposals for additional federal pre-trial detention beds or local concerns with the negotiated cost for prisoner beds. Some of these officials disagreed with the prisoner rate negotiated by my staff. I always kept an open mind, hearing the concerns of the officials. Some jail rate proposals required the assistance and approval of the OFDT. My office forwarded those proposals to the OFDT office to resolve.

I had another detention matter that was elevated to my attention from the U.S. Marshal in the District of Arizona. I became friends with this Marshal during my days as the Assistant Director for the Judicial Security Division. The detention issue involved the County Jail in Yuma, Arizona. The Sheriff of the county was seeking a rate increase for the federal prisoners in his jail. The Marshal informed me that there was no movement on the written request for a rate increase, and the Sheriff was getting a little bit agitated. The Marshal also let me know the Sheriff was going to call me, or the agency Director. I appreciated the heads up from the Marshal. I always advised the District Marshals and Chiefs at our agency management conferences to let me know if they had any issues with my division, so I could look into the issue and get it addressed and resolved. I further told the agency leaders, if I could not get the issue resolved, taking the matter up the chain was understandable.

During this time I selected a new Chief of the Inter-Government Agreement Program. I made an inquiry with this manager about the Yuma county jail rate increase, and let the manager know I wanted her team to work on the request and resolve it. Additional time passed by, and I did receive a call from the Sheriff, and spoke with him regarding his concerns. I told him I was looking into the matter and would call him back. After checking with the Program Chief I was told there were concerns with the request from the county for a rate increase. I asked the Program Chief to bring me the file to review and I reviewed the file. The Program Chief let me know that the OFDT Chief who approved all substantial Inter-Governmental Agreements did not approve the rate increase based on a formula used to develop detention per diem rates. It took me a little time to work with the Chief from the OFDT on the rate increase. However, the request was approved after some good negotiations. The county did not get the exact rate they wanted, but did get a fair rate increase.

I was also receiving information on the Witness Security Program as the agency Director and other staff made the Congressional notification to move the Witness Security Program from the Investigative Services Division to form the Witness Security and Prisoner Operations Division. I was working on my strategy on how I was going to lead and manage two Programs, both of which were formerly divisions at one time. I decided to have the two Division program senior leaders report directly to me. I also decided to meet weekly with key staff for joint division meetings to discuss general management matters. When necessary, I met with Witness Security Program leaders separately due to the sensitive nature of some of the issues within that program.

On March 5, 2005, the Marshals Service received Congressional approval to move the Witness Security Program from the Investigative

Services Division. The program move formed the Witness Security and Prisoner Operations Division (WSPOD) under my leadership. I did not like the abbreviations WSPOD as I thought it was out of sync with other division abbreviations such as JSD for Judicial Security Division, ISD for Investigative Services Division or MBD, Management and Budget Division. After a couple of meetings with my boss the Deputy Director, I was surprisingly able to get his support to use the abbreviation WPD for Witness Prisoner Division, using 3 letters like the other divisions. I was now busy leading these two critical Marshals Service program areas. My previous background in leading protective operations programs with the Judicial Security Division, and my previous experience working in the Prisoner Services Division on detention matters, greatly benefited me with my new assignment.

I received extensive briefings from all Witness Security Program leaders and managers and reviewed their biographies to know their experience and backgrounds. I took some time to work on my assessment of the Witness Security Program reviewing files, inspections and audits. I also interviewed all managers, and various Inspectors in the program. Conducting assessments of programs, divisions or offices I was assigned to lead, is a critical part of my business plan for good leadership. After my assessment was done, I knew my work was cut out for me to lead a strategic revitalization effort to assist the Witness Security Program. The revitalization effort was needed to increase morale, develop an internal division advance annual training program, enhance structure and partnerships, obtain additional resources, and re-focus existing resources to move the program forward. This effort was important to continue to do the excellent work the employees were committed to doing to protect witnesses for the Department of Justice. I used my existing toolbox of leadership and protective operations experience to assist the Witness Security Program to address the needs of the employees and the program. I went to work to build a good plan to assist both the Prisoner Operations and Witness Security

Programs move forward with operations and personnel management. I was ready to continue to lead with a strategy, and a tactical plan. All I needed was a good division strategic plan.

As with my former division, the Judicial Security Division, I created an Oversight Team to assist me with leading this new dynamic large division with two Marshals Service operational programs. I selected a manager already on staff to lead the Oversight Team and gave the manager guidance on what I wanted from the Oversight Team. My guidance included developing a Strategic Planning Committee to establish a division strategic plan. The guidance further included bringing all division managers to an offsite location for a strategic planning session with a focused agenda. I worked closely with a Witness Security Program Chief Inspector creating another committee to work on the annual advance professional development training program and a curriculum. The Advance Training program required all program operational personnel to receive training at an offsite training facility. These were all successful steps I took while leading the Judicial Security Division.

I was very excited about the future of my new division with the two programs. I was also receiving requests from various countries and Embassies asking for training assistance to start Witness Security or Protection Programs. Two of the requests came from the Embassy in Bangkok, Thailand and the government of the Bahamas. I traveled to assist officials in Thailand and the Bahamas in May and July 2005 respectively. Both of these trips were successful. I put in long hours with numerous meetings and gave presentations and briefings on Witness Security and Protective Operations. I took a Chief Inspector with International experience with me on both of these trips. These two trips set the tone for dozens of international trips I participated in as the Assistant Director for Witness Security, assisting with the protection of justice and protection of witnesses. I will briefly discuss both of these trips before moving on to the next chapter. The first international trip I took working on behalf of global

Witness Security was to Bangkok, Thailand. That trip was a very long trip, as it took a day to fly to Bangkok. It was a day I saw daylight for nearly 24 hours as my subordinate Chief Inspector and I flew out of Dulles Airport in the Washington DC area going West by Northwest heading to Narita, Japan. The flight to Japan was nearly 15 hours. We had a 3 1/2 hour layover at the airport in Narita and then boarded our flight to Bangkok, Thailand. The flight to Bangkok was just under 8 hours. By the time we got to our hotel at the Hilton, it was nighttime and we both were very tired. The one good thing about the long day of flying is we were flying business class. We were allowed to fly business class since the first leg of the flight was more than 12 hours, and we did not stay overnight in Japan.

The service in business class on All Nippon Airways was outstanding. I love fish and, they were serving fish and sushi for just about all meals. After arriving at the Hilton hotel and getting a bite to eat, we called it a night and retired to our rooms. We wanted to get a few things done the next day, which was a Sunday before our business meetings the next day on Monday at the U.S. Embassy. This was a 10-day trip filled with various meetings including a two-day forum with judges, prosecutors and law enforcement personnel. There were a number of enlightening presentations and briefings during the two-day forum. My Chief Inspector and I gave remarks and answered questions both days. The meetings I attended were informative, and I enjoyed meeting the fine professionals and executives working in Thailand. I established a very good relationship with a tailor shop and had several suits made in Bangkok. One of the tailors came to the United States to sell tailor made suits. I hosted him a few times at my home inviting friends and colleagues over to be measured for tailored shirts and suits. This international trip on behalf of Witness Protection set the tone for my 9 years leading the Witness Security Division. My longest assignment working in the United States Marshals Service is the 9 years I served leading the Witness Security. Using a golf term, I labeled the last 9 years of my career as the back 9. I did not want to serve in any other capacity at the division level, with the exception of Investigations before moving on and retiring from the Marshals Service.

My second international travel assignment was to the Islands of the Bahamas. I selected the same Chief Inspector who accompanied me to Thailand to travel with me on this trip. I also took my wife and daughter Morgan to the Bahamas. I paid for their travel and expenses with personal funds as I always did when they accompanied me on my official travel assignments. This was a 5-day trip and I was scheduled for several meetings on several Bahamian Islands. This trip was no vacation. After arrival to Nassau or Paradise Island as it is called, my wife, daughter, and the Chief inspector were met by police officials from the Bahamas Police Department and transported to our hotel near the Atlantis Resort. After getting checked in to our hotel, my family and I went out for a walk and located a nice restaurant to grab dinner. We were impressed by the size of the amazing Atlantis Resort, which was within walking distance to our hotel. The island was beautiful and the weather perfect. None of us in our little traveling group had ever been to the Bahamas before. We arrived on a Saturday evening, and I had Sunday to relax and get ready for meetings Monday morning.

The same police officers that greeted us at the airport picked my Chief Inspector and I up from our hotel for our meetings. Our meetings on Monday lasted all day. That evening after arriving back at our hotel, we were told that we had a flight the next morning at 6:30 am to the large island of Grand Bahama. We were informed that we were scheduled for a series of meetings including a forum where I was the key speaker. We made our flight that morning. The session went well. There were questions not only about Witness Security, but also about Court Security. The Court Security questions were easy for me to answer. I had six years of experience working in the Judicial Security Division as a Program Chief and Assistant Director. I enjoyed meeting the Bahamian judges and was captivated by the court's British influence.

My days started early and ended late. We flew back to Nassau Monday night arriving about 9pm. I had another trip the next morning to travel to another island called Eleuthera. Eleuthera was another beautiful island. I met dozens of Bahamian police officers that were assigned to protect witnesses. I gave a presentation and held a question and answer session. I was impressed by the commitment of these officers to secure witnesses, and listened to the trials and tribulations they had in trying to get the job done. I heard several officers say that financial resources were a major impediment to doing their job. Some officers mentioned they spent money out of their own pockets at times to help their witnesses remain safe. I have learned in my understanding of protecting witnesses, that it takes support and commitment from political leaders to have a good successful witness security program. Along with the political support, it takes funding and compartmentalization, meaning everyone involved should not know or have access to all of the relevant program information. It also takes good vetting of those involved with the program for program security and integrity. In the years to come, I briefed this information over and over again to countries around the world trying to start or enhance witness security programs. During this trip, I traveled to several islands in the Bahamas and met and spoke with hundreds of Bahamian officials. There was one town I was especially happy to visit. The Bahamian officers assigned to work with me, made sure my Chief Inspector and I visited a town as a part of our visit. The town is Jonestown. I took a photo with our group in front of a sign at the entrance to town with the words Jonestown. With Jones being my last name, I enjoyed the fact the Bahamian officers made sure I got to see and visit Jonestown, Bahamas.

I worked many long hours and stayed an extra day with my family to spend some time while not working on the beautiful island of Nassau. My family and I wanted to check out some of the activities at the Atlantis. My good friend Joe Alexander, an editor of this book, told me about one of his best friends he played soccer with in their younger days. His friend was a successful businessman in the Bahamas. Joe contacted his friend and made a connection between us. His good friend and his business partners owned a small island near Nassau. My family and I took a ferryboat to the island from Nassau as part of a tourist package to hangout on the island, and enjoy festivities that included getting in the water with stingrays. The small island was very pretty, and the half-day trip to the island and back was very nice. The two Bahamian police officers assisting me on the trip were very helpful and made sure they were available if I needed them. I saw one of them again, at the last International Witness Protection Symposium that I will discuss later in another chapter.

This was a very progressive and informative business trip. The officers I worked with during this trip briefed me about crime in the Bahamas. We had discussions about very dangerous organized drug criminals who had potential witnesses willing to testify against the organizations killed. These officers impressed upon me the importance of having a good witness protection program. I did my best to assist the Bahamian officials with their witness protection program. I made some good friends with law enforcement officials and prosecutors from the Bahamian Attorney General's office. I got to see two of the prosecutors again when they visited the Washington DC on two occasions after my visit to the Bahamas. This was the start of many years of service helping to promote justice and witness security in the United States, and countries around the world through training, consultations, and symposiums. The last nine years of my career, or the back 9 as I noted earlier, sent me to many corners of the world.

CHAPTER FIFTEEN

Leading Witness Security, Hiding Them-Not Finding Them

As I continued to work with the Witness Security Program and the Prisoner Operations Program, I knew I had to keep working on developing a good strategic plan that captured all of the Department of Justice critical requirements in protecting witnesses. This was not a problem. The program operators were getting the job done. However, they needed a good strategic plan adding resources, enhancing capabilities and good senior executive leadership. These requirements were vital to the continued successful operation of the Witness Security Program. I was happy to provide the senior executive leadership, and other strategy and planning requirements to get the job done more effectively and efficiently.

I spent plenty of time during 2005 learning as much as I could about the Witness Security Program along with working on a number of detention management issues. I wanted to fully understand the Witness Security Program to assist me with developing a strategic plan that added significant value to the program. Developing an advance professional training and development program for the operational employees under my leadership was critical to enhancing the program and moving it forward. I put a committee together to work on a curriculum of training to get our first year of training moving. I gave the committee guidance on critical criteria I thought was needed for the training program. As a military person, I had experience with a training concept called crawl, walk and run. The professional development program started with a one-week crawl session for all operational personnel. As a part of the training, I had an evening dinner program with a speaker toward the end of the week. I divided my operational personnel into 4 groups, to attend 4 training sessions. This was the first phase of the professional advanced training that was labeled the crawl phase. The 4 training sessions for year one was well received by all operational personnel. The training allowed the operational personnel to address critical issues and requirements for the program, while also affording them needed time to network.

As 2006 approached, I was still focused on enhancing the Witness Security Program, focusing on increasing program accountability, program expansion, and obtaining resources. I was also working on a couple of major detention projects. One of the projects led me to Las Vegas, Nevada. The Marshals Service district office in Nevada needed additional detention pretrial bed space and requested a meeting with my staff and I, along with the Federal Detention Trustee and her staff. The Marshals Service district office was losing some its pre-trial detention jail space from the city of Las Vegas. The city of Las Vegas had an initiative to clean up its downtown area arresting drunks and others for crimes committed downtown. The city needed its local jail space for arrested local downtown offenders. Members of my staff and I traveled to Las Vegas for a series of meetings with our federal partners, the Chief Judge, U.S. Attorney, U.S. Marshal and Chief Deputy Marshal. The Federal Detention Trustee and her staff also traveled to Las Vegas for the meetings.

The day after our arrival, we met with the Mayor of Las Vegas, Mayor Oscar Goodman and his key staff to negotiate with the city seeking their support to allow the Marshals Service district office to continue to use the allocated local detention beds. I enjoyed meeting with Mayor Goodman who called himself the "Happiest Mayor Alive." We were not able to get the Mayor to give in on the detention bed issues, but the meeting did go well. We ended up discussing other alternatives for additional pre-trial bed space for the district office. Those of us traveling to Las Vegas along with the local U.S. Marshal and Chief Deputy U.S. Marshal attended another meeting the next day with officials from Clarke County Nevada. This meeting was to discuss a proposal to build a pre-trial detention center outside of Las Vegas. This proposed detention facility if approved, benefitted not only the District of Nevada with pre-trial detention needs, but also provided pre-trial detention beds to the district of Arizona. The District of Arizona was also in need of additional pre-trial detention space. The trip to Las Vegas was a productive trip. The meetings ended with some good detention possibilities to assist the Districts of Nevada and Arizona. After returning to my office, I received a nice note from Mayor Goodman thanking me for attending the meeting and for the small Marshals Service memento I gave him.

Leading the Witness Security Program was starting to take more of my time. I felt I had a good handle on the Prisoner Operation's Program and national detention matters. The Witness Security Program needed more of my time as the program had some serious challenges with resource shortages in some of the functional areas, and needed some other professional enhancements. I was committed to turning those issues around and upgrading the Witness Security Inspectors who at one time were thought of as the crème of the crop in the Marshals Service. However, as years passed, the program lost star status, and did not have strong support and advocacy to move forward. My job as the boss of Witness Security was to re-establish the Witness Security Program's luster and star status and be a very strong advocate for the program.

For the rest of 2006, my focus was to enhance the program in many areas developing strategies and tactics to move all areas of the program forward. In March 2006, the 9th Director of the Marshals Service was appointed. The U.S. Marshal from the Eastern District of Virginia, a career Deputy Marshal was nominated and confirmed as Director of the agency and appointed by President George W. Bush. I met with the new Director and briefed him on the status of both of my programs with an emphasis on many needs of the Witness Security Program. The new Director pledged his support of my efforts to bring change and enhancements to the Witness Security Program. I continued with the Witness Security Program's professional development program working with my staff on the second year of our operational Advance Training program. The second year of the professional development program was the walk phase, and was focused on operations. Things were starting to look up for the program and our strategic planning and tactics were gaining traction and paying off. The strategic plan for my division covered both programs charting our direction and efforts to secure witnesses, and federal pre-trial detainees, while also locating much needed pre-trial jail detention space.

My Oversight Chief coordinated a very good strategic planning session at Shepardstown, West Virginia. All division managers were required to attend and work on our strategies and efforts to continue to improve both the Witness Security and Prisoner Operations programs in support of the U.S. Department of Justice Strategic Plan. My key staff and I put in plenty of time working on the agenda and identifying speakers and presenters for the strategic planning session. I met a tremendous lady during the first year of the operational training program for my Witness Inspectors. This lady was an excellent facilitator, and I was able to collaborate with her and her boss for her assistance with our strategic planning session. This fantastic professional was the final piece needed for the strategic planning session.

I wanted this session to be perfect. I wanted the strategic plan to chart the way forward for the division and it's two programs for several years. I cannot overemphasize the importance of a very good strategic plan to any organization as the organization seeks to improve, obtain resources and adequately use those resources to get the job done. Our strategic planning session had speakers and presenters from the Marshals Service Office of Congressional Affairs, Management and Budget Division, Office of General Counsel, a Presidential Appointed United States Marshal from a Southwest Border district, and the Department of Justice Office of Enforcement Operations. I also gave a presentation outlining my vision for both programs.

During the strategic planning session, one of my regional Chief Inspectors asked why we were starting to do more in support of international requests for training assistance and that this assistance was taking resources away from the domestic program and using those resources in other countries. The Witness Security Program was starting to provide more support to other United States agencies and programs such as the Department of State, and the Department of justice Overseas Prosecutorial and Development and Training Division. I let the Chief Inspector know I appreciated the concern, and support for the missions we were participating in, which at the time included assistance to Serbia, Colombia, Thailand, the Bahamas and a couple of other countries. I informed the Chief inspector and others at the session that the support and assistance we provided for International Operations was minimal and requested by other United States organizations. I further added that the support was for a worthy cause to assist countries trying to enhance their justice system, and that some of the countries had become allies or partners with the United States in pursuit of justice.

Additionally, I emphasized that our employees who were on these training teams, gained invaluable added experience with the training and tactics they provided to the officers in the countries assisted, but also added skills to our program. The strategic planning session went very well. We charted our direction and growth for both programs for the next few years. During this time I continued to consult with Mr. Gerald Shur, who was of tremendous assistance to me with both the domestic Witness Security Program, and Witness Security matters in various countries around the world.

During the first year of working as the Assistant Director of Witness Security, I worked with a Chief Inspector who had an idea about hosting an International Symposium on Witness Security. I liked the idea, and put in some time working on the proposal with the Chief Inspector, and a couple of other division personnel. We developed a plan to have the initial Symposium in Washington DC at a local hotel. We put together a Symposium theme, and developed presentations to support the theme. We identified a few good speakers including former Judge and Federal Bureau of Investigations Director Louis Freeh, and Gerald Shur the Founder of the Witness Security Program. The Director of the Marshals Service approved our Symposium plan proposal. The Witness Security Program partnered with the Department of Justice Overseas Prosecutorial Training and Development Division, and we had an exceptional Witness Security Symposium in September 2006, attended by about 26 countries. This was the first of five outstanding annual Symposiums on Witness Security. I will discuss International Symposiums on Witness Security in more detail in the next chapter. The budget for the First Symposium was very manageable. My staff and I did not have to travel, and we worked with the Marshals Service conference and hotel coordinator taking advantage her contacts and negotiation skills. We were able to obtain below market hotel rates for our guests who had to travel to Washington DC.

During 2006, my staff and I continued to work on a number of operational issues in both the Witness Security Program and the Prisoner Operations Program. I worked many hours on upgrading my Witness Security Inspectors from their journeyman grade level to the grade level of other operational Inspectors. I met often with my staff, staff from the Director's office, Human Resources Division, and the agency financial managers on tactics and strategies to get the upgrade accomplished. These meetings involved a number of discussions mostly on the financial impact of the upgrade. My staff and I had to revise and enhance the position description of duties for the Witness Security Inspectors. Meeting after meeting on this issue showed support and progress to complete the upgrade. However, other meetings left me in a quagmire wondering if my promise to accomplish the upgrade might fail. However, I always remember one of my Grandfather's quotes that he must have picked up from the late legendary football coach Vince Lombardi. My Grandfather always said to me "Winners Never Quit, and Quitters never win." I use this quote often and seriously believe in the saying. I continued my efforts to lead and work on this very important upgrade for the Witness Security Inspectors.

As 2007 arrived, the Marshals Service Director approached me one day in early 2007. He told me he had met the Secretary General of INTERPOL Mr. Ronald Noble. My Director further told me that Secretary General Noble heard about the success of the first International Symposium on Witness Security, held in September 2006, and was very interested in partnering with the Marshals Services to host another International Symposium on Witness Security at INTERPOL in Lyon, France. INTERPOL stands for the International Criminal Police Organization and was established in 1923. I was very interested in collaborating and working with INTERPOL to have the Second International Witness Security Symposium. I made plans to travel to INTERPOL to meet with key officials to work on having the Second International Witness Security Symposium at INTERPOL. I traveled to France with a Chief Inspector who I knew well from our time working together in the United States Virgin Islands. This Chief Inspector had been working in the Witness Security Program for a few years. He had been promoted as a Supervisory Deputy Marshal in a district office in one of the Carolina districts. He was promoted again to the position of Chief Inspector in the Witness Security Program. The Chief Inspector and I traveled to Lyon, France on a Monday night arriving in Europe on Tuesday. We grabbed dinner and rested for the night before starting our various meetings at INTERPOL on Wednesday and Thursday. We had to travel back to the Washington DC area on Friday morning. We had to get a lot accomplished in a couple of days.

We had a number of meetings with individuals working at INTERPOL including Protocol, Logistical, and Security officials. The INTERPOL facility is a large and magnificent facility. Everyone treated my Chief Inspector and I politely. We attended the INTERPOL session meeting with all 188 Member Countries. Secretary General Noble convened the general session meeting. The INTERPOL meeting was very informative as there were a number of power point presentations by speakers who discussed important INTERPOL issues and matters. I was allowed 15 minutes on the schedule to discuss the Witness Security Symposium I was proposing to be held later in the year at INTERPOL. I was appreciative of the opportunity to address this outstanding body of International law enforcement professionals informing the group about the first Symposium and our expectations for the Second Symposium. I found the 188 Member Countries and the INTERPOL leadership to be very supportive of the Second International Symposium on Witness Security at INTERPOL. I met with Secretary General Noble spending a little time with him discussing the Witness Security Symposium purpose and objectives.

The other meetings at INTERPOL that my Chief Inspector and I attended went well. We were both excited with what was offered by INTERPOL in a partnership to hold our Second Symposium in France. Lyon is a beautiful and historic city south of Paris. My colleague and I stayed at a very nice hotel the 3 nights we were in Lyon. We enjoyed some of the local French cuisine and took early morning walks at the National Park and Zoo that was across the street from out hotel. We met and worked with the hotel management to negotiate the cost of rooms to house all of the attendees for the Second Symposium. Things were shaping up exceptionally well for this event. I had good expectations this was going to be an outstanding Symposium allowing many countries with Witness Protection Programs at various stages of development to come together to learn and network. The Chief Inspector and I returned home with an agenda and a purpose to bring this International event together at INTERPOL in the fall of 2007.

CHAPTER SIXTEEN

Creating Global Witness Security Alliances with International Symposiums

In 2007, I had my hands full leading two major operational programs under one flag or division. I was working diligently in support of both the Prisoner Operations and Witness Security Program. I linked both programs together for strategic and tactical planning, and linked the operational personnel on the Prisoner side with the Advance Training program developed for the Witness Security Inspectors. We kept some of the training compartmentalized due to separate missions. However, general training activities such as shooting on the firearms range, driving on the tactical driving range, and other activities were combined.

My Oversight Team, International Team, and I were working on the logistics and program for the Second International Symposium on Witness Security. As I noted in the previous chapter, the Second International Symposium was scheduled for the fall of 2007 at INTERPOL in France. My staff and I were in close contact with the Protocol Specialist at INTERPOL. The Protocol Specialist was a pleasure to work with. He was a critical and very important partner during the planning of the Symposium. At this point the Symposium did not have a budget, and my staff and I had to work very hard to develop and secure a budget obtaining the necessary funding. We were able to obtain partial funding from our Symposium partners at INTERPOL. The U.S. Department of Justice Overseas Prosecutorial Development and Training Division (OPDAT) was already working with and sponsoring a number of countries that were planning to attend the event. With funding assistance from OPDAT and INTERPOL, along with utilizing funding from my division work-plan, we were almost at the budget bench mark needed to successfully pull off this huge event. We were about $25,000 short of our budget target. I decided to request the $25,000 from the agency Director. As I mentioned, our Director approached me letting me know INTERPOL was interested in partnering with us for this event. The Director supported my request and had our Budget Division forward the $25,000 to my division. The Second Symposium planning was going well.

I established biweekly meetings with my key staff working on the Symposium, and tasked the responsible Chief Inspector to create a bi-weekly bulletin on the Symposium's progress. The bi-weekly bulletin was a very helpful management tool to list and track various tasks. We shared the bi-weekly bulletin with the Director's Office to keep the Director and his staff informed on the status of the Symposium. I anticipated the Director's interest in attending this major event. The Second international Symposium planning was moving along, and everyone involved with the project was excited by this endeavor. I selected what staff from my division was going to travel and participate in the Symposium. I also decided we needed a security team from my division to attend the Symposium as well to partner with INTERPOL law enforcement officials to provide security for this event. We had a number of things moving with this event. I wanted the event to be a perfect forum for networking and discussing witness security and other critical law enforcement issues and trends affecting the various countries that attended. I challenged my staff to develop recommendations for the Second Symposium Theme. I always liked having a theme, and knew that the theme set the tone for the agenda.

I was also receiving recommendations from OPDAT and INTERPOL for some agenda topics to consider. I approved the theme of "Witness Security/ Protection: A Critical Law Enforcement Tool in a Global Age."

The Symposium was scheduled for September 2007 at INTERPOL. By the summer of 2007, we had just about everything in place including the theme, agenda, program, list of attendees, and keynote speakers. I decided to ask the Founding Father of the American Witness Security Program Mr. Gerald Shur if he could attend the Symposium as a guest and speaker and give the opening address to the attendees. I knew that having Mr. Shur give the opening address, would be a big hit with all in attendance. Mr. Shur related he could not attend the event in Europe. I asked him if he would consider allowing me to film a presentation by him so that I could take the video clip of his presentation and make it part of our Symposium program. Mr. Shur agreed and he and I set a date to have his presentation filmed at his home. I had my staff procure a film company and went to Mr. Shur's home, and filmed his presentation. The presentation by Mr. Shur was a very good 45-minute opening address. Our plan was to kick-off the Symposium with the Gerry Shur video.

My staff and I invited speakers from OPDAT, The United States Attorney from the Northern District of Illinois, and the Associate Director of the Criminal Division Office of Enforcement Operations, U.S. Department of Justice. For our Symposium Dinner Program, I invited Mr. Howard Safir to be the speaker. Mr. Safir was at the time CEO of his business and the Former Commissioner, New York City Police Department. Mr. Safir was involved with the Witness Security Program when he was a Senior Executive working with the United States Marshals Service. My staff and I secured speakers and presenters from Serbia, Latvia, the Netherlands, and the Slovak Republic. As September arrived things were in place for the Symposium. We shipped all our supplies and equipment to INTERPOL. We coordinated with INTERPOL to make sure we had Interpreters, as most of the Symposium presentations would be in English. We needed Interpreters and technical equipment. INTERPOL had plenty of experience hosting meetings with language barriers, and had the Interpreters and technical support we needed. This was another logistical matter we could cross off our list after we identified the funding to pay the Interpreters.

On Sunday September 2, 2007, my division Advance Team and Security Team arrived at INTERPOL as scheduled. The main party, which I was in, traveled for the most part together, flying out of Washington DC Dulles airport to Europe. We had a connecting flight to Lyon, France. After arriving in Lyon Monday September 3, we were greeted by members of the Advance Party and Security Team, and transported to our hotel. We coordinated a van transportation service to pick up Symposium attendees to transport them to the hotel. The hotel was in walking distance to INTERPOL. We had a very nice opening reception on Tuesday evening. The Symposium started on Wednesday September 5, and ended Friday September 7, 2007. The Director of the Marshals Service arrived Tuesday, September 4, with his family and security team in time to make the opening reception.

After the Symposium registration, opening remarks by me, INTERPOL Secretary General Ronald K, Noble, Marshals Service Director John Clark, the Deputy Director of OPDAT, and the Associate Director, Office of Enforcement Operations, the group photo and a break, we watched the Gerald Shur video. As I anticipated, the video was a huge success setting the tone for the Symposium. We were off to a great start for a great event. The next 3 days were incredible as the Symposium was outstanding. We had thirty-nine countries and 4 International Organizations participating. Some of the countries in attendance were Albania, Austria, Colombia, Canada, El Salvador, Denmark, Croatia, Israel, Kosovo, Latvia, Chile, Thailand, Sweden, Kenya, Indonesia, and United Kingdom. The organizations in attendance included, United Nations Office on Drugs and Crime, International Criminal Court, United Nations International Criminal Tribunal, and the Organization of American States.

Most attendees including my staff traveled home Saturday morning, and my team arrived home Saturday afternoon as the time difference was 6 hours between Europe and the east coast of the United States. This event was talked about and praised for months. I knew that the concept of the Marshals Service coordinating and having an International Symposium on Witness Security should continue. The Second International Symposium presented an opportunity for me to meet new friends such as an official from the Attorney General's office in Kenya who let me know Kenya had started a Witness Protection Program, the District Attorney's office in Panama, and Chiefs and Deputy Chiefs of Witness Protection Units from Estonia, the Netherlands, Poland, Latvia, France, Finland and other countries.

I enjoyed seeing other friends I had and worked with such as my good friends from Serbia, Israel and Colombia. After returning home, I held an After Action Review with my team on the Symposium to determine what if anything we could do to make the event better. The only thing that we could come up with to do better was to have more speakers and presenters from other countries, and less speakers from the United States, which I concurred with. I decided to pursue having a Third Symposium on Witness Security the next year.

As 2007 came to a close, I participated in Marshals Service Strategic Planning meetings to consider a reorganization of the agency. As 2008, approached, it appeared imminent to me that the Marshals Service reorganization was going forward, and some division's structure and titles were going to change. The Prisoner Operations Program was going to become its own division again, and so was the Witness Security Program. The reorganization created 6 operational divisions and 6 administrative divisions including the creation of an Associate Director for Operations and an Associate Director for Administration. These two new positions were responsible for leading the operational and administrative divisions. I actually thought I might be considered for one of these two newly created positions as I had led three Marshals Service major operational programs and divisions: Judicial Security, Witness Security and Prisoner Operations. I was also the second most senior executive. What I soon found out was I was not going to be considered for either of the two new positions. The Director knew what two people he was going to select to fill the positions, which is a Director's prerogative. I was fine with remaining the head of the Witness Security Division, as I had more work to do to move the division and program forward. The reorganization was implemented in April 2008. I was designated to continue to lead the Witness Security Division. I said goodbye to the great employees and friends in Prisoner Operations. I knew I would still see them around our offices at Marshals Service Headquarters. This reorganization did not have much of an effect on the 94 Marshals Service District offices.

I went to work with my staff to plan the Third International Symposium on Witness Security. I was interested in going back to INTERPOL in Lyon, France. I traveled back to Lyon, France with a new Chief Inspector assisting me with division International activities to meet with Secretary General Ronald Noble and his staff to propose having another Symposium at INTERPOL. Secretary General Noble after consulting with his staff agreed to host the Third International Symposium back at INTERPOL. The planning phase was on again to have the next Symposium and expand on the success of the Second International Symposium on Witness Security/ Protection. The planning and format to have this Symposium was much easier this time around as we had the blue print for success. I was also still focused on domestic Witness Security operations including working on infrastructure enhancements and assisting with the professional development of all division employees. Training and mentoring have always been important to me, and I continued with various training programs for division employees. The Advance Training program was ongoing, and my staff and I worked on the next year's training plan for the operational staff. The Advance Training was always very good and well received by the Inspectors.

My team and I continued to work on the Third International Symposium on Witness Security, and I approved the Symposium theme "Witness Security/Protection, a Key Partner in the Judicial Process." I felt this was an excellent theme as it was in my view, true that protecting witnesses is key to upholding the judicial process. Without witnesses being able to testify in our court system, criminals and criminal organizations would be out of control, and the judicial process could not administer justice. With this theme in place, my staff and I started building the agenda to support the theme. We again obtained the support and partnership from OPDAT, enabling the three organizations that held the Second International Symposium on Witness Protection to again work together to have another great event. I made a request to the Director, and Deputy Director of the Marshals Service, and counterparts working in the Marshals Service Financial Services Division, that my division needed a budget specifically for Symposiums. They all agreed, and my division received a budget for the International Symposiums. This helped tremendously with our Symposium financial planning. I was a good steward overseeing financial work plans entrusted to me, and had a good record as an executive and senior executive with managing resources. I was pleased that my division started receiving agency annual funding for the Symposiums.

We scheduled the Third International Symposium on Witness Security and Protection for October 30, 2008. For this Symposium we had more international speakers and presenters, and had more involvement from the international community on the agenda. The exact same format for the Second International Symposium was used for the Third Symposium. We used the same hotel, which as I previously mentioned, is nearby INTERPOL. We again selected a security team, and an advance team to travel ahead of the main party. We had a social event on the evening of

October 29th, with the Symposium occurring on October 30th and October 31st. The event closed on Friday October 31st. The same speakers gave opening remarks as we had for the Second Symposium with the exception of OPDAT. For this Symposium, the Director of OPDAT gave opening remarks instead of the OPDAT Deputy Director. We had speakers and presenters from INTERPOL, Serbia, Canada, Australia, Spain, United Nations Office on Drugs and Crime, and the International Criminal Court along with the Federal Bureau of Investigation.

I obtained another video from Mr. Gerald Shur. For the second year in a row, I went to Mr. Shur's home to film his presentation. I also used the same film company as before. I again anticipated Mr. Shur's presentation would be a huge success to start our Symposium. I was right. His video presentation was a resounding huge success. Many people in the delegation wanted copies of Mr. Shur's presentation. However, I did not let anyone have it. Requests for Mr. Shur's presentation occurred at the Second Symposium as well. I did not provide copies of Mr. Shur's presentation at that Symposium either. The Director of the Marshals Service attended the Symposium again accompanied by his security team.

The Honorable Ann Claire Williams, United States Circuit Judge, from the U.S. States Court of Appeals 7th Circuit was Symposium Dinner keynote Speaker. Judge Williams who I have known for many years, gave a wonderful presentation on "Collaboration and Rule of law: Lessons from Africa". The presentation was thought provoking, and well received. Judge Williams has done some great work in Africa, which I was aware of. I anticipated her presentation was going to be a good fit for the Symposium. The Third International Symposium on Witness Security/Protection was just as outstanding as the Second. INTERPOL is a wonderful venue, and I appreciate the support, friendship and partnership extended by INTERPOL Secretary General Ronald K. Noble, and his outstanding team. Delegates attending the Symposium came from the same countries as the Second International Symposium. The Third International

Symposium was larger as the word must have got out as to how great the second Symposium was. Many additional countries attended the Third Symposium. The Delegation included representatives from the Czech Republic, Belgium, Kyrgyz Republic, Republic of Costa Rica, Republic of Macedonia, Republic of Lithuania, Republic of Moldova, Romania, Turkey and Brazil. Officials from Brazil mentioned to me during the Third Symposium, that they were interested in hosting a Symposium. I let these officials, and the delegation know, that I would take the request into consideration, when we started planning the Fourth International Symposium on Witness Security.

It was very good to see friends from Israel, Serbia, the United Kingdom and others. I met many new friends and colleagues from Brazil, Bulgaria, Macedonia, Moldova and other countries. This was another meaningful International event that was a huge success, and well received by all in attendance. Our Serbian colleagues hosted an evening reception after the Symposium Dinner at the hotel. This reception was referred to as the "Serbian Café." The "Serbian Café" turned into a popular forum after hours at future hotels where we lodged for Symposiums. The Serbian Delegation brought their favorite beverage from Serbia for Symposium attendees to enjoy after hours. At this Symposium, a second International bilateral agreement was signed adding two additional countries to the agreement. The first bilateral agreement between several countries desiring to work together was signed at the First International Symposium on Witness Security/Protection in Washington, DC in the fall of 2006. The countries attending the First International Symposium on Witness Security were expanding their witness protection efforts.

The Third International Symposium on Witness Security and Protection ended, and everyone returned home safely. My staff and I held another After Action Review on the Third Symposium. We did not come up anything we could have done better with this event. Our Symposiums were very popular in the Witness Security family worldwide.

In December 2008, I was very happy to see that my very close friend and colleague, Herman Brewer got promoted to the Chief of Internal Affairs and Inspections. At the time of his promotion, he was serving as the Assistant Chief Deputy Marshal in Puerto Rico. As I previously mentioned, Herman was my old fugitive apprehension partner back when I was a Deputy Marshal in Chicago. It was good to have Herman, his wife and younger kids close by again. We always kept in touch, and supported each other over the years. Herman had been trying for quite some time to obtain his promotion to GS-15, and after several years and many attempts he finally had a breakthrough and was promoted. As I will discuss in the last chapter of this book, it can be very challenging and difficult for minorities to get promoted to the top tiers of the Marshal Service. I count my many blessings that I was able to breakthrough a difficult system, fighting my way to the Senior Executive tier. I had my challenges as well. But thanks to God's grace, I was able to compete, work hard, and have excellent mentors to guide me. Now I had two of my longtime best friends and colleagues, Herman Brewer and William Walker living and working in the Washington DC area. I was blessed to have these guys close by to spend quality time with, and continue our great friendship in the same area.

Things were going very well with my division and our domestic operations as we entered 2009. The implementation of the division strategic plan was going very well along with our advanced training program for my Inspectors. My staff and I started planning for the Fourth International Symposium on Witness Security/Protection. The planning for this Symposium went well as we implemented the same protocols as we did with the past two Symposiums. I received another proposal to hold the Fourth International Symposium on Witness Security/Protection from officials in Brazil. I had to carefully consider this request, as I anticipated having the next Symposium in Brazil might limit the participation of our European colleagues. Having the Symposiums in Europe at INTERPOL was cost efficient for our European Delegates. It cost more to travel from Europe to Brazil, and I anticipated the European Delegation attendance would drop off. My staff and I had to do more logistically for the Fourth International Symposium on Witness Security, as we did not have OPDAT as a sponsor or INTERPOL to host the event. The Director of OPDAT related for budgetary reasons, OPDAT could not assist financially, but would participate. I was thinking that we needed another Symposium location somewhere other than Europe. I was considering Brazil, Costa Rica, and Panama.

Our Colombian colleagues had also mentioned hosting a Symposium on Witness Security during one of my visits to Bogota in 2008. My staff and I did some research into possible Symposium locations, and Brazil was starting to win out for the bid to host our next Symposium. The Resident Legal Advisor working in Brazil for OPDAT was very supportive of having the event in Brazil. The Resident Legal Advisor kept expressing that the Brazilian law enforcement officials and prosecutors were eager for us to hold the Symposium in Brazil. I had a new Program Chief promoted from within my division and assigned to lead our International Operations efforts. He was also pushing for Brazil. I thought about the various choices and decided Brazil was where we were going to hold the Fourth International Symposium on Witness Security. Now it was just a matter of picking a location in Brazil.

My Chief of International Operations, my Oversight Team Chief, and other key division staff members were asking me to consider Rio de Janeiro. I had never been to Rio, but did not think it was a good location in Brazil to have our Symposium. I thought there were too many distractions in Rio de Janeiro, and began to look for other options in Brazil. The Resident Legal Advisor contacted my Chief of International Operations and recommended Salvador, Brazil as a good location to have the next Symposium. As I studied Salvador, Brazil, I learned that it was a major slave port off the western coast of Africa, and that Salvador, is a historic geographic area on the eastern coast of Brazil. I also learned that Salvador, Brazil has a large population of African descendants and the population still spoke with African dialects. The OPDAT Resident Legal Advisor worked in Rio de Janeiro, and had participated in a conference in Salvador, Brazil at a very nice resort. She made it clear to me she would work very closely with us if we selected Brazil. With the Resident Legal Advisor's commitment of her support, and the support of other Brazilian law enforcement officials and prosecutors, I was convinced we were going to have another world class Symposium. I briefed my Director on my decision to take the next Symposium to Brazil, giving him my justification and selection criteria. The Director gave me the go ahead to proceed with having the Fourth International Symposium on Witness Security in Salvador, Brazil.

My staff and I employed the same tactics and planning as we used for the other two overseas Symposiums. I again asked my division managers and key support staff for recommendations for a Symposium Theme. I enjoyed the ideas put forward by my staff for the Symposium themes. My Chief of International Operations was working very hard as this was the first Symposium where he was the actionable executive reporting to me. He heard from many people about how great the last two Symposiums were that were held at INTERPOL. He knew this Symposium had to be as good or better as the last two, or at least very close. He was recently promoted and I let him know this Symposium was very important, and we had to work harder to pull off a great event, as we did not have the usual assistance of our past partners. What we did have was a very successful blueprint to work with as we had a great deal of success with the prior events especially the two Symposiums held at INTERPOL. My new Chief of International Operations was on point and focused as we worked closely together to make the Fourth International Symposium another huge success. Our Symposium Theme was Witness Security/Protection: A Bridge From Investigations to Prosecutions, Combatting Organized

Crime and Gang Violence. I loved this theme. I thought it was perfectly suited to focus on global Organized Crime and the rise of Gang Violence worldwide. The Fourth International Symposium on Witness Security/Protection was to be held at Praia do Forte, Brazil near Salvador, Brazil from September 16 to 18, 2009. We would have to fly into Salvador, Brazil and take a 45-minute ride to Praia do Forte.

As we moved forward with this event, I received bi-weekly status reports of progress and the number of attendees registering to attend. I was a little concerned that our attendance for the Symposium might drop off. As I anticipated, the European commitments to attend this Symposium dropped off. My International Chief of Operations was trying his best to encourage me that the attendance was going to pick up. He kept telling me that the Brazilians were expected to have a very large delegation in attendance for the event. I was not convinced at the time that attendance for this Symposium was going to be at the same level as the previous Symposiums because the number of registered attendees was low. I was starting to second-guess my selection of going to Brazil. After a couple more weeks, the Symposium attendance started to pick up. The reassurance about attendance by my International Chief and his assistant was not well received by me initially, but after the Brazil delegation started registering for the event, the attendance was picking up. As with any event, you coordinate with the hotel and vendors and project a number to attend. As I mentioned earlier, I anticipated a significant decline in attendance by our European colleagues due to the location. For these colleagues to get to Lyon, France, was pretty easy. Some of these attendees drove to Lyon, France, while others took the train or took short airplane rides. As I was keenly aware, getting to Brazil was not that easy or cost effective for many of the European Symposium Delegates. The European colleagues who attended the Symposium in Salvador, Brazil included the United Kingdom, Spain, Kosovo, Italy, Germany, and Finland.

For the Fourth International Symposium in Brazil, we welcomed attendees from Cameroon, Kenya, Zambia, Portugal, Saint Kitts and Nevis, Mexico, Chile, and Ecuador. This Symposium was attended by over one 100 Delegates from 21 countries. The Brazilians sent a delegation of 54. For the American Delegation, we flew from Washington, DC to Miami, Florida and from Miami to Brasilia, Brazil. We stopped in Brasilia staying on the same plane and continued to Salvador, Brazil. The Captain of our flight was a great guy who upgraded me, and one of my Inspectors to first class. The Captain is an author of Children's books and offered my Inspector and I copies of his children's books. He told us he was going to mail the books when he returned home. The Captain did send us copies of his children's books, which were very nice. My daughter liked her books.

Getting back to the Fourth International Symposium on Witness Security, we put together a very nice agenda with several excellent speakers and presenters. The Symposium had presentations from a Judge from Australia representing the New South Wales Mental Health Review Tribunal, the Head of the Witness Protection Unit in Colombia, along with the Department of Justice Program Manager stationed in Colombia, an official representing the United Nations Office on Drugs and Crime, officials from Brazil, and the United States including the U.S. Department of Justice Bureau of Prisons Forensic Psychologist, the Office of Enforcement Operations and I. This Symposium was outstanding. My Chief of International Operations and the OPDAT Resident Legal Advisor did an outstanding job with the coordination of this event. My division team including Bernadine Jordan-Howard and others were superb with logistics, and this Symposium was just as exceptional as the two preceding Symposiums held at INTERPOL.

I was excited to spend some good time with my good friends and colleagues from Israel and Serbia. The "Serbian Café" opened again in Brazil, and as a very close friend and advisor often says to me "a good time was held by all." I met the Head of the Kenyan Witness Protection

Program becoming friends with her. The Head of the Kenyan Program is a hard worker with a good vision for her program. However, she needed assistance to move the program forward. Little did I know, I would see her soon as I was invited by the United Nations Office on Drugs and Crime to be the Keynote Speaker for the First Eastern African Witness Protection Conference a couple of months after the Symposium in Brazil. Everyone made it home safely from Brazil and my Symposium staff and I had our usual After Action Review, which went well. The Fourth International Symposium on Witness Security/Protection was perfect.

I was content with where the Marshals Service was at with working with our International partners collaborating on witness security matters. I was also very gratified with the state of our witness security domestic operations program including our strategic planning, program enhancements and deployment of resources. I was almost finished with accomplishing all of my plans and goals in my journey as the Assistant Director for Witness Security. However, I wanted to complete a few more things focusing on both Domestic Operations and International Operations. I wanted to help Kenya, and continue working with Witness Protection Programs in Israel, and Colombia. I received requests to help Guatemala and Trinidad develop their Witness Protection Programs.

The end of the year 2009 was outstanding for me professionally. However, in my personal life in my marriage, things were not going well. I was invited back to Chicago in October 2009, to be inducted in my High School Hall of Fame for Professional Life Achievement as an alumni quarterback. I traveled back to Chicago for the recognition ceremony, which was held at halftime at a homecoming football game at Gately Stadium on the far south side of town. It was good to be back at Gately Stadium, a stadium I played in a few times. The ceremony at halftime was nice. I and three other alumni of Carver High School (now called Carver Military Academy) received our plaques and letters inducting us into the school Hall of Fame.

As I mentioned earlier, I received an invitation to be the keynote Speaker in Nairobi, Kenya for the United Nations Office on Drugs and Crime, First Regional Conference on Witness Protection For East Africa. I was very happy to receive the invitation and obtained approval from my boss to attend as the Keynote Speaker. I had always wanted to go to Africa, and now I was going to Kenya in an official capacity to speak at a significant event on a continent known to many African Americans as the homeland. The Conference was held on November 12th and 13th, 2009 in Nairobi, Kenya at the Safari Park Hotel and Casino, a very large and nice complex in Nairobi, Kenya. I decided to take my Chief of International Operations with me and another Chief Inspector I worked with when I arrived in Witness Security in March 2005. This Chief Inspector had very good working relationship with staff working for the United Nations Office On Drugs and Crime (UNODC). In my opinion, this trip was the trip of a lifetime for my team and I.

I make it no secret that of all my travels on behalf of the Marshals Service, this was my best trip and one for the memory. Why? Because of the importance of helping Kenya a country that attended a couple of our International Symposiums to enhance their Witness Protection Program. Additionally, the Kenyan Witness Protection Program Director is a very intelligent and kind lady. I was aware from my contact with U.S. Circuit Judge Ann Williams, that Kenya like many countries in Africa made progress with protecting the rights of women from rape and other travesties. I started to embrace a quote from my Chief of International Operations, "we were changing the world one country at a time."

I had a huge dilemma with the trip to Africa. I found out from a good friend that her father had passed. He was originally from Mississippi, but was a long time Chicago area resident. His funeral was during the time of my scheduled trip to Nairobi, Kenya. My heart was very heavy, as I had become very close to him. I stopped by his home to see him almost every time I was home in Chicago. We sometimes watched Chicago Cubs baseball games on television together and he often told me how proud he was that I was a good father to my kids and a hard worker. He knew while I was back in Chicago, I visited with my Grandfather before visiting with him, and he appreciated that. I was extremely torn between going back to Chicago for his funeral and taking the trip of a lifetime to work with and assist Kenya. I prayed about the situation, and it came to me that he would have wanted me to go to Kenya. I had a gut feeling his preference for me was to keep my commitment to participate in the very important First Witness Protection Conference in Kenya. I made plans to travel to Kenya taking along with me the Chiefs I mentioned. My team and I flew to Europe and then boarded our next flight to Nairobi. We flew eight hours to Europe, and then eight hours to Kenya. During a 20-hour period we were on three different continents.

We were very happy to arrive in Nairobi and take a cab to the conference hotel. The Conference in Kenya was outstanding. The Attorney General at the time in Kenya, Amos Wako gave the opening address at the conference. My keynote presentation was "The Role of Witness Protection in the Fight Against Organized Crime." I took great pride in my remarks, giving a well-received speech. I also participated in a panel question and answer session with the Head of the Kenyan Witness Protection Program and members from the UNODC. I enjoyed meeting and taking a photo with Amos Waiko the former Attorney General of Kenya. I also enjoyed seeing and working with my friend and colleague the Head of the Kenya Witness Protection Program. She is a tremendous person and professional. At the hotel after the session on the first day of the conference, there was an outstanding African dance performance put on for attendees of the conference with various local foods prepared on a fire pit or large grill near where we were seated. Everything was delicious. My team and I enjoyed the very nice program of African Dance. The Friday session was also exceptional with speakers and presentations discussing Best Practices and Challenges in Witness Protection, Setting

Up a Witness Protection Program, Protecting Witnesses in West Africa, the Challenges of Protecting Witnesses and Victims in Africa, and the Rwanda Experience. My team and I were called on to provide input on various Witness Protection subjects and issues.

After the conference ended, my team and I wanted to get some shopping in for souvenirs. The Head of the Kenyan Witness Protection Program took us shopping to a couple of venues including an open-air market. We picked up some nice souvenirs and were constantly approached by local vendors knowing we were shopping and spending money. The next evening on Saturday, November 14, we were scheduled to leave Kenya to travel back home. We decided to go to an Elephant Orphanage and a Safari before leaving Nairobi. We had to be ready at 6:00 Saturday morning for the day's events, which included the main event, the safari. We also had to be ready to leave for the airport around 6:30 that evening for our first flight to Europe. The Head of the Kenyan Witness Protection Program was very kind to us coordinating our Saturday activities. We were ready to roll at 6:00 on Saturday morning after only getting a few hours of sleep the night before.

Our driver for the day's activities seemed to be a hospitable gentleman. He talked about his family, and President Barack Obama saying he was from the same village in Kenya as President Obama's Father. The driver said he was very happy that President Obama visited the village where he and the President's father were from. It was good to talk with the driver and enjoyable spending time with the Head of the Kenyan Witness Protection Program. We went to the National Park and took in the Safari first, which was very exciting. We saw all kinds of animals including Giraffes, Zebras, rhinos, elephants and deer. We wanted to see the King of the Jungle, the lion, but did not see one.

We also went to the elephant orphanage, which was also interesting. When we got back to our hotel we only had time to eat before taking a taxi to the airport to fly out. I remember we had dinner at a pizza restaurant at the hotel and then took our taxi to the airport. We were all very tired and slept the entire taxi ride to the airport. The taxi driver woke us and said we were at the airport. I remember telling my team that if the driver was a bad guy, he could of taken our sleepy behinds anywhere. We traveled home connecting through London where we had a 6-hour layover. I did get some sleep on the flight from Nairobi to London. We sacrificed our last night's sleep in Kenya, however, we knew it was worth it, and we never ever complained. All I can say is what a great trip it was. We returned safely home and got back to our families and work.

In January 2010, I traveled to Trinidad and Tobago to participate and speak at a Witness Protection Training Program my division was conducting. My division worked closely with and became good friends with our colleagues from Trinidad and Tobago. This was another interesting trip. I returned home to the Washington DC area, which had several days of snowfall. I had to shovel snow like many others in the area for several days. I remember trying to make it to a Georgetown University Men's basketball game, but had not cleared my driveway enough to get out. I watched the game with my daughter Morgan on television. President Obama and Vice President Biden both attended the game. I did not know it, but things were about to get real difficult for me personally with my marriage.

In 2010, I went to work with my staff on the Fifth International Symposium on Witness Security. We did not know it at the time that this was going to be the last Symposium under my tenure as the Assistant Director and maybe in the Marshals Service. My staff and I again used the International Symposium playbook to have the Fifth International Symposium on Witness Security. I wanted to have the conference either in the Caribbean or Central America based on the countries we assisted, were assisting, or planning to assist such as the Bahamas, Trinidad and Tobago, Jamaica, St. Kitts and Nevis, and Guatemala. I decided after considerable thought to bring the Symposium back to the United States. I chose Miami,

Florida as the location for the Fifth International Symposium On Witness Security/Protection. We picked the dates of Wednesday, September 15, 2010, and Thursday September 16, 2010 with an opening evening reception on Tuesday, September 14, 2010. I approved the Symposium Theme of "Leveraging Technology and Other Resources in Witness Protection." Again the Marshals Service was hosting this event without a co-sponsor or partner. The good thing was we had a budget to host the Symposium, and we knew that Miami, Florida was a very attractive venue for our worldwide colleagues to join us for the Symposium.

My division had our next strategic planning session in San Diego, California in August 2010. I did not attend the session in person, but participated by teleconference with my input. I discussed my division priorities, which were in direct support of our core mission and strategies for success. With God's blessing, I overcame a tremendous personal domestic situation, and was very much engaged in the operations of my division. The Fifth International Symposium on Witness Security Symposium was rapidly approaching. The Symposium had a heavy focus on technology with plenty of presentations discussing various technology applications regarding witness protection. My division again used the same blue print as we had before with our International Symposiums. We coordinated with the local U.S. Marshal's district office and the local police department for additional support. My executive team, and I expected attendance for this Symposium to be very high based on the location. We negotiated a below market lodging rate with the Fontainebleau Hotel in Miami. This hotel went through a tremendous renovation project and was in my view a 5 star hotel. The hotel management was very cooperative with our requests for extra considerations regarding room rates, security considerations, and space for our Symposium.

I decided again to have our own security team to make sure our security protocols were in place. This Symposium was very well attended with the largest level of attendance of all prior Symposiums. I attribute the very high attendance to the location and the past successes of the Symposiums. We used the same plan and protocols to have this Symposium. It was another huge success. At the time, I had a very unsupportive chain of command as far as my direct supervisor who was formerly a colleague. However but I managed to work around his lack of support. Just about all of the regulars attended the Fifth and last International Symposium on Witness Protection. For this Symposium I did not travel to the home of Mr. Gerald Shur. My staff and I decided we had a very full agenda focused on technology issues for the two-day event. I did not know the federal government budget situation was going downward with political struggles. As I mentioned earlier, this was going to be the last International Symposium on Witness Security under my leadership as the division Assistant Director.

As September 2010 arrived we were prepared to put on the Fifth International Symposium. We sent our advance team initially, with the main party to follow a couple of days later, including the Director of the agency and his contingent. I arrived with my division's main party and we were picked up and driven to the conference hotel. I made a visit to the hotel months before to check out the venue and approve it. The Fontainebleau hotel is a large first class facility with various shops and restaurants, and a top class club. Everyone who attended the Symposium loved the hotel. The only complaint was the cost of some of the items at the stores and shops. Many of the usual attendees made it to this event. We had the Symposium Social Event and Welcome Reception on Tuesday evening, September 14th. The event started with registration on Wednesday morning September 15th followed by welcome and opening remarks at 9am. My good friends and colleagues in charge of the Israeli Witness Protection Program, Canadian Witness Protection Program, Australian Witness Protection Program, and Serbian Witness Protection Program, in addition several other Witness Protection Chiefs were present including the Head of the Witness Protection Unit in the Netherlands, and the EUROPOL Witness Protection Project Manager.

The Symposium speakers included the U. S. Attorney for the Southern District of Florida, Mr. Wilfredo A. Ferrer, Marshals Service Director John F. Clark, myself, the Technical Operations Chief from the Marshals Service Tactical Operations Division, the Caribbean Regional Coordinator for the Department of Justice Overseas Prosecutorial Development Assistance and Training Division, the Head of the Witness and Victim Protection Unit State of Brandenburg, Germany, Head of the Dutch Witness Protection Unit, the EUROPOL Witness Protection Project Manager, Technology Executives from the United Kingdom, and several American based technology corporations. The Thursday evening dinner speaker was Mr. Evan Ratliff from Wired Magazine who traveled from New York. Mr. Ratliff gave a very good presentation on a project and story he did where he dropped out of society for a while and challenged readers to find him as he traveled around the country. As a part of his project, he occasionally used social media to leave clues, but kept moving around the country. As I mentioned, the presentation was very good and interesting. On Friday, most of us traveled home. A number of people stayed in Miami for the weekend taking in the sites and other attractions.

October, November, and December of 2010 was pretty much uneventful both domestically and internationally. During this time frame, the Office of Enforcement Operations received a new Senior Executive who took a very active role in the Department of Justice Witness Security Program.

CHAPTER SEVENTEEN

Witness Security and Protection
My Mission Accomplished

In December 2010, the Marshals Service received a new Director. The Obama Administration appointed Stacia Hylton as the agency's first female Director. Stacia Hylton was the 7th agency Director I worked for during my Marshals Service career. I worked for the Marshals Service under Director Hylton's leadership another 3 years before I retired. The year 2011 was pretty much a regular year with the exception of my division's involvement with training operations in Mexico and Guatemala, and my visits to my Regional Offices and the EUROPOL Conference in Budapest, Hungary. During this time period I had joint legal custodial custody of my daughter Morgan, and was enjoying every day I could spend time with her. She and I have an exceptional relationship. I have outstanding relationships with my older children too, but I recognize my civilian and military careers took me away from my older children more than the norm, and my divorces did not help the situations. I did well with my careers, but not that well with marital family life. I feel some of the requirements of my careers with the military and law enforcement caused some distance in my marriages. However, I have always loved my kids and remain close with them. Having

Morgan gave me another chance to be the father I was not while pursuing my career goals.

In May 2011, I traveled to the EUROPOL Witness Protection Conference in Budapest, Hungary. I missed the EUROPOL Witness Protection Conference the year before in Dubrovnik, Croatia due to my domestic situation. In 2011, with that situation behind me, I was looking forward to traveling to Budapest. I traveled with a Chief Inspector and one of my Senior Inspectors. I was looking forward to seeing good friends from the European Witness Protection family along with friends and colleagues from Canada, and Australia. I was asked to give a presentation for the conference. The EUROPOL Witness Protection Project Manager always treated me with honor and valued my experience and commitment to Witness Security and Protection. Budapest is a beautiful city and the Capital of Hungary. The Danube River separates the old cities of Buda and Pest. These cities were separate cities prior to becoming a single united city in 1873 according to Wikipedia. Residents of Budapest informed me of the remarkable history of their city during my visit. I always loved learning about history, and found Budapest to be a very interesting European city. I enjoyed the food as the EUROPOL Witness Protection Project Manager selected an exceptional restaurant in the hills of Budapest for the conference dinner. I enjoyed the Hungarian stew known as Goulash along with other very tasty local dishes. I located a couple of Russian Nesting or Babushka dolls for my youngest daughter Morgan and my college daughter Ashley. I have always loved and been fascinated by culture and customs of the local people when I visit their countries and I enjoyed the EUROPOL conference and the city of Budapest. After a very successful conference, my team and I returned home to the states resuming our normal duties.

I had set several professional goals for the rest of 2011. One goal was to continue my division's professional development program with our advanced training. Another goal was to continue to my efforts upgrade our Regional Office Administrative Officers. An additional goal was to start visiting a couple of the Bureau of Prisons Protective Custody Units. The Bureau of Prisons controlled and operated the Protective Custody Units for protected witnesses working in partnership with the Department of Justice Office of Enforcement Operations. I wanted to visit some of the Protective Custody Units to fully understand the operation of the units and hear some of the concerns of protected witnesses in the units. With respect to my planned upgrade of my division's regional Administrative Officers, the federal government was under a hiring freeze with threats of furloughing federal employees or reducing their 40-hour a week work schedule. Budgets were being reduced and the federal government was labeled as having too many employees, and unnecessary programs. I anticipated I was not going to be able to upgrade our division Administrative Officers based on the overall status of federal budgets. These employees are very hard working public servants and are under paid. This should be corrected as soon as possible. I hope those that are assigned to lead the Witness Security Division, will continue to work diligently to upgrade these fine employees. This was one major goal I was not able to accomplish. In my view federal government employees have been made scapegoats by those in political positions, using annual federal appropriations for political positioning.

I had my division's 2011 advance training ready to go with an appropriate training curriculum and the training was cancelled due to fiscal constraints, which I understood. If you cannot keep employees working, training must be discarded, especially advance training. I was able to start my visits to the Bureau of Prison Protective Custody Units where witnesses cooperating with the federal government are held while sentenced to serve time in prison. A protective custody unit is a prison unit inside a prison. I requested and obtained the Department of Justice Office of Enforcement Operations, and United States Bureau of Prisons approval to visit Protective Custody Units. During these visits some inmates in the units complained about various issues or perceived promises they felt went unfulfilled by the government. The visits were interesting, as these protected witnesses had valid, and some not so valid issues to report.

I was very content with my division's performance with domestic and international operations. The division was not perfect, but it was operating at a very high level. Our international footprint during my leadership had expanded dramatically worldwide. As a Senior Executive, I accomplished what I estimate is 95% of my goals for the Witness Security Division. The division expanded in regions, expanded in top tier leadership positions, expanded in Case Management personnel, growth in journeyman grade structure, tremendous growth in international training and operations with, an exceptional strategic plan, and a professional development training program. I was elated with the status of the Witness Security Division.

I applied for and was accepted to participate in the Federal Bureau of Investigation National Executive Institute Class 34. This is a well sought after executive police training course the FBI hosts and coordinates along with their National Academy course at Quantico, Virginia. The National Executive Institute is offered to law enforcement senior executives at the local domestic and international level. The FBI National Academy is offered to a similar group of police professionals but at the command level of law enforcement departments and agencies. I am pretty certain my good relationship with the FBI Training Academy attributed to my selection to be in the National Executive Institute Class 34. The course was held in three separate week intervals. The first week's session was held at Quantico, Virginia in April 2011. The second session was normally held in Australia, but was held in the Washington DC area in June 2011, at a hotel due to federal government budget constraints. This change of venue for the second session broke the hearts of many of us in the class, with the exception of the colleagues in the class from Australia. The third and final session was held at Gettysburg, Pennsylvania where we walked and subsequently rode a horse over the battleground at Gettysburg.

Our class consisted of law enforcement Chiefs, Deputy Chiefs, Sheriffs, and Superintendents from across the United States, London, Ireland, Australia, and Canada including FBI Special Agents in Charge of various offices and one Assistant Director with the United States Marshals Service. I was only the third United States Marshals Service employee to be selected to attend the National Executive Institute, and the only career employee to be selected to attend this outstanding senior executive training course. The other two employees were politically appointed Deputy Directors of the agency. The FBI NEI had outstanding speakers and authors giving lectures and presentations. Our class received plenty of leadership books to read. This was the second training course I attended with the Federal Bureau of Investigation. In December 2008, I attended and participated in the FBI Leading Strategic Change course in Chicago, Illinois at Northwestern University Kellogg School of Management.

Getting back to protecting witnesses, I worked closely with the new Department of Justice Office of Enforcement Operations Director and his Deputy Director on various program related matters. We were starting to work on and review highly sensitive witness cases involving terrorism related cases. The new Director and I acknowledged and agreed that we needed to handle these cases differently. We were engaged with the Federal Bureau of Investigation on developing new protocols for terrorism related cases.

In the middle of 2011, I was called to a meeting with my Director and tasked with working on a strategy to help Mexico develop its first formalized Witness Protection Program. The Attorney General of Mexico at the time, Ms. Marisela Morales traveled to the United States a week or so prior to my meeting with my Director, to meet with United States Attorney General Eric Holder. The purpose of her meeting was to ask for assistance with establishing a Witness Protection Program in Mexico. This training initiative in Mexico was a high priority for Attorney General Holder, and passed on to my Director and then passed to me. After I received my task to start the training program, I decided to use the same blue print I had implemented in Colombia for this new initiative in Mexico. My International Chief Inspector and I went to work on this initiative using our road map or blue print already in place to develop plans to get the new task of helping Mexico start it's Witness Protection Program.

We worked closely with the new Office of Enforcement Operations Director and his Deputy Director on various issues important to the start of the training program. I traveled to Mexico City and Cancun Mexico on business trips working with the Government of Mexico on their efforts to get their Witness Protection Program going. I assigned a Team Chief to be the actionable manager for this tasking and I provided that Chief support and guidance for this new very important mission. This new project required similar tactics and strategies as the program I was involved with in Colombia for many years when that country had very serious violent murders of witnesses and officials trying to uphold justice.

There was no doubt in my mind that we could handle this new assignment. My focus was on the safety of my division personnel conducting training in Mexico. The team chief I selected to lead this assignment was one of my dependable and dedicated Senior Inspectors who assisted with other training operations in Spanish speaking countries. This Senior Inspector mentioned to me on another international assignment when we were both overseas at INTERPOL that he wanted to continue to assist me, and our division with any training opportunities we had. I did not forget what the Senior Inspector told me. I had the Inspector travel to my office in the Washington DC area to discuss this new very critical mission requirement in Mexico. The Senior Inspector was honored at the opportunity to assist the Government of Mexico (GOM), and accepted a leadership role for our operations in Mexico. My office worked very closely with the United States Department of Justice Office of Enforcement Operations Division, Overseas Prosecutorial Development and Training Division, and the Government of Mexico's Prosecutor General's Office known as the PGR.

My division had been engaged with training operations in Colombia for a number of years. My division was also working with Guatemalan officials on a training assignment in Guatemala. We were working with Guatemala for a year. Now we were working on another strategy to work with and train hard working dedicated officers in Mexico in protective operations and witness protection. This was a very interesting new assignment. I worked closely with my key staff and we developed a superb training program for the Mexican Witness Protection Program that included several phases starting with basic techniques, followed by advance techniques and administrative training. The first session for the program started in August 2011. I traveled to Mexico City, Mexico to be a speaker at the graduation program. In November of 2011, I was invited to be a speaker and serve on a panel with the Department of Justice Office of Enforcement Operations, Department of Justice Overseas Prosecutorial Development and Training Division, and officials from The Mexican PGR unit and leaders of the GOM Witness Protection Program in Cancun, Mexico. I was surprised the meeting was being held in Cancun, Mexico. I had never been to Cancun, Mexico before. I had heard about the beauty of Cancun and looked forward to participating in the conference.

I traveled to Cancun, Mexico with my Chief of International Operations and another Senior Inspector to participate in this very important conference on Witness Protection and the Prosecution of cases involving protected witnesses. This conference had a focused agenda and despite the beautiful resort location, our few days there started early and lasted late into the evening. I gave a speech about witness security and protection. I participated on a panel answering questions about various protective witness situations. We had a magnificent gathering in the late evening after the first day of work, and I had the opportunity to spend time with several PGR attorneys attending the conference. Many of the conference attendees were attorneys, including the Director of the GOM

Witness Protection Program. OPDAT sponsored the conference and it was an outstanding conference.

My last major challenge other than the day to day activities of leading the domestic witness protection program, and making certain the domestic program did not lose a witness to harm, was helping the great country of Mexico start its Witness Protection Program working side by side with the Director of the Office of Enforcement Operations, various dedicated officials in OPDAT, and other Marshals Service personnel assigned to work in and assist Mexico. I was very happy that the Mexico initiative was gaining traction. My training teams and my Chief Inspector with responsibilities for our ground operations in Mexico were doing a wonderful job, and well received by everyone they worked with in Mexico. Failure has never been embraced by me as an option with any mission or task I have had in my career working for the Marshals Service or the Military. I always preferred to have an exceptional and challenging plan with solid alternate plans to accomplish objectives. I was very pleased with our plan of operation in Mexico and our personnel involved.

In the fall of 2011, I received notice from the Department of Justice Office of Inspector General that the Witness Security Program was going to be audited by one of their regional offices. Audits of programs under my leadership have never been an issue or a worry for me and always welcomed. I had experienced audits while serving as an Assistant Director for Judicial Security, and as a Chief Inspector for the Prisoner Services Division. One of my leadership procedures is to audit my own division or office, or request an audit of my division. I have always wanted to make sure my staff and I were compliant with agency policies and procedurals, and if we were not, I was more than happy to embrace corrective action and constructive recommendations. This audit did not just involve the Marshals Service Witness Security Program operations, but it also involved the Department of Justice Office of Enforcement Operations. As mentioned earlier, the Office of Enforcement Operations or OEO has the authority to authorize witnesses to be accepted into the Witness Security Program and terminate witnesses for cause removing them from the Witness Security Program. The Marshals Service Witness Security Division operates the program providing all required security related services.

As the year 2011 was closing, I was invited to participate and speak at the United Kingdom Caribbean Overseas Territories, and Bermuda Witness Protection Workshop from November 15th to the 17th in Miami, Florida. I took my Chief of International Operations with me to help with the presentations and dialogue. I gave a presentation on the Management and Implementation of Witness Protection. My Chief of International Operations and I gave a case Study presentation on International Witness Protection relocation issues and challenges. Countries attending this well put together workshop were from Anguilla, British Virgin Islands, Bermuda, Cayman Islands, Montserrat, Trinidad and Tobago, Turks and Caicos, United Kingdom, and Canada's Royal Canadian Mounted Police.

My division training plans and operations in Colombia were still under way and going well. In 2012, I traveled again to Colombia to visit my training team and staff. I participated in the last week of training addressing the Colombian law enforcement officials and participating in a driving range course. I had been involved with training plans and operations with the government of Colombia since 2001, and was extremely pleased at the changes in the country from a security stand point, including the development of the Colombian protective operations program which assists and enhances justice.

During 2012, my division and I worked very closely with the Federal Bureau of Investigation, and the Office of Enforcement Operations on Witness Security terrorism related cases. The Department of Justice Office Inspector General's (DOJ/OIG) general audit of the program had stopped. The Inspector General's office started to focus on cases dealing with terrorism for the purpose of making sure the Department of Justice had appropriate protocols in place to monitor these cases.

My senior staff and I met with the DOJ/OIG audit team often to work on a list of recommendations the DOJ/OIG developed for better coordination between DOJ entities dealing with witness security terrorism related cases. As I noted earlier, this was something my office, the Office of Enforcement Operations, and the Federal Bureau of Investigations were already working on, but now had a major push from my Director and senior Department of Justice leadership to resolve coordination issues on these cases at a faster pace, which we did. With close coordination with the Department of Justice Office of Enforcement Operation, my office and the Federal Bureau of Investigations National Joint Terrorism Task Force (NJTTF) and Terrorism Screening Center (TSC) put together joint protocols to focus on this category of witness security cases. I developed a very good working relationship with Federal Bureau of Investigation over the years and looked forward to the opportunity to work closely with the FBI NJTTF and TSC.

CHAPTER EIGHTEEN, LAST CHAPTER

My Retirement from Federal Service

Working with Department of Justice Overseas Prosecutorial Development and Training Division or OPDAT has always been enjoyable. OPDAT is a critical international training program for the Department of Justice and in my estimation, a tremendous partner to the international community assisting various countries around the world with training programs enhancing the judicial process of the host nation. I cannot think of a time when I received a call or written request where I was reluctant to support OPDAT or a country requiring training assistance or consultation. The fine professional attorneys, program managers, and other employees working for OPDAT all deserve tremendous recognition and applause for their efforts in promoting and expanding justice in various countries worldwide. It has been a pleasure to serve and work with OPDAT.

Likewise, working with the United Nations Office on Drugs and Crime or UNODC has been an memorable experience. UNODC and its employees, like those working in OPDAT, are also hard working very dedicated professionals supporting justice and human rights all over the world. I appreciate the partnership and support of those working for the UNODC. It was my pleasure to work with UNODC in Spain, and in Kenya. UNODC has partnered with a number of organizations including the United States Marshals Service to make a different in people's lives no matter where they live or come from. Having UNODC attend and participate in the Marshals Service Witness Security Division International Symposiums was very important to me. I know firsthand that UNODC is a first class worldwide meaningful organization.

I also enjoyed working with the EUROPOL, Witness Protection office, and the EUROPOL Witness Protection Project Manager. The EUROPOL Witness Protection office focused mainly on issues affecting European countries, but also were great partners in support of various other witness protection and security professionals such as colleagues in Canada, Australia and the United States. I served on a EUROPOL Witness Protection advisory committee along with personnel representing Canada, Australia, and several other European countries. The EUROPOL Witness Protection Office did not have conferences for a number of years until their conference in 2009. Prior to 2005, my division working with OPDAT, and INTERPOL had been the entities bringing many nations together to address and work on Witness Protection and Justice Sector security issues. As I noted earlier, the International Symposium idea was brought to my attention by one of my subordinate Chief Inspectors prior to his retirement.

I worked on several witness security cases that were brought to my attention. My role as the Assistant Director was usually in an oversight capacity. In one case, the division review team discovered one witness was requesting and receiving 80 Viagra pills a month, which was at federal government expense. I asked a subordinate manager why the Witness Security Inspector working with the witness had not stopped this abuse with the pills. I was pretty sure no person should be taking 80 Viagra pills a month. At best, I was thinking if a person was active each day of the month, the maximum should be 30 pills a month. I tasked the Chief Inspector responsible for the Inspector signing off on the 80 pills a month, to put a stop to it. As it is commonly known, the Witness Security Program supports witnesses with health issues providing medical assistance. However, allowing a witness to obtain 80 sexual enhancement pills each month was abuse, and that was halted. I believed that this witness was most likely adding to his income by selling the pills. I always received a good laugh from groups when I give presentations or speeches about Witness Security and discuss the Viagra case.

In another case, a witness became romantically involved with a new lady friend. The witness had to be terminated from the program as he disclosed he was in the program to his new paramour, a serious violation to his agreement to be in the program. In another case, a witness decided to opt out of the program after a young adult child of the witness got arrested. The witness did not wish to be relocated again, which is the choice of each witness entering the program. The Witness Security Program is known as a program of last resort. No one can be forced to enter or stay in the program.

It was during this time, I started to realize I was just about done with what I could do for the agency and the Department of Justice I served and loved for over 26 years. I started wondering what was next for me career wise. I did not think my agency would assign me to lead the Investigative Operations Division. The Investigative Operations Division was the only major operational division I knew I would enjoy leading and serving in. My first love in the Marshals Service was hunting and finding criminal fugitives. I had tremendous success conducting and leading fugitive investigations. I also knew my agency was not willing to appoint me to the Deputy Director's position, which I had been passed over for a couple of times for more junior Senior Executive employees. I knew I was at the highest level of non-political positions. To go higher in the agency required a Director who embraced working closely with an accomplished African American.

One thing I can say from my many years of experience with my agency is that it can use some help and strategic guidance appreciating and elevating minority employees who deserve the opportunity to serve at the highest levels of the agency. Former agency Directors Eduardo Gonzalez, and John Marshall and former agency Acting Director and Acting Deputy Director Louie McKinney were long gone, and with them went many opportunities for many minorities to serve at the highest levels of our agency. I made my break through to the Senior Executive Service 15 years ago. My promotion to the Senior Executive Service tier as a career Deputy Marshal must have been the limit, as there was only one other African American law enforcement Senior Executive appointed after me prior to my retirement from the agency. This Senior Executive only served in the position a few years before having to retire due to attaining mandatory retirement age. Within the last few years the agency elevated a Hispanic male to the Senior Executive tier. In my opinion and observation, having an extensive knowledge of the federal government and many federal agencies, the United States Marshals Service, the oldest federal law enforcement agency, lags extremely behind many federal law enforcement agencies with minority employee development, to include the placement of these hard working and deserving employees in high-level positions.

I did have aspirations during my long tenure as an Executive and Senior Executive for the Marshals Service to serve as our agency Director or Deputy Director. I came to realize that the last earned promotion I received, was my selection in 2000 by then Director John W. Marshall to the position of Assistant Director. I remember reading General Colin Powell's book My American Journey. General Powell mentioned in his book that his last earned promotion was to the rank of Colonel. General Powell also mentioned that a promotion in the military after obtaining the rank of Colonel was more political, and depended on who you knew and who liked you. In the United States Marshals Service, it is my position that the last earned career promotion is to the position of Assistant Director.

After obtaining the rank of Assistant Director, to go any higher in the organization such as Associate Director, Deputy Director or certainly Director, it is political. The Director of the Marshals Service for the most part controls who will be selected for the positions of Deputy Director, and Associate Director. However, if the President, Vice President, Attorney General or Deputy Attorney General have someone they want placed in those positions, the Director of the agency would most likely have to accept that person. I reached as high a level as I could as an Assistant Director, and I accomplished plenty.

There were two additional things related to Witness Security that I wanted to complete and get behind me before I retired. As I mentioned in the last chapter, I wanted to visit a couple of Bureau of Prison Protective Custody Units, and also visit Guantanamo Bay. Like many people, I had heard much about Guantanamo Bay and was very interested in seeing the terrorist prisoner security operation conducted by the military. In the fall of 2011 and the spring of 2012, I did visit two Bureau of Prisons Protective Custody Units after coordinating with the Office of Enforcement Operations and the Bureau of Prisons. Both of these visits were very insightful. I got to meet and speak with several protected witnesses in these units. I enjoyed meeting with the professional Federal Bureau of Prison personnel, discussing their interaction with protected witnesses. As I mentioned in an earlier chapter, most witnesses because of their significant criminal past have to serve time in the federal penitentiary before entering into the Witness Security Program. At both Protective Custody Units I visited, I listened to complaints of witnesses. The complaints very similar to complaints I have heard from other incarcerated inmates in penal institutions such as lack of medical support, time computation complaints, and lost files. One inmate did not like his institution job, saying he was only given "bullshit" jobs making only $10 a month. Some prisoner witnesses complained of food issues saying there were not enough food alternatives.

Another prisoner witness related the institution did not have cottage cheese and he was a type 2 diabetic. Another prisoner witness related he wanted to be transferred to another institution as he reported seeing another prisoner witness that he was familiar with. Another prisoner witness serving a life sentence related he was having problems getting visitors cleared. He further adding he had the same problem in a jail under Arizona Maricopa County Sheriff Joe Arpaio. Another prisoner witness wanted to know when he could speak with his wife. Another prisoner witness related he did not get the reduced time from testifying against a prisoner charged with murdering Chandra Levy in the Washington DC area, a case I was familiar with. While one other prisoner witness related he wrote President Obama in an effort to get his time reduced. Lastly, another prisoner witness related he had child custody issues saying his wife abandoned their kids. The visits to the Protective Custody Units were very interesting as I got to hear directly from prisoner witnesses about issues they were having.

Guantanamo Bay or GTMO was important to me as my division supported a military operation working with the Office of Military Commissions. Terrorist detainees are held in custody and subject to military Combatant Tribunal proceedings. I took a 2-day trip to GTMO in August 2012 to visit the site. I met officials in command of GTMO and the detainee operation. I departed Andrews Joint Air Force Base in Maryland on a 737 jet with other military officials, non-government organizations, and victims of the deadly cowardly terrorists act committed on September 11, 2001. After arriving at Guantanamo Bay, I was greeted by members of my division and a Navy Rear Admiral lower half, an equivalent of a one star Army General. I learned that there is a Commander of Base Operations, and a Commander of the Detainee Operations. I was treated very well by the Commanders on base, and spent some good time with the Rear Admiral who was in charge of Detainee Operations. I received briefings, and a tour of the detainee operation.

As a retired Military Police Soldier and Officer, I was extremely proud to see Army Military Police professionals handling business with security operations securing terrorist enemy combatants. I had lunch at the base dining facility with the Rear Admiral, and dinner at a GTMO local restaurant. I met several very good military and GTMO Task Force personnel. I developed a friendship with a gentleman I will name as Johnny. I found out that Johnny lived about 7 miles from where I live. We have been to each other's residence. As I mentioned earlier, visiting GTMO was rewarding for me. I wrote a White Paper in 2010 for the Obama Administration with possible solutions for closing GTMO, and moving the enemy combatant detainees to alternative secure sites. This is a document I still have. I never submitted the document to the Obama Administration.

My last international trip prior to my retirement from the Marshals Service was to Belgrade, Serbia. I was invited to be a speaker and panelist in a Balkan Regional Witness Protection Conference in Belgrade. I accepted the trip, and traveled to Belgrade with my Chief of International Operations. I had been invited to go to Serbia to participate in Witness Protection forums, but I always sent a representative. This time I went and participated myself. This trip was a Department of State sponsored trip, and was coordinated by Department of Justice officials in Belgrade assigned to Serbia to assist with various projects including Witness Protection. Several regional countries were invited and participated in the conference. I gave my presentation and participated on a panel with my Chief of International Operations. It was good to work with and spend some time with my good friends from Serbia. As I mentioned earlier my good friends from Serbia were the sponsors of the "Serbian Café" in the evenings during our International Symposiums. I enjoyed my trip to Belgrade.

I decided to retire from federal service in December 2013 to pursue another adventure. After much prayer, discussions with family, friends and other loved ones, I decided run for the office of Sheriff of Prince George's County, Maryland, a county I resided in for 18 years. I retired from the United States Marshals Service on January 11, 2014 as one of the longest serving leaders of Witness Security having led the program for 9 years. I hope you have enjoyed reading about my endeavors in law enforcement and the military. My career with the Marshals Service did go full circle or

360 degrees as I went from hunting and finding fugitives and criminals, to hiding them for the past 9 years of my federal law enforcement career. As you can see from reading this book, I traveled the world speaking and consulting about protecting witnesses. My face and name became known in many international networks from my service and accomplishments on behalf of witness security, working for my agency, the Department of Justice, and the United States Department of State.

Serving for 26 ½ years with the oldest federal law enforcement agency the United States Marshals Service, and working in the United States Department of Justice has been very rewarding to me. I count my many blessings. I have served our government and the American public well. I seek to continue serving in public safety but hope to do so returning to the local level. Please wish me well in my journey to continue to serve. I am looking forward to going full circle one more time returning to community based public safety.

Abbreviations

ATF, Bureau of Alcohol Tobacco and Firearms

CNN, Cable News Network

C130, Four-engine turboprop military transport aircraft

DC, District of Columbia

DEA, Drug Enforcement Administration

DOJ, Department of Justice

ECQ, Executive Core Quality

FBI, Federal Bureau of Investigation

FTO, Field Training Officer

GTMO, Guantanamo Bay

HRD, Human Resources Division

HWY, Highway

IRS, Internal Revenue Service

INTERPOL, International Police

I-75, Interstate 75

I-95, Interstate 95

MCC, Metropolitan Correctional Center

NOBLE, National Organization of Black Law Enforcement Executives

OCDETF, Organized Crime Drug Enforcement Task Force

OEO, Office of Enforcement Operations

OPDAT, Overseas Prosecutorial Development and Training

ROTC, Reserve Officer's Training Corps

U.S., United States

WANT II, Warrant Apprehension Narcotic's Team (Second Fugitive Operation)

WITSEC, Witness Security Program

The Jones for Sheriff of Prince George's County, Maryland Campaign
Kick-Off Event, March 2014 in Hyattsville, Maryland

Election Day in Ft. Washington, Maryland, Prince
George's County with Herman Brewer

Jones Family Members

In 2003 with Associate U.S. Supreme Court Justice Stephen Breyer

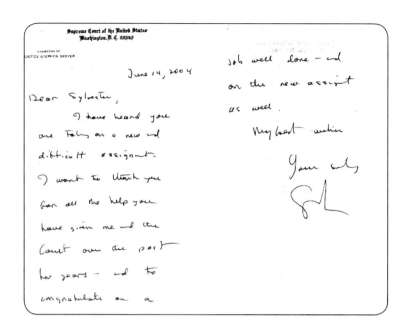

Note from Associate U.S. Supreme Court Justice Stephen Breyer

As a three year old boy in Chicago, Illinois

In St. Croix U.S. Virgin Islands as a Captain and Company Commander of the 661st Military Police Company during a parade in 1995

Making a presentation at the Second International Witness Security/ Protection Symposium, INTERPOL, Lyon, France, September 2007

As Assistant Director for Witness Security with Gerald Shur, Founding
Father of the American Witness Security/Protection Program at
a U.S. Probation Conference in South Carolina in 2011

Giving opening remarks at the Fifth International Witness Security/
Protection Symposium, Miami, Florida, September 2010

Making a presentation at the Fifth International Witness
Protection Symposium in Miami, Florida September 2010.

1989 at the Wall as it is starting to come down between East and West
Germany as a First Lieutenant with my Army Reserve Unit the 308th
Civil Affairs Group supporting the Army's 8th Infantry Division

As a Chief Inspector with American Activist and Author Ruby
Bridges at U.S. Marshals Service Headquarters in 1997

Five years old in Chicago.

As a Deputy Marshal in 1989 with Virginia State Troopers and other
Deputy Marshals in southwest Virginia working the Pittston Coal Strike

As a Deputy Marshal in southwest Virginia working
the Pittston Coal Strike in 1989

March 1991 in Kuwait City with a Kuwaiti Army General
after U.S. Forces pushed Iraqi Forces out of Kuwait

February 1991 preparing to lead a tactical convoy from Al Jubayl
Saudi Arabia to Kuwait as part of the effort to Drive Iraqi forces out
of Kuwait in support of Operation Desert Storm as a member of the
432nd Civil Affairs Company attached to the Army's 7th Corps

March 1991 in my sleeping quarters Kuwait City

In 2003 at my home as a Lieutenant Colonel getting ready to
attend a District of Columbia National Guard formal event as the
Operations Officer for the 260th Military Police Command

1985 on duty as a Police Officer with the Markham Police Department

In July 1981 as a Private with the 933rd Military Police Company with the Illinois Army National Guard after completing Army Basic Training and Military Police School returning to my former employer, Bank Marketing Association with the company CEO In Chicago, Illinois

As a Deputy Marshal in 1989 in Southwest, Virginia working the Pittston Coal Strike. As a Deputy Marshal in 1989 in Southwest, Virginia working the Pittston Coal Strike.

As a Supervisory Deputy Marshal in 1995
at my desk in San Juan, Puerto Rico.

On a Safari after being the Keynote Speaker for the United Nations
Office on Drugs and Crime, First East Africa Regional Conference
on Witness Protection, November 2009 in Nairobi, Kenya

At a National Organization of Black Law Enforcement
Executive's National Conference in July 2008

With my late Grandfather William A. Jones June 2013
along with Eugene Shaw in Markham, Illinois

With my late Grandfather William A. Jones and A.
Howard, June 2013 in Markham, Illinois

As Assistant Director for Judicial Security in 2001 at my
desk at U.S. Marshals Service headquarters.

With my Mother Cheryl circa 1991 in South Bend, Indiana

In 2008 with William Walker at an Alpha Phi Alpha Fraternity
Incorporated - Xi Alpha Lambda Chapter Black and Gold Ball, Fairfax, VA

June 2014 with my daughter Ashley at her
graduation from Texas State University

In Chicago November 2014 for my daughter Erika's wedding
with Erika, Sylvester Jr., Ashley, and Morgan

October 2009 at a social event for the Fourth International
Witness Security/Protection Symposium in Salvador, Brazil

INDEX

CPSIA information can be obtained
at www.ICGtesting.com
Printed in the USA
FFOW04n0038031115
18256FF